Praise for
FOOD FC
M000203501

"Bell's absorbing account is neither Halloween fantasy nor tabloid frenzy, but a major contribution to the study of New England folk beliefs.... [H]is tales, stripped of Dracula's Eastern European trappings, give a deeper and more somber meaning to the overgrown fields and their enclosing stone fences, to the derelict farmhouses and their sagging barns, of rural New England."
—Michael Kenney, *The Boston Globe*

"An elegantly spun, crisply written and carefully researched book.... *Food for the Dead* is filled with ghostly tales, glowing corpses, rearranged bones, visits to hidden graveyards, and references to writers like Robert Frost, H. P. Lovecraft, and Amy Lowell.... Bell reveals the powerful roots of folk ideas, the importance of community and prophetic dreams, the pull of legend and blood.... But most of all he reveals the darker designs behind old stories and the ineluctable fascination of the living with the dead. This is a marvelous book, which can only disturb our own darker dreams."
—Sam Coale, *Providence Journal*

"The 'vampire' threat here has little in common with your garden-variety Dracula, the fanged menace of Transylvania; these quiet apparitions are in some ways more macabre.... Bell himself is a talented stylist, and academics working in folklore and myth will find his study a refreshing departure from the dry fieldwork ordinarily on offer."
—*Publishers Weekly*

"Eerily interesting exploration of the 18th- and 19th-century New England folk custom of digging up and burning recently deceased family members to ensure they weren't vampires.... Bell goes beyond the Dracula stereotype to unearth a creepy aspect of early America that few today remember."
—*Kirkus Reviews*

"This highly-skilled piece of research unravels a New England mystery, and accomplishes it with much success. One of the best books I've read this year and extremely well-written."
—Al Klyberg, former director of the Rhode Island Historical Society

"A candidate for best title of the season.... Bell's intriguing book, the result of two decades of active research, is at once a lively source for rough legend and rigorous scholarship, because while the writer shares a wealth of passed-down stories, he also gets to the roots of them."
—William Ruehlmann, *Virginian-Pilot*

FOOD FOR THE DEAD

On the Trail of New England's Vampires

MICHAEL E. BELL

CARROLL & GRAF PUBLISHERS
NEW YORK

FOOD FOR THE DEAD
On the Trail of New England's Vampires

Carroll & Graf Publishers
A Division of Avalon Publishing Group Inc.
161 William St., 16th Floor
New York, NY 10038

First Carroll & Graf cloth edition 2001

First Carroll & Graf trade paperback edition 2002

The poem "The Griswold Vampire" (pp. 176-177) by Michael J. Bielawa originally appeared in the Summer 1995 issue of *Dead of Night*. It is reprinted here by courtesy of the poet.

Book design by Michael Walters; Stonewall illustration by Simon Sullivan

Frontispiece art (p. ii) courtesy of Culver Pictures, Inc.

Map of "Vampire Incidents in New England" (p. xiv) copyright © 2001 by Jeffrey Ward

Library of Congress Cataloging-in-Publication Data is available.

ISBN: 0-7867-1049-7

Printed in the United States of America
Distributed by Publishers Group West

She bloom'd, though the shroud was around her,

locks o'er her cold bosom wave,

As if the stern monarch had crown'd her,

The fair speechless queen of the grave,

But what lends the grave such lusture?

O'er her cheeks what such beauty shed?

His life blood, who bent there, had nurs'd her,

The living was food for the dead!

—From the May 4, 1822,

Old Colony Memorial and Plymouth County (Massachusetts) Advertiser

To my parents,
Lester M. Bell and Sarah Elizabeth Jackson Bell

CONTENTS

ACKNOWLEDGMENTS

Over the twenty years that I have been following the vampire trail in New England, I have received the kind assistance of many individuals and organizations. I would like to thank the interns who worked with me and the Rhode Island Folklife Project: Joe Carroll, James Clements, Dawn Dove, and Brian Hokeness. Mary-Lou Haas Fidrych was my Administrative Assistant for many years; she was an enormous help as well as a great companion on legend trips. I owe a debt of gratitude to all those whom I interviewed for this project; I will always treasure the generosity and hospitality of Everett Peck and the late Margery Matthews. Thanks to Joe Uscio, whose research into Rhode Island's supernatural realm helped me appreciate the importance of genealogy. Many scholars and colleagues located and passed along references that opened new trails, including Jane Beck, Nick Bellantoni, Mary Deveau, Ruth Herndon, Robert Mathiesen, William Simmons, Paul Sledzik, and John Sterling.

Without exception, the staff of the many institutions that I visited in my search for documentation were helpful and friendly. I would especially like to thank the following: The Rhode Island Historical Preservation & Heritage Commission; The Rhode Island Historical Society Library; John Hay Library at Brown University; Rare Books and Special Collections Department of the Countway Library of Medicine; Archives of the City of Boston; and the Massachusetts State Library. Frank Iacono, of the Rhode Island Department of State Library Services, always went beyond the call of duty to locate obscure and scarce materials.

I would like to acknowledge the generous support of the National Endowment for the Humanities, under whose funding the fieldwork and research for this project was begun.

The manuscript for this book was prepared using Nota Bene's Scholar's Workstation 5.5, a seamless suite of software for writing, research, and managing bibliographies and notes. Thanks, Nota Bene, for facilitating an often daunting task.

My wife, Carole O. Bell, has given generously of everything it's possible to give, from encouragement to ideas to editing.

I am especially indebted to my editor, Philip Turner, who never gave up on this project.

PROLOGUE

Folklorists, like vampires, are doomed to a dual existence. Vampires are both dead and alive; folklorists are both participants and observers. I was introduced to this dualism in the classroom of the late Wayland Hand, the personification of a gentleman and scholar. Impeccably attired in a jacket and tie, he looked a bit out of place at UCLA in the late '60s. Every first-year graduate student in the Folklore & Mythology Program was required to take Wayland's class in folklore bibliography. Each classroom session began with a mimeographed annotated bibliography on the topic of the day. Wayland would go down the list, discussing each volume—its genesis, contents, relative merits and demerits, and where it fit into the world of folklore scholarship. Often he would relate obscure anecdotes about the authors. Sounds deadly, does it? It wasn't, because Wayland not only *knew* the lore, he *treasured* it. When he spoke of Pertinacious Kobolds and other mischievous spirits, they became distinct beings with personalities.

My epiphany came the day Wayland told us about the disappearance of giants from Europe. This was not a rapid, catastrophic event like the extinction of the dinosaurs. It was, rather, a more lengthy demise with the final death blow administered by the Industrial Revolution. As Wayland talked about the giants, I noticed that he stopped looking at us, and his eyes seemed to focus somewhere beyond the windowless walls of our Bunche Hall classroom. His voice, naturally soft, grew softer. He spoke about how Christians stigmatized the giants as devils, in league with Satan. He described how industry's widening circle of smoke and clamor finally pushed the giants from their homes. His voice dropped to a near whisper, and I'm sure I saw tears well up, as he described how the giants shrank, deeper and deeper into the forests and caves. Demonized, and no longer able to find refuge, the giants vanished. When Wayland concluded, it dawned on me that he wasn't talking only about giants no longer appearing in the *folklore record*. He was describing the *extinction of a species*. I thought, this is incredible: Wayland Hand, a meticulous, reasoning scholar—a *professional folklorist*—actually believes in giants.

Some introspection led me to conclude that those two words—professional folklorist—embody opposing perspectives. "Folklore" suggests the stuff of youthful play and fantasy (though I and other folklorists take issue with this narrow view), while "professional" is what grown-ups aspire to become—capable, proper and, above all, rational. All professional folklorists are to be found somewhere, perhaps wavering, along this continuum. Dualism is reflected in our principal technique for acquiring primary data, "participant-observation." We interact with "informants" (an unfortunate term) and join in their activities to learn and understand from the insider's point of view. But, at the same time, we are interpreting these experiences through the lens of folklore theory. We are simultaneously part of, yet apart from, what we study.

The use of the term "vampire" also reflects the insider/outsider duality. Insiders, the New England families and communities involved, never used the term. Following the vampire trail, I discovered that a vampire is much more complicated and interesting than simply a corpse who returns from the grave to suck the blood of the living. When I, or anyone else, refers to a corpse that was exhumed as a "vampire," it is good to keep an open mind.

I've grown to accept my two folklorist personae, and I've given them names. Dr. Killjoy Rational III is the observer/scholar. His title indicates his credentials and standing in the academic community; the suffix "III" suggests his intellectual descent, linking him to a longstanding tradition of scholarship. Killjoy's rationality often keeps impulsiveness at bay. On the other hand, Mike (who is, I like to believe, the natural me) is willing to suspend his disbelief because he wants to participate wholeheartedly, without reservation—sometimes without premeditation. He tends to be open and trusting, perhaps naive at times.

The vampire journey that fills this book was undertaken, interpreted, and written by both Mike and Dr. Rational, frequently in perfect harmony, occasionally not. Even when their presence is unacknowledged, you can be sure that they both are on the page, engaging in an ongoing dialogue. Wayland Hand did not set me out on the vampire trail—that was done by another remarkable man, Everett Peck, who lives on the opposite coast. But Wayland gave me the wherewithal to follow the trail, and the courage and wisdom to allow Mike to accompany Dr. Rational.

Michael E. Bell
Pawtuxet Village
Independence Day 2001

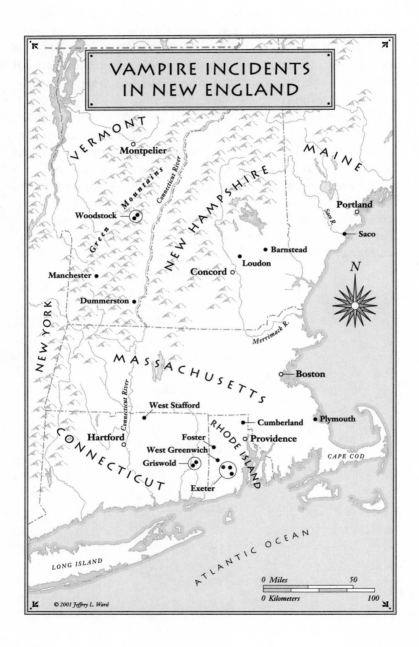

VAMPIRE INCIDENTS
IN NEW ENGLAND

CHAPTER 1
This Awful Thing

I hated to admit, even to myself, that I was excited by the prospect of interviewing Lewis Everett Peck, an Exeter, Rhode Island, farmer and descendent of Mercy Brown, who was probably the last person exhumed as a vampire in America. By 1981, I had been a folklorist for more than a decade and had hundreds of interviews under my belt, but no one had ever told me a vampire story based on personal experience. Of course, like most modern Americans, I have a familiar, comfortable relationship with vampires—but these are fictional vampires. Their existence requires us to suspend our disbelief, whether we're watching a movie, reading a book or looking at an ad for beer or batteries. Peck was going to tell me about a vampire who actually existed—a relation, no less—not some cardboard cutout, B-movie actor, or figment of an author's imagination.

Exeter is only a thirty minute drive from my home base of Providence; it seems light years removed culturally. Halfway into this short ride, I left Interstate 95 and began to notice the rubble stone walls stretching for miles in every direction. Overgrown and seemingly in the middle of nowhere, they are a silent reminder of the once-prosperous farms—true plantations, really, relying on the labor of black slaves and indentured Indians—that began to fade after the American Revolution.

Exeter is a wide town, bumping against Connecticut on its western edge and stretching eastward almost to Narragansett

1

Bay. Its northern border slices off the lower third of Rhode Island, identified as Washington County on maps but known by everyone as South County. In colonial times this "Narragansett Country" was a no-man's-land fought over by Rhode Island and Connecticut. When Rhode Island eventually gained control by royal edict, the colony gratefully named it King's Province, which yielded to King's County. Washington replaced King after the break with England, but the area was—and still is—called South County by the locals.

South County's climate is harsh but, moderated by the waters of Narragansett Bay and the Atlantic Ocean, conducive to good farming. Its rocky soil is among the most fertile in New England. Plantations that began to bloom in the late 1600s reached their zenith by the mid 1700s, occupying anywhere from 500 acres to twenty square miles each. The "Narragansett Planters"— gentlemen owners including the Hazards, Robinsons, Gardiners, Reynolds, and Congdons—grew crops of corn and hay for their large stocks of dairy cattle, sheep, hogs, and horses, all under the direction of a tenant "husband man" and his crew of paid laborers, indentured servants, and slaves. A typical agreement between owner and tenant might stipulate that ten acres be cleared for meadow each year and that stone walls be constructed.

On the same land that supported gentlemen farmers who bred the famous Narragansett Pacer—a marvelously light-footed saddle horse with an easy gait, extinct by 1800 because the breeding stock was sold to meet the overwhelming demand— isolated "Swamp Yankees" literally carved out their homesteads by hand. Stones that could be moved were hauled, with the assistance of animal power, to the perimeter of the field where they were eventually transformed into a dry (unmortared) rubble wall. Larger rock outcroppings remained, forcing the neat, straight rows of corn to temporarily break apart and coalesce on the other side, their undulations a visible reminder that nature can never be totally subdued. This fragmented landscape of fields framed by meandering stone walls emerged from the interaction between unrelenting natural forces and the tenacious Swamp Yankee. The man I'm going to interview, known as Everett to friends and neighbors, is one of these tough, hard scrabble farmers whose work never seems to end. What they lack in formal education is more than offset by resourcefulness and plain common sense.

Like his South County ancestors, Everett is independent and self-sufficient, raising much of his own food. He has a large garden (which provides vegetables for canning), makes his own apple cider vinegar and elderberry wine, raises pigs (his brother slaughters them, he makes the sausage) and wild turkeys, and still uses many home remedies passed down from older generations.

As I pulled into the dirt driveway of Everett's isolated farm at the end of Sodom Trail, four St. Bernards greeted me, leaping and slobbering on my small car. I rolled down the window just far enough to ask if it was safe to get out. A middle-aged man of medium build, dressed in gray cotton work shirt and pants, pointed to one of the dogs and said, "Well, better let me get this one here." I was relieved when Everett put all four in the pen.

He led me into a cozy living room heated by the wood stove in the adjoining kitchen, much appreciated since it was chilly for mid–November. He motioned for me to sit on the couch, then eased himself down next to me. On a small table was a pile of clippings and other documents. Everett pulled out a yellowed clipping, containing printed text, photographs, and a map, and handed it to me, asking, "Can you find where you are?"

Why did I have the feeling that I was back in third-grade geography? My eye was attracted to a road outlined in red. "Is this Sodom Trail, down here?" I asked.

"Sodom? Oh, I got that in red? Yeah. What's it say there?" he asked, pointing at a photo caption.

I read from the clipping, "Half a mile from here, in a locality called Sodom, is the site of what is claimed to have been among the first cotton or woolen mills established in this state. Structures now as seen in the past. Only two families reside in the hamlet."

Everett broke in, "Yeah, and I'm one. Now, this is when?"

Locating the date at the top of the clipping, I answered, "1896."

"Well, in 1981, I happen to be the only one left," Everett said. He laughed and I felt I had just passed a test.

Everett's speech is forthright, with a snap and edge to it. Hearing him talk is the auditory equivalent of biting into a crisp, cold Macintosh apple. As I was soon to learn, he is also a wonderful raconteur, steeped in local history, with a repertoire that includes personal experiences and anecdotes, family tales, and local legends. Everett describes himself as a Swamp Yankee and jack-of-all-trades. I found out that Everett is a master of understatement—and as shrewd as any Yankee ever was.

What does he do besides farm? "Anything!" he exclaimed. "I hunt up boundaries. And boundary disputes—I got a couple lawyers I do research work for. Done it all my life! Write deeds myself. I'm a notary and everything. Done it ever since I was twenty years old, at least."

As far as Everett is concerned, he is simply carrying on with his family's traditions. He said: "We were a poor family. My family were farmers. That was the source of their income. But they also did logging and wooding. You had to get your money 'cause things was needed. For an example, water power ran the mills around here. But if it had a dry spell—no water—you didn't work in the mill. So you went out and picked blueberries or you did something else. Same with the whole family. We were farmers. But we did logging. We did woodwork. And we sold wood. And we cut posts. And we had cattle. And we had horses. We had everything. We were just regular New England farming, country people. On one side of my family they had a little money. On the other side they had nothing. And they all worked together."

This cooperative self-reliance extended to medicine, too. "If we had poison ivy, we got a herb, indigo. We steeped, we bathed in it. Or, if you cut your foot on a piece of tin or a piece of glass—'cause we were barefooted—you made a poultice. You didn't go down to the doctor and get a tetanus shot, or whatever they got down there to give, an antibiotic of some nature. We made poultices. Sometimes it was bread and sugar."

As an aside, Everett explained: "Today's bread won't do it.

You've got too many chemicals in it," before continuing with his contrast between then and now. "Sometimes they used salt pork. Wrapped a finger up. Salt pork and bread on it and it draws. We did our own medication, lots of times. And they did the same. They were experimentin'—same thing. Today everybody goes to a center somewhere, or they all got doctors. Everything is done, today, differently than it was then."

Swamp Yankee. Like other regional, racial, or ethnic labels, Swamp Yankee suggests a bundle of stereotypical traits: shrewd, penurious, independent, imaginative (often to the point of exaggeration), approachable, but curt and cantankerous. Playing it close to the vest, a Swamp Yankee overstates the mundane and downplays the extraordinary. Although a person like Everett may use the term to refer to himself or his family, and wear it proudly, he may resent its use by outsiders.

Theories about how the term came into use have faded into legend, varying from place to place. It has been suggested that Swamp Yankee is New England's equivalent of the Western "Squaw Man"—an insulting reference to a man who married a Native American or lived among them. Another supposition is that those addicted to drink had to pursue their vice outside the respectable confines of town, so they took to the swamps to indulge themselves. Their straight-laced and sober neighbors began calling them "Swamp Yankees." One explanatory story substitutes the weakness of fear for the vice of drink. In Thompson, Connecticut—or New York City, depending on which version you accept—several townspeople fled to the outlying swamps to avoid the invading British during the Revolutionary War. When they returned, the folks who stayed behind chided them as being "Swamp Yankees." The term followed these newly designated Swamp Yankees as they migrated to other parts of southeastern New England.

Some of the family stories shared by Everett are remarkably similar to these Swamp Yankee tales. "There's a place over here in Exeter," Everett began, pronouncing it 'Egster', "we call Ephraim's Bedroom. I had a relative—and I can't truthfully tell

you his last name, it could'a been Reynolds, but I don't know—
but his first name was Ephraim, and he didn't want to go to war,
so he hid. And he went up in the cave and he stayed there until
the war was over. And his girlfriend would sneak him food, and
he had a spring right there by the cave. And they've called it, in
the family, Ephraim's Bedroom ever since."

I asked Everett which war Ephraim was hiding from and he
responded, "What was it that was between the states here?"

"The Civil War?" I suggested.

"Civil War, yeah."

Everett's tag to the story also connects it to the drinking associated with Swamp Yankees: "The last thing that lived there, probably thirty years ago, was this great big bird. He had a wing spread
about ten feet. Yup. And this great big bird . . . he laid this egg.
And, of course, my people drink a little, you know. [So they] gig-
gled and laughed about it and finally my old man went up and
shot it. And he had it tacked up, with wings spread, on the barn
door there for a while, and then they took pictures of it. I don't
know where in the hell the pictures are."

Everett also shared some family information that completed
his connection to all three speculations concerning the origin of
Swamp Yankee. Late in our conversation, when we were discussing Native American sites in the town, Everett interjected:
"Now! Be honest with ya, I'm part Indian. Not from here. Don't
know. Couldn't tell ya. No way a findin' out. My great-grandmother was a full-blooded Indian. . . . You know, back when we
were kids, if you had any Indian you weren't recognized too
good, you know. People'd bother you. You didn't tell nobody you
had Indian blood in you." Laughing, Everett matter-of-factly
observed: "That's the way it was when we were little. They didn't
like you too well."

One of Everett's anecdotes, which he shared after I had
turned off the tape recorder, summed up his Swamp Yankee heritage. During the blizzard of '78, when Everett was serving as
vice president of the town council, he learned that other members of the council, presumably vying for his position, were

gaining favor with local voters by riding on the town snow plows. Being snowed in, Everett couldn't take advantage of this publicity stunt, so he devised an alternate plan. Phoning people in town and asking them if the snow plow had been by yet, Everett was able to plot each plow's progress. Then he would phone people on the next road, informing them that the plow was on its way.

"They thought I'd sent it over. Never said I did—never said I didn't, neither," Everett explained. His smile and sparkling blue eyes showed he still relished the memory of how he claimed the other council members' share of goodwill as his own.

Everett thumbed through the pile of clippings next to the couch, pulled one out and handed it to me. A two-part headline topped the article, which had appeared in a local newspaper the week of Halloween two years before. The smaller type read: "They burned her heart . . . " and underneath, in large bold letters, was the question: "Was Mercy Brown a vampire?" Flanking the article was a photograph of Everett in his work clothes standing next to Mercy's gravestone, looking at the camera and pointing to his left. The caption reported: "LEWIS PECK of Sodom Trail, Exeter, stands at the grave of Mercy Brown (left) in the Chestnut Hill Cemetery, Exeter, pointing to the rock where the corpse's heart was burned in 1892. Ancestor's [sic] of Peck's performed the hideous act to rid the body of what they believed was a vampire." The caption reading "Lewis" instead of "Everett" revealed that its author was an outsider.

In a polished, self-assured performance that suggested he had told this tale many times, Everett began to tell me the story of Mercy Brown. "Mercy Brown was a relative. I can't tell you right now how we're related, but we are related. My mother's mother was a Brown. And it was told to me as a kid, you know, from my mother. Uh, Decoration Day was one of the big days, and Children's Day was one of our big days around here."

Everett, sitting next to me on the couch, turned his head toward me—an outsider—to explain how anyone could be enthusiastic over some minor holiday. "You didn't go very far around here, you know." On Decoration Day, now known as Memorial Day, children accompanied their parents to the cemetery behind the Chestnut Hill Baptist Church to place flowers on the graves of their relatives.

"The Brown cemetery is at what we call Shrub Hill—Chestnut Hill, used to be. All the family is buried there, practically. And at that place there is the church and a Grange Hall. In them days, we had one-room schoolhouses. Graduation was called Children's Day at the Grange Hall. The various school districts, single-room schools, would meet in June for graduation, and it was called Children's Day. When we went to Children's Day, or when we went to any celebration there, we were instructed by our parents—mother—when we were playing, 'Don't go over the wall and don't go where that rock is. Stay away from there. Don't you touch it, now, because of this awful thing that took place years ago.' "

Everett paused—I think he was checking to see if he had my undivided attention, which he did—then continued: "So, anyway, over there was this stone and there'd been several in the family, they had, uh, come down with some disease. Young and old! All of a sudden! And anything that they did didn't seem to stop it. Even those that didn't even live here, as far away as Ohio!"

"In the same family?" I asked.

"In the same family. Brother! Was comin' down with the same sickness. So, there was twelve men, as it's told to me, of the family that was left. They got together and they figured it was all their turn. This is it! And they got together and they took a vote, what to do. And they dug up one grave, not several. They dug up Mercy. For some reason they picked her, because there was something there that led it to that. Then, they dug her up and she had *turned over in the grave.*"

With his characteristic soft-spoken understatement, Everett interjected, "Well, right away, there's a lot of problems there," before continuing. "So they took her out and they cut her heart out. There was blood in the heart. Well, they decided they had to kill it, so they started a fire, not far from the grave—there was this rock here—and they burnt the heart, took the ashes and done something with 'em. I don't remember that stuff there. Them rocks there is what I was told—and my brothers and sisters—don't go over there and play around. Stay away from there. Stay away from the whole thing! That was the attitude of my mother, bringing us children up. But anyway, it seems as if that's what took care of it."

Seeming to anticipate my next question, Everett jumped in with an explanation. "You know, years ago you didn't have medicines, you didn't have nothin'. You had to figure out your own. They were self-independent people, everybody that lived here. There was no such thing as relyin' on somebody. You did it yourself."

I think Everett also needed to explain without resorting to the supernatural, and as much to himself as to me, how Mercy might have turned over in the grave. "Now, let me say one more thing on this. During my time—not their time, you know—when I was younger, a lot of people was buried and they never was embalmed. Today, you're dead when you're in the ground, because if you're not, they finish killing you when they embalm you. Years ago, you wasn't embalmed. You're dead, you're dead; and you're down in the ground, buried. And then—I'm sure you've studied it—then, you know, a natural death doesn't happen in a few minutes. It sometimes takes years. For an example, your fingernails and your hair—an animal or a person that is not embalmed, but buried—will still grow. Hair will grow and so will fingernails. Now, when this Mercy Brown was buried, there was no embalming. It's possible she weren't quite dead when they put her in there. Why was she turned over? Everything today is different than it was years ago."

Everett took the newspaper clipping that had been resting on my lap and held it up as he continued. "Now they have gone further, some of these, and hunted up dates and different things that I wasn't told and I can't tell you whether it's . . . you know, but, anyway. That is, in general, what happened. They even found the names of the brother, Edwin, and the father's name and some of the pieces that I didn't even know."

Turning back to the clipping and shaking it for emphasis, Everett said, "Now, what they do here, they change this around as if *I* believe in vampire. Now, that ain't what I'm saying'. I'm just revealin' what *they* believed and how they had to handle their own problems, see?"

"Do I believe?" Everett asked rhetorically. "I believe my mother. I believe the family did what they did." "Do I believe in vampire?" he repeated, adding the crucial word. "No. No, I don't believe in that. I'm not sure they did, but they had to come for an answer. And it turned out that maybe that was the answer. And some of them old people probably died with that in their mind, that they did the right thing."

Everett handed the clipping back to me so that I could see for myself and confirm his indignation. It was obvious as I read through the article that its author had indeed "hunted up dates and different things." He also at least implied that Everett, and practically everyone else in Exeter—past and present—believed Mercy was a vampire:

> Rhode Island's past hides many dark things but few are as chilling as what they did to Mercy L. Brown—and why.
>
> Mercy died, apparently of tuberculosis, in January 1892, and her tombstone can still be seen among those of generations of Browns in Exeter's Chestnut Hill Cemetery.
>
> But the pious epitaph on Mercy's stone has been thoroughly and cleanly erased.
>
> Mercy was a vampire.
>
> So her family and fri[e]nds believed, at least, and what they did about it is a matter of public knowledge.
>
> Mercy's brother Edwin was a strapping young man of 18, known as a person not usually subject to illness of any kind.
>
> In the fall of 1891, however, Mercy and Edwin

10

both became ill. The boy went off to Colorado, where he recovered. His sister eventually was carried to her grave by the illness.

Edwin returned to Exeter still in weak health, and when his condition became worse and stumped the doctors, a council of family and friends was called.

Why was such a strong young man's life draining away? Why had the same thing happened to Mercy only a few months before?

Whether by blind ignorance or horrified piety or something of both, it was unanimously decided that something hideous was at work on the family.

Nothing less terrible than a vampire was sucking their children's blood and taking their lives with it.

Because it seemed that the Browns were the only family being preyed upon, they came to the conclusion that the vampire spirit must be inhabiting the corpse of one of [t]he deceased members.

With Edwin finally conceding to the plan, three bodies were disinterred and examined for signs of the vampire.

To their infinite horror, Mercy's body, which had been buried for nearly three months, still had blood and seemed unnaturally preserved, with color still in the cheeks.

With minds frozen, the Brown men removed the corpse's heart and burned it on a rock that can still be seen near the grave.

They considered this not only a destruction of the vampire spirit inhabiting the body but also as an antidote for Edwin, whose doctor had prescribed the ashes to cure his illness. Edwin died shortly thereafter.

Lewis Peck of Sodom Trail, Exeter, is a descendent of those who performed that act on a grey March day in 1892.

"My grandmother was Brown," he says, "She and my mother always taught us never to touch that gravestone (Mercy's)."

Peck tells visitors about Mercy Brown only if they ask.

"I think almost everyone in Exeter today knows about Mercy. And a lot of people believe she was a vampire."

He himself had a frightening experience at the grave in the early 1960s.

"I was in back of the (Chestnut Hill Baptist) Church hall with a friend of mine. It was about 11:00 p.m. and suddenly we saw this great big ball of light right over Mercy's grave. I was scared to death—I've never seen anything like it before or since."

Peck says he later heard that psyc[h]ic phenomena of this type take place when there has been violence done to a gravesite.

"I don't know whether I believe she was a vampire or not," he says, "but my people did that awful thing.

"I don't know what I believe."

Everett's indignation seemed justified. For one thing, his unsolicited defense of the Browns and their neighbors as independent and self-reliant rang truer than either of the newspaper's alternative explanations. Neither "blind ignorance" nor "horrified piety" fit what I knew about the character of Exeter Yankees. As for "a vampire was sucking their children's blood," nowhere in Everett's tale was such a scene depicted or even suggested.

Taking my cue from this realization, I asked Everett, "Did they call them vampires in the story when you heard it?"

"No! No, it wasn't designated as a vampire. It was just, you don't go over there handlin' it and you leave it alone because this awful thing that had to be done."

Everett paused and looked down at the floor for a moment; he seemed to be replaying some memory. "Oh, yeah, I've been in places, people say, 'Here comes the vampire man.' And they go all through it, and, 'Ha, ha, ha.' It doesn't bother me because I don't ask them to believe it. I don't care if they do or not."

"When did they start calling it vampire, anyway?" I asked.

"I don't even know that. No. No, my grandmother and my mother never mentioned the word. I'm fifty-two years old and I never heard anybody talk about vampire until we got into *this . . . stuff . . . here.*" He provided emphasis by jabbing a finger at the words in the article.

Perhaps responding to the skepticism he had come to expect after countless repetitions of this story (even though I was *not* incredulous and hoped I didn't appear so), Everett volunteered some corroboration.

"And there's an old man livin' today who can remember one of the twelve. He's in his nineties. And his name is Brown. Reuben Brown."

Everett recalled being interviewed by a local television station some years back: "I told them just as it was told to me. So I said to the Channel 6, I said, 'If you really . . . think that I'm far-fetched here, well, there's one man livin' today that would tell you, 'cause my grandmother an' him is the same age (but she's dead).' But I says, 'You'd better call 'im, 'cause he may put you off the place. Maybe he won't talk to you.' So they call 'im and he says, 'Well, come on!' So they went down an'—an' he's in his nineties—an' he tol' 'em. He says, 'Yuh.' And they asked him if he *believed* in it and he said, "Tain't what I believed in, it's what *they* did.' You know, that was his answer." The fact that this was also Everett's "answer" certainly wasn't lost on me.

There was no way I could leave without inquiring about the ball of light reported in the newspaper article. Did they get that right, or was it just journalistic hype?

Everett's response indicated that, although the article's dating of the incident in the early 1960s was too late, the other essentials squared with his memory.

"My mother died, 47 years old, on her birthday. I was fourteen," Everett began. "Years later—well, couldn'a been too many, I was a young fella—my brother and I, we were out riding around one night, with a Model A coupe, you know. And it leaked a little bit, so we went up there to the pump, water pump; pump up water and put it in the radiator. And we swung around just right between that Grange Hall and that church, and 'course there's your cemetery over that wall and there's Mercy, the Brown cemetery, there. We saw a ball of fire, about that size—the size of a football. It was so bright that it was blue tinted. And I'd say it'd been off the ground, maybe as high as this table. 'Course we got outta there. I don't know what it is. Doesn't make any difference. We start down the road to a farmer, which is a different cousin—they're all dead now—and we were quite excited and told about it. And they laughed and said, 'Yeah. Other people have seen it. Yeah, they've seen it. You must be up around Mercy Brown's cemetery.' And that's about as far as I understand it, to be truthful, authentic about the whole thing. I have told this to several. And I've been asked several times to tell it, and didn't tell it because I didn't feel like talking. So, we go from there."

"So, you're riding around in this Model A and you stopped to get water and you see this ball of fire. What were you thinking?"

"It was time to get out," Everett responded, with his restrained smile again hinting at understatement. "That was the first thing. You weren't going to stay there. We were—I could have been, I might have been sixteen. Not old enough to have my license. If I was old enough, I didn't have my license. Neither one of us. 'Course we had our father's car and we weren't supposed to have it. But you know how kids are. Kind of country folks, and there weren't many houses here in them days, you know, like there is now. So, we just take a little ride now and then. Well, we did go out, but the radiator kept leaking, see, that's why we was in there. There's a hand pump out there where you get water. That's how we spotted that light over the fence. But other than that, I have never seen nothing. I go there, quite often. I go there at Halloween times . . . watch it [Mercy's gravestone], because somebody's gotta bust it, break off a hunk, tip it over. You know, Halloween time, I've gone there and set in the cemetery and wait for somebody to put their hand on it and I'd holler at 'em."

Everett was clearly angry and sad as he described some of the negative attention that Mercy's grave attracts. People were taking chips from the stone as mementos, and some were even placing tape recorders (which Everett referred to as "electronic soundin' devices") in her grave. Bewildered, this down-to-earth Yankee said, "They say they hear things. Well, now, damn, you ain't gonna hear nothin'. I don't imagine . . . there may not even be bones left!"

Everett shook his head and added: "Halloween night we had a cop there. This year, we had a cop up there. We had a town sergeant stay half the night. And people were comin' in around midnight to do something! Who knows what they're doin'?" (In 1996, Mercy's entire gravestone disappeared. What seemed most mysterious was that the stone was stolen in August, not October. Less than a week later, the stone was recovered.)

Everett then deftly tied together some of the threads that had been introduced but left dangling. With the following anecdote, he elegantly connected Halloween, legend trips (more about this later), supernatural occurrences, and journalists: "I had some reporters call me up one night, around Halloween. They wanted to know a whole lot about it, and I had decided I would explain a little. They wanted to meet with me, two girls. I met at the church. It was raining a little bit and they wanted to know if we could walk out and take a look at it. And I said, 'Sure.' So they walked ahead of me. And, when we got to the grave, they said, 'We don't see nothing wrong here.' And I said, 'Yeah, well look down and you'll see there's a light burning in her grave.' And, of course, they looked down. There was a light burning in the grave there, top of the grave. And they about panicked. Well, obviously, somebody had been there, prior, that night. And they had put in one of these little objects that glow at night—for a joke!"

I wondered if Everett knew of any other similar cases in the area. He nodded and said: "There was another family that experienced this same thing. Which would be about, I would say, close to a mile east of where this other one took place. There was another one, I've been told—which I didn't know at the time. I've heard of this since these paper clippin's. 'Cause I get letters from everywhere."

Everett made it plain before I left that afternoon that I had been a privileged guest: he had shared his knowledge of Exeter and his family with an outsider. Although I knew I wasn't the "someone" he referred to in the following explanation, I still felt a sting of recognition. Silently I vowed that I wouldn't betray his implicit trust in me.

"See, we don't have no true history of the town of Exeter. Out in the safe I probably have got much as anyone, and I won't hand it out. I wouldn't hand it out for a lot of reasons. And, uh, one of the reasons is, it's against my grain to have someone come into town, be here six months and know the whole town. And when you go to explain something, they treat you as if, well, who's this guy? Who's that fat old guy, he don't know nothin'. You know, and that—that don't go good. And so I decided when they come here, I didn't tell everything, just enough to let 'em know we *did* know, and that's it."

Everett laughed and added a final, chilling comment in reference to a well-known radio personality and writer of local history. "Fact, this mornin's paper, the writer, found her dead, in this mornin's paper. And I says, 'Well, I don't wish anybody dead but I ain't gonna cry over that one.' " And he laughed again.

Driving back to Providence I was on automatic pilot with my mind turned inward. Was Everett telling me just enough to let *me* know that *he* knew? How much of Everett's incredible story was true? If based on fact, how widespread was this practice? Was it confined to just this one family—tainted as was Poe's House of Usher or cursed with a "family peculiarity" like the bosom serpent in Hawthorne's short story—or had it occurred in other families, as Everett vaguely suggested? My folklorist's instincts—my academic training combined with years of fieldwork—told me that Everett's family tale grew out of an actual event, a conclusion reinforced by the newspaper clipping that Everett had shown me. I didn't have even the whisper of an inkling that the next two decades would find me absorbed, part-time but passionately, in an ever-widening search; that an amazing puzzle would evolve piece-by-piece, sometimes frozen for months, sometimes developing at a hectic pace. At this moment, my main concern was to find evidence of what really happened to Mercy Brown and her family in 1892. With a start, I snapped out of my trance as I realized I had arrived at the Old State House on Benefit Street, my home base. On the way back, I hadn't seen a single stone wall.

CHAPTER 2
Testing a Horrible Superstition

EXHUMED THE BODIES.
Testing a Horrible Superstition in the Town of Exeter.

BODIES OF DEAD RELATIVES TAKEN
FROM THEIR GRAVES.
They Had All Died of Consumption, and the Belief Was That
Live Flesh and Blood Would Be Found That Fed Upon the
Bodies of the Living.

With this front-page headline the *Providence Journal* introduced the Brown family to the world on Saturday, March 19, 1892. The melodrama didn't surprise me. Nor was I surprised, after reading the article following my interview with Everett, that the newspaper questioned the cultural refinement of those who exhumed the bodies. But I was taken aback by the harshness of the tone. I wondered what animosities had simmered beneath the surface more than a hundred years ago. Further investigation would show me that Mercy Brown's exhumation was a small skirmish in a much larger war of civilization versus superstition. And this war itself had several local fronts that pitted town against country, commerce and industry against agriculture, and urban Providence against the rural towns in southern and western Rhode Island. But I'm getting ahead of myself.

Despite the caustic tone of the *Journal* article, I was very pleased to find that Everett Peck's tale was grounded in history—not so much because it validated my instincts, but more because it presented a challenge that combined all of the elements that had steered me toward my rather off-beat profession in the first place. Looking at the front page of the *Providence Journal* assured me that Mercy Brown's story was not a dead end.

I was setting off on a trail that had no map, precisely where I wanted to be.

I expected the newspaper accounts of Mercy's exhumation to include much more detail than Everett's story, and I was not disappointed. As any folklorist knows, repeated oral recountings of a story, especially across generations, tend to smooth it out, eroding information not vital to its central plot. Beyond the details, such as names and dates, though, some of the discrepancies between Everett's rendition and the newspaper accounts are striking. The newspaper reported that the bodies of George Brown's wife and both daughters were unearthed—and there was no mention of Mercy having changed position in the grave.

Everett told me that "they dug up one grave, not several. They dug up Mercy. For some reason they picked her, because there was something there that led it to that . . . and she had turned over in the grave."

He said that Mercy's heart was cut out, then "they burnt the heart, took the ashes and done something with 'em. I don't remember that stuff there."

According to the newspaper, both the heart and liver were removed and burned, "and to make the cure certain the ashes of the heart and liver should be eaten by the person afflicted." Dr. Harold Metcalf, the medical examiner for the towns of Exeter and North Kingstown, whom the newspaper reported as being at the scene to evaluate the situation, did not know whether or not Mercy's gravely ill brother, Edwin, had ingested the ashes.

The *Journal* reporters fleshed out the Brown family tragedy with an abundance of detail acquired through interviews and research. In December of 1883, Mary Eliza, the wife of George T. Brown, a respected farmer in Exeter, Rhode Island, died of consumption, the term in common use for tuberculosis at that time. (I use the term "consumption" when I am referring to the sickness as it was understood in its historical context and "tuberculosis" when referring to the disease as it is understood in a biomedical context). Seven months later, his twenty-year-old daughter, Mary Olive, succumbed to the same disease. Within a few years, his only son, Edwin, gradually began losing his strength, color, and appetite. Alarmed, Brown took Edwin to the doctor, knowing painfully well from his recent experiences that a diagnosis of consumption was probably a death sentence. Edwin was sent to Colorado (not Ohio, as was implicit in Everett's story) in the hope that a change of environment would affect a cure or at least slow the course of the disease. When it became obvious that Edwin was getting worse, not better, he returned to Rhode Island. By this time, Brown's daughter, nineteen-year-old Mercy Lena, was obviously ill, too. Her consumption was diagnosed as the "galloping" variety, and she quickly passed away and was entombed in the family vault on Chestnut Hill (or Shrub Hill as it was then called by the locals) in January of 1892.

With no other hope to save his family, and urged by friends and neighbors, Brown turned to a folk remedy. An unidentified "local correspondent" for Rhode Island's largest newspaper told the following "story of the call for Dr. Metcalf to hunt out the vampire, and what occurred when the graves were searched":

"It seems that Dr. Metcalf attended Mercy Lena Brown during her last illness, and that a short time prior to her death he informed her father that further medical aid was useless, as the daughter, a girl of 18 or 19, was in the last stages of consumption. The doctor had heard nothing further from the family until about a year ago, when a man called on him and stated that Edwin A. Brown, a son, was in a dying condition from the same disease, and that several friends and neighbors fully believed the only way in which his life could be saved was to have the bodies of the mother and the two daughters exhumed in order to ascertain if the heart in any of the bodies still contained blood, as these friends were fully convinced that if such were the case the dead body was living on the living tissue and blood of Edwin. The doctor sent the young man back, telling him the belief was absurd. Last Wednesday the man returned and told the doctor that Mr. Brown, the father, though not believing in the superstition himself, desired him to come up to satisfy the neighbors and make an autopsy of the bodies.

"On Wednesday morning [March 17], therefore, the doctor went as desired to what is known as Shrub Hill Cemetery, in Exeter, and found four men who had unearthed the remains of Mrs. Brown, who had been interred four years [she had been dead for nine years]. Some of the muscles and flesh still existed in a mummified state, but there were no signs of blood in the heart. The body of the first daughter, [Mary] Olive, was then taken out of the grave, but only a skeleton, with a thick growth of hair, remained.

"Finally the body of [Mercy] Lena, the second daughter, was removed from the tomb, where it had been placed till spring. The body was in a fairly well preserved state. It had been buried two months. The heart and liver were removed, and in cutting open the heart, clotted and decomposed blood was found, which was what might be expected at that stage of decomposition. The liver showed no blood, though it was in a well-preserved state. These two organs were removed, and a fire being kindled in the cemetery, they were reduced to ashes, and the attendants seemed satisfied. The lungs showed diffuse tuberculous germs.

"The old superstition of the natives of Exeter, and also believed in other farming communities, is either a vestige of the black art, or, as the people living here say, is a tradition of the Indians. And the belief is that, so long as the heart contains blood, so long will any of the immediate family who are suffering from consumption continue to grow worse; but, if the heart is burned that the patient will get better. And to make the cure certain the ashes of the heart and liver should be eaten by the person afflicted. In this case the doctor does not know if this latter remedy was resorted to or not, and he only knows from hearsay how ill the son Edwin is, never having been called to attend him."

Despite Dr. Metcalf's assurances that the condition of Mercy's corpse was not unusual, "attendants" at the scene burned her heart and liver to ashes on a nearby rock. Edwin was said to have drunk the ashes in water shortly thereafter.

Just what was this disease, consumption, that was killing Edwin after taking down his mother and two sisters? If you set out to invent a baffling disease, you could hardly do better than tuberculosis. Multifaceted and constantly in motion, it is difficult to diagnose and often confused with other diseases. Although the name "tuberculosis" first appeared in print about 1840—in reference to the small nodules, or tubercles (from the Latin meaning swelling), that appear on the diseased tissues of those afflicted—the infectious organism, *Mycobacterium tuberculosis humanis*, was not discovered for another forty-two years. Tuberculosis has been known under a variety of names during its long history, including phthisis, Scrofula, asthenia, tabes, bronchitis, inflammation of the lungs, hectic fever, gastric fever, and lupus. It was also known as the great white plague, after the typical pallor of its victims. Prior to the twentieth century, it was most commonly called consumption, a term that also was applied to practically any chronic respiratory infection that produced coughing, expectoration of mucus, and aches and pains of the chest.

Tuberculosis most often involves the lungs, but it can attack the entire body. When resistance to infection is particularly poor, it can spread in a "miliary" pattern, where small granulomas (about the size of millet seed, thus "miliary") are transported from the site of primary infection through the blood and establish lesions in other tissues and organs. The disease may occur in the bones (mainly the thoracic and lumbar vertebrae, known as Pott's disease), genital tract, urinary tract, gastrointestinal tract, adrenals (destruction of the cortex leads to Addison's disease), heart, cerebrospinal nervous system, and the cervical (neck) nodes (known as Scrofula). Common symptoms include wasting fever, night sweats, breathlessness, pain in the side or shoulder, cough, abundance of sputum, and blood spitting.

A Neolithic grave, dating from 5000 BCE, near Heidelberg, Germany, contains the earliest evidence of tuberculosis in humans. Documentation from both mummies and tomb paintings shows that it was a common disease in Egypt by 4000 BCE. Tuberculosis was the subject of a hymn in the *Rig Veda*, a sacred text of India dating from 2500 BCE. About 460 BCE, Hippocrates identified phthisis as the most widespread disease of the times, noting that it was almost always fatal (and he warned his colleagues against visiting patients in late stages of the disease since their inevitable deaths might damage the reputations of the attending physicians!).

Detailed anatomical and pathological descriptions of the disease, and observations of its infectious nature, had to wait until the late seventeenth century. In 1679, Sylvius became the first to identify tubercles, and their progression to abscesses and cavities, as a consistent and characteristic change in the lungs and other areas of consumptive patients and, in 1702, Manget described the pathological features of miliary tuberculosis. An edict issued by the Italian Republic of Lucca in 1699 states that, "henceforth, human health should no longer be endangered by objects remaining after the death of a consumptive. The names of the deceased should be reported to the authorities, and measures undertaken for disinfection." English physician Benjamin Marten was the first to connect the pathology of tuberculosis to a possible method of contagion. In his 1720 publication, *A New Theory of Consumption*, he speculated that the disease could be caused by "wonderfully minute living creatures," which, once they had gained a foothold in the body, could generate the lesions and symptoms of the disease. He conjectured that "it may be therefore very likely that by an habitual lying in the same bed with a consumptive patient, constantly eating and drinking with him, or by very frequently conversing so nearly as to draw in part of the breath he emits from the Lungs, a consumption may be caught by a sound person."

Despite the high level of insight displayed by the likes of Marten, Sylvius, and Manget, those attempting to cure the disease were still grasping at straws. Early reported "cures" from physicians included warm sea air, milk from pregnant women, seaweed placed under the pillow, cold baths and deep breathing. Most of these proved to be fruitless, and it would be many years before any real cures could be found. Ancient literature, including the Bible, discloses that many people believed consumption was a form of punishment.

The introduction of the sanatorium was the first effective treatment of tuberculosis to gain wide acceptance. Hermann Brehmer, a German botany student suffering from tuberculosis, was instructed by his doctor to seek out a healthier climate. He travelled to the Himalayan mountains where he could pursue his botanical studies while trying to rid himself of the disease. He returned home cured and began to study medicine. In 1854, he presented his doctoral dissertation bearing the auspicious title, *Tuberculosis is a Curable Disease*. In the same year, he built an institution in the Alps, amidst fir trees, where patients were provided fresh air and wholesome food. His sanatorium became a model of treatment that spread throughout Europe and North America. In one of the most remarkable stories in the history of medicine, the sanatorium's nearly global reign as the most successful treatment for tuberculosis lasted almost one-hundred years.

In the meantime, advances in understanding the nature of the disease accelerated. In 1865, the French military surgeon Jean-Antoine Villemin demonstrated that tuberculosis could be passed from humans to cattle and from cattle to rabbits. On the basis of this revolutionary evidence, he postulated a specific microorganism as the cause of the disease, believing that he had established the contagious nature of tuberculosis, thus disproving the centuries-old belief that it arose spontaneously in each affected organism. But his report was little regarded and most people continued to believe that consumption was inherited, or at least predetermined.

All of this should have changed on March 24, 1882, the day bacteriologist Robert Koch announced that he had identified the organism responsible for consumption. When Koch presented his findings to the Berlin Physiological Society, showing that he had found the tubercle bacillus, had succeeded in cultivating it, and could infect animals by inoculating them with it, he confidently asserted, "In the future the fight against this terrible plague of mankind will deal no longer with an undetermined something but with a tangible parasite." But people, especially Americans, were wary. The *New York Times* took six weeks to acknowledge his work, and then poked fun at his discovery by suggesting that if human trousers were inoculated, people would be protected from broken legs. As encouraging as things looked in 1882, by the time Eddie Brown had contracted consumption, any optimism had been dampened by the failure of bacteriologists to deliver the cure that Koch's discovery seemed to promise. Koch certainly would have been disappointed had he known that it would be another sixty years before the tangible parasite, and not just its symptoms, was dealt with effectively.

The war on consumption enlisted an eclectic army of physicians, clergy, businessmen, community activists, and social reformers. By 1889, the National Tuberculosis Association, having fully accepted that tuberculosis was not directly inherited and was, therefore, preventable, set out to educate the public about bad food, impure air and unhealthy drinking water. People were advised against overcrowding in the home and working too hard. But the measures available to doctors were still modest. Improving social and sanitary conditions and ensuring adequate nutrition were all that could be done to strengthen the body's defenses against the tuberculosis bacillus. Sanatoriums provided a dual function: they isolated the sick, the source of infection, from the general population, while they enforced rest, which, together with a proper diet and the well-regulated hospital life, promoted the healing processes. A further significant advance came in 1895 when Wilhelm Konrad von Roentgen discovered x-rays, enabling the progress and severity of a patient's disease to be accurately followed and reviewed.

Despite these concerted efforts and significant discoveries, progress toward a cure was slow. Though many procedures were followed in attempting to control it, tuberculosis seemed to be an unstoppable disease. From the opening of sanatoriums until the 1940s, mainstream medical treatments included the use of iron salts, sodium chloride, calcium chloride, chlorine gas, and iodine. For a time, copper and gold salts were used even though they proved to have little or no value and, worse, also caused injuries to other parts of the body and the skin. After Forlanini observed that lung collapse tended to have a favorable impact on the outcome of the disease, a lung would be artificially collapsed under medical supervision (often through surgery), then rein-flated in the hope that this procedure would somehow rest the infected lung. On some occasions, ribs were removed, allowing pressure to be taken off the infected lung. Between 1910 and 1920, Calmette and Guerin developed a weakened form of *Mycobacterium bovis* (a close relative of the human bacterium) to produce Bacille Calmette Geurin (BCG). Beginning in the 1930s, BCG injections were administered to confer immunity and to help control the spread of tuberculosis.

In industrialized countries, tuberculosis did decline steadily in the first half of the twentieth century as the public became better educated in how the disease functioned and governments took steps to improve housing and alleviate poverty. Then, in the middle of World War II, came the breakthrough that would pose the greatest challenge to the germ that had threatened humanity for thousands of years—chemotherapy. The first trials of drug treatments for tuberculosis were carried out in the early 1940s with sulfonamides. Streptomycin was discovered in 1943, and the first patient was treated successfully with it the next year. Multi-drug treatment became standard within a decade, following the recognition of drug resistance when patients were treated with only one agent. It had taken a few thousand years to understand the full nature of tuberculosis. Only when antibiotics became more sophisticated did a real cure seem achievable. Between 1945 and 1960, progress to control the disease was remarkable, and the many sanatoriums began to close.

Eddie Brown, however, was born into a world of medical uncertainty and transition. In the years following the Civil War, the biomedical paradigm was consolidating its authority in the realm of medicine. By the close of the century, it was well on its way to doing away with the medical pluralism that had been the norm for most societies throughout history. In complex societies, such as America, empirical, lay, indigenous, and magico-religious traditions had provided alternative ways of dealing with sickness and healing. Nineteenth-century America had inherited a mixture of approaches based on astrology, religion, and folk cures. Unchallenged for centuries was the ancient Greek doctrine advanced by Hippocrates that the human body, like all of nature, was regulated according to the interaction of four basic elements. Nature was governed by the four elements of air, fire, water, and earth, and the human body was controlled by the interplay of the four "humors" of phlegm, choler, bile, and blood. Ill health resulted when these fluids or vapors got out of balance. To restore balance and good health, doctors would purge the digestive tract with cathartics and emetics or bleed the patient. The concept of "vitalism" posited that blood, the "paramount humor," contained the essence, or vital spirit, of the creature in which it flowed.

For the office of physician or doctor formal training was practically nonexistent. Barbers routinely performed surgery, sometimes bleeding patients to the point of death to get rid of "bad humors." Contagious diseases decimated populations which, in desperation, tried whatever remedies were offered, from roots and herbs to magical incantations. While the actual source of plagues, such as black death, malaria, cholera, yellow fever, and smallpox was unknown, there was no lack of scapegoats to accept the blame. Unseen demons were exorcised and suspected witches were tortured and burned.

About 1840, a surgeon described the medical profession:

> "It was heroic, it was murderous. I did not know anything about medicine, but I had enough common sense to see that physicians killed their patients, that medicine was no exact science, that it proceeded empirically and that it was preferable to put one's confidence in to nature and not in to the dangerous skill of physicians."

Indeed, illnesses ran their natural course and most of the afflicted survived, whether or not they received treatment.

New England has had a long (and continuing) history of self-treatment and treatment by lay healers, relying mainly on herbs and readily available household ingredients. The *New Guide to Health* by Samuel Thomson (1769–1843), a New Hampshire native, was enormously popular and ran through dozens of editions. Thomson prescribed the use of a small assortment of easily available and affordable ingredients. Democratizing medicine under the slogan, "Every man be his own physician," Thomson is credited with establishing America's first significant home-grown healing system. Itinerant healers worked the circuit throughout America, and even Europe, in the eighteenth and nineteenth centuries. They set up shop in town, advertised in local newspapers and broadsides (most of their ads included testimonies from cured patients), and moved on when business dropped off or, not infrequently, when run out of town by officials or dissatisfied clients. The following list of self-proclaimed specialists suggests the inclusive and unsettled nature of the healing profession at the time: physicians, surgeons, oculists, aurists, bonesetters, animal healers, botanic/Indian healers, pharmaceutical peddlers, medical electricians, and apparatus healers, cancer curers, and dentists and surgeon-dentists. But New England never warmed to itinerant healers, as a scholar of New England culture noted:

> New Englanders gathered to elect magistrates, to execute criminals, to ordain clergymen, to raise meeting houses, and to train militias—and not much else. Mountebanks, platform healers, Indian doctors, and herbalists may have been reduced to soliciting door-to-door and tavern-to-tavern in an informal underground network far removed from public acceptance and recognition.

While epidemics of consumption have ebbed and flowed for thousands of years, the disease began an alarming increase around 1730. By 1800, one of every 250 people in the Eastern United States was dying of the disease, accounting for almost twenty-five percent of all deaths. It remained the leading cause of death throughout the nineteenth century and well into the next. The symptoms of consumption progressed from a suspicious cough to the recurring hemorrhages that signalled certain death. The cough, frequent and bothersome in its early stages, became chronic with hollow rattles. An initial ruddiness of the face gave way to a deathlike pallor, which, at the very last stages of the disease, was masked by a glowing feverish flush. The mucus discharge changed color and texture from green to blood-streaked. As hemorrhaging became more frequent, the bloody discharge was measured first by teaspoons, then by cups.

Difficulty in diagnosing the disease facilitated its transmission and also led to identifying the "galloping" variety that Mercy

Brown and many others were supposed to have contracted. In many cases, a person could live a normal life, with little evidence of disease, right up to the final months or even weeks. Observers, alarmed at the apparent swiftness of the disease's course, failed to realize that it had been working, covertly, slowly and inexorably, to destroy its host over a period of years.

Consumption, perhaps better than any other disease, exemplifies Susan Sontag's assertion that "feelings about evil are projected onto a disease. And the disease (so enriched with meanings) is projected onto the world." Reflecting their own predilections as well as the attitudes of society at large, doctors, moralists, and reformers never seemed to tire of offering "explanations" for how one acquired the disease. Too much sex, overindulgence of food, drink or tobacco, unconventional behavior, lack of exercise, and even "a passion for dancing" were regarded as causes for consumption during the nineteenth century. The year that Mercy's body was exhumed, a physician wrote that the constitutional predisposition to tuberculosis "appears to be built up with equal certainty by impure air, drunkenness, and want among the poor, and by dissipation and enervating luxuries among the rich." If that were the case, then Mercy must have been deluged with impure air, for, certainly, she was no drunk, nor did she suffer from poverty or the overindulgences of wealth. Pragmatic physicians looked to the environment rather than behavior. In a speech to the Boston Board of Health in 1872, Henry I. Bodwitch discussed the geographic correlations of consumption. He argued that living in cold and damp places was the major cause of consumption. John Baron, whose *Illustrations of the Enquiry Respecting Tuberculosis Diseases* was published ten years later, seemed to echo Bowditch when he cited "cold, moisture, and bad food" as the major causes.

What cures and hope for recovery were medical practitioners offering their consumptive patients? If you judge by sheer numbers and kinds of treatments, they offered a great deal. But if you measure the effectiveness of these treatments, then, unfortunately, they were still groping in the dark. Under the heading

"Therapeutics" in the index to a recent book on the history of tuberculosis, the following subheadings indicate the great variety of approaches for treating the disease: bleeding, blistering, climatology, diet, drug regimens, exercise, leeching, open-air treatment, open health resorts, opium, poultices, purgatives and emetics, rest cure, sanatoriums, voyages for health.

In his *Consumption Curable, A Practical Treatise to Prove Consumption A Manageable Disease*, published in 1841, J. S. Rose advocated exercise (he specifically mentioned running), healthy living and diet, and attending to business where possible. Specific remedies recommended by others included shutting patients up in a closed room, removing them to distant climes, frequent horseback riding, incision of the chest wall to produce collapse of the lungs, inhaling warmed air followed by rubbing the chest with sulfuric acid, taking a solution of brown sugar in water, and, of course, the ubiquitous bloodletting or phlebotomy. In his fascinating book on blood, Douglas Starr observed that twenty-five hundred years is a long time for a useless practice, such as bloodletting, to endure. But, as he also pointed out, "It is important to realize in retrospect how paltry were the tools that doctors had available. Disease had always been frightening, a mystery, and practitioners had no idea how to control it. Bleeding gave them a sense of control, a feeling that they could do something, anything." Looking at the range of choices available through the medical establishment, it is not difficult to understand why some families turned to alternatives. And it is no wonder that George Bodington wrote, in 1840, that "consumptive patients are still lost as heretofore. They are considered hopeless and desperate cases by most practitioners, and the treatment commonly is conducted upon such an inefficient plan as scarcely to retard the fatal catastrophe."

Tuberculosis has been labelled "a disease of incomplete civilization." Civilization brought industrialization and urbanization, creating crowded and generally unhealthy environments. Incomplete civilization failed to eliminate the conditions favorable to the spread of tuberculosis. And it failed to achieve the implicit promise of civilization to find a cause and cure for all of humankind's afflictions. Medical science failed to understand and successfully treat microbial infection and contagion, not for lack of trying, but simply because they had not assembled the necessary body of clinical research. To be sure, the mortality rate of consumption had dropped by the end of the nineteenth century. But, as the following observation in the introduction to *Tuberculosis in Massachusetts*, published in 1908, implies, it was prevention, not cure, that reduced that statistic: "The former high mortality from consumption in Massachusetts and other New England states is well known. It was at first attributed to the severity of the climate, but later rather to various unhygienic conditions, such as vitiated air, poor food, and damp soil, and before the discovery of the active agent of the disease the mortality had been greatly diminished by improved hygiene."

Despite abundant speculation on causes and cures, and an endless number of remedies and treatments suggested by folk healers and establishment physicians alike, being diagnosed as a consumptive prior to the twentieth century was essentially a death sentence. In 1840, a physician wrote that cures for consumption "are scarcely ever heard of, and never expected. Despair seems to have taken full possession of the medical profession as regards this destructive disease." When consumption appeared in a community, there was genuine cause for alarm—and fear. Paul Barber, in his excellent book on vampires, wrote about the "sheer terror" that prompted people to seek—and find—vampires, as their friends and neighbors were "dying in clusters, by agencies that they did not understand." Death appeared to be contagious. MY NEIGHBOR DIED—AM I NEXT? Even though death is as inevitable now as it was then, it is hard for us to understand this fear of death because "epidemics do not usually rage out of control, at least in industrialized countries. Moreover, we have well-established methods to control them. We are no longer obliged to mythologize them in the same way," Barber wrote. Of course, today we would legitimately consider a fear of vampires to be irrational. But aren't we afraid of contagion? Fear of the dead may just express a broader notion of contagion—one that could include revenants as well as microbes—than the one currently holding sway.

Eddie Brown was on the brink of death in March, 1892. He first "began to give evidence of lung trouble" about two years before Mercy's death. According to a local newspaper, this "young married man of good habits" grew worse until, "in hopes of checking and curing" his disease, "he was induced to visit the famous Colorado Springs, where his wife followed him later on." Eddie Brown thus became one of a horde of health seekers flooding the arid climes hoping to be cured. The stimulus that attracted consumptives living in the cold, damp Northeast was, itself, largely folklore. The virtues of the "Western Eden" were extolled by a steady stream of personal experience stories and exaggerated anecdotes, passed along by word-of-mouth. The vigorous, outdoor way of life, combined with the healthful climate, would turn emaciated, diseased easterners into rugged, beefy mountain men. Entrepreneurs joined forces with railroad companies, empowered by the completion of the transcontinental railroad, to create new cities founded on the pursuit of healthiness. Begun in 1869 and fueled by a combination of folklore and boosterism, in a mere ten years, Colorado Springs was transformed from a desolate, semi-arid tract of several thousand acres into a fashionable, tree-lined health spa of three thousand residents.

Alas, Eddie was not to be one of the magically transformed. On February 26, 1892, Eddie's hometown newspaper published this notice:

> Our young fellow townsman, Eddie Brown, who has been tarrying at Colorado Springs about two years in pursuit of health, but without success except temporarily at times, has returned to R.I. accompanied by his wife, she having been with him a good part of the time to nurse and cheer him. They remained abroad until it became evident he could derive no more benefit there and then sadly and gladly started

> for their old home in Exeter, arriving at Wickford
> Junction per midnight train from Boston, the 23d
> inst. We learn that for the present they will stop with
> Mr. and Mrs. Willet Himes the parents of Mrs.
> Brown.

Eddie's coming home to die, and choosing who would attend to him, or "watch" with him, in his final days, was an important and long-standing social ritual. New England families did whatever was necessary to keep a loved one from dying alone. Those chosen to be "watchers" considered it a privilege. Neighbors took turns at the sickbed so that exhausted family members could sleep. "Watchers could administer medicine when needed, but, far more important, they provided a continuous comforting presence—as well as witnesses who could quickly gather the family around if death seemed imminent." Today, weakened social ties and fear of contagion have stigmatized the seriously ill. No longer "enmeshed in a web of concern," they are banished to hospitals where their care is delegated to strangers.

As the outcome of Eddie's condition became increasingly evident, George Brown faced a difficult decision. Would he "satisfy his neighbors" by having the bodies of his wife and two daughters exhumed and examined? We know that he did; the question is why. I arrived at a satisfying answer by assuming that (1) the people of Exeter (absent evidence to the contrary) were reasonable and rational human beings, and (2) nineteenth-century Americans were no less intelligent than their present-day descendants. It's easy to be lulled into the unsubstantiated belief that we are smarter than our ancestors, simply because we have access to the vast store of knowledge that has been assembled over the last century.

When I view this event through the eyes of George Brown, his son, and his neighbors, I will not put words into their mouths; and I will be cautious about putting thoughts into their heads. What I offer below are interpretations derived from a number of sources, with a New England and Rhode Island focus. Histories, genealogies, accounts from newspapers, medical history and the anthropology of healing, and studies of tuberculosis, folk medicine, and folk culture all have contributed to my understanding of what happened in the Exeter graveyard on March 17, 1892. The crucial event in that drama was George Brown choosing a course of action. I viewed his decision in relation to what that he surely must have felt: uncertainty, fear, desperation, community, hope, resolution, healing.

Residents of late nineteenth-century Exeter did not know that consumption was caused by a microscopic organism, they had never heard of, much less seen, a germ. Their doctors talked to them about catching it from other people and about family tendencies. Other healers in the region—lay, irregular, folk—had their own opinions. Some insisted that regular doctors could not cure this disease with their ordinary treatments because its cause was not ordinary. While most people didn't put much stock in the old wives' tales, they were cautious about outright rejection of received traditions. One point everyone seemed to agree on: they had attended too many funerals of family and friends, seen too many die before their time. When they asked how such things could happen, most received no answer. Disease and death were facts of life. Maybe only God knew why or where it would strike next.

Consumption was killing more people than any other single sickness. Nobody could do much to stop it. Sometimes a person who came down with it was fired from his job; sometimes he couldn't even get a haircut or shave because the barbers were afraid they'd get it, too. I cannot fault Brown's neighbors for worrying about consumption. Three of his family were dead from it, and one had a bad case. Everyone had seen it take hold in a family. And it might not stop after it killed them. It might spread to another family.

There were no disinterested bystanders in this community of less than a thousand people. Those who knew the Brown family were concerned about Eddie's health. When he returned from Colorado Springs, the local newspaper wrote: "If the good wishes and prayers of his many friends could be realized, friend Eddie would speedily be restored to perfect health." Neighbors were also worried about the wider implications of his illness: that it might become a full-blown epidemic. In helping the Brown family solve its problem they were protecting their own families. Theirs was a community where consensus took priority over rules and regulations administered by outside officials. The family and neighbors would consult to decide on a course of action— just as Everett Peck had told me during our interview.

Some of George Brown's friends dropped by to talk about how they might help Eddie get well and also stop the consumption from continuing on. Perhaps one of Brown's acquaintances told him about a problem he'd had in his own family some years back, and how he finally tried an old remedy that he concluded had saved the life of his family. When Brown heard about the procedure, he found the idea repulsive, and didn't think there was anything to it. His hometown newspaper reported that "the husband and father of the deceased ones has, from the first, disclaimed any faith at all in the vampire theory." Even the largely disapproving *Providence Journal* acknowledged that Brown had "no confidence in the old-time theory." But Brown agreed to talk it over with Eddie. After all, it was Eddie's life that was at stake. Father and son probably addressed several questions: Are there any other options? What if the old theory really works but we don't try it? Can we turn our backs on our friends and neighbors? What do we have to lose? Reluctantly, they agreed to let their friends undertake the procedure. Brown made it plain that neither he nor Eddie would be present.

Brown wanted to save the last remnant of his family. He could not rest knowing that he had not exhausted every possibility. How could he face the guilt if he said "no" and the epidemic continued? Brown and his community seemed aware that the disease could be transmitted from person to person, even though they did not understand how that occurred. So, there was an unspoken, tacit obligation to his family and his community to stop the contagion by whatever means were available. As head of the family, the decision rested with him. It is well-documented that people under emotional stress will turn to solutions not sanctioned by official systems more readily than they would if free of such pressure. It is clear that George Brown did not believe anyone in his family was a vampire. In characterizing the motivation for his course of action, we would be on firmer ground by substituting for "belief" one or more of the following terms: hope; desire; acquiescence; assent; possibility. These may be related to the concept of belief, but certainly do not require its existence.

In March, a young acquaintance of George Brown informed Dr. Harold Metcalf that Eddie was close to death from consumption. He told the doctor that "several friends and neighbors" were convinced that the bodies of Brown's wife and two daughters must be exhumed and their hearts examined. He said that any heart filled with blood must be destroyed because it was "living on the tissue and blood of Edwin." Dr. Metcalf dismissed the young man, telling him the belief was absurd. The same emissary returned to tell the doctor that Brown, "though not believing in the superstition himself, desired him to come up to satisfy the neighbors and make an autopsy of the bodies." Metcalf attended the "autopsies" in his official capacity as the Medical Examiner for the towns of North Kingstown and Exeter.

Thousands of years of Indo–European folklore have etched certain concepts into our culture. The blood is the life. The spirit is in the heart. Disease is an evil spirit that can infect even the innocent. Fire is cleansing. Like cures like. Embedded in myths, folktales, legends, ballads, proverbs, funeral customs, death rituals, and folk medical practices, these folk ideas are not "primitive survivals from a lower level of culture," as many nineteenth-century folklorists and anthropologists argued. Even now they continue to function in everyday life, subtly shading our orientation to the world. Beyond our awareness, taken for granted, or ignored, they may nevertheless initiate strategies for solving problems. George Brown shared in this inherited tradition. In his time and place, he was aware of two options. One, based on these familiar and ingrained concepts, though intellectually implausible and certainly abhorrent in implementation, offered a possible solution. The other said, in effect, stick with the medical establishment and choose death. Although the nineteenth century witnessed significant advances in the biomedical understanding of tuberculosis, they did not save Eddie Brown and thousands like him. By March of 1892, when Eddie's mother and sisters were exhumed, he was too far gone for any available treatment to work. He was just twenty-four years old when he died on May 2nd.

If we broaden our conception of healing beyond its strict biomedical borders, we might conclude that a family and community were healed even though the patient died. Folk medicine is successful because it treats the community along with the patient. The patient is not regarded as an autonomous organism requiring a cure. He or she is an integral part of a community, and a death is a loss to the community, a disturbance of the normal rhythm of life. The community enterprise—the community itself—is endangered. The practitioner must reunite and heal the broken community.

The *Providence Journal* was not so charitable in its assessment of this community.

> The shocking case of exhumation in one of the border towns of this state last week is, after all, only a rather more than usually striking illustration of a truth which cannot be denied, that the amount of ignorance and superstition to be found in some corners of New England is more than surprising to one who comes into contact with it for the first time. There are considerable elements of rural population in this part of the country upon which the forces of education and civilization have made scarcely any impression.

Superstitious, ignorant, uncivilized. These harsh labels seem unjust. It is possible for a reasonable community to accommodate magical acts. I think George Brown realized what role he was being asked to play and why. He knew that no one else could give his son, his family, and his community (himself included) what they required at that moment. Singled out by circumstance to be a folk healer, he reluctantly assented. There was nothing magical in George Brown's pragmatic decision.

CHAPTER 3
Remarkable Happenings

Sylvia Tory lived alone in a small cabin deep in the Ministerial Woods. The former slave was a "sibyl or fortune-teller or prophetess or spirit-medium or witch, just as one's fancy might call her," according to "Shepherd Tom" Hazard. The irony of an African-American fortune-teller living on lands granted in 1668 "to preach God's word to the inhabitants," was less than apparent in South Kingstown, Rhode Island, as Shepherd Tom and his two young companions paid a visit to Sylvia to have their fortunes told on a Sunday afternoon in 1820. With her head back and eyes shut, Sylvia spent an hour telling the fortunes of Hazard and Charles Barker—"more in truth than fiction," as far as Hazard could discern. "But when she came to Adam Babcock (then in robust health)," Hazard wrote, Sylvia's fluent predictions ceased abruptly:

> . . . not a word could he get from the old shriveled, gray-headed crone save, "Don't you by no means go east," which Sylvia repeated as often as Adam pressed her to say more, for some half a dozen times, without a word's addition or subtraction, "Don't you by no means go east!" which made Adam *mad*, but still he offered to pay her his quarter, the same as we did, which she persistently refused to accept, and on my asking the contrary old critter after Adam had gone outdoors, why she would not

tell him his fortune, the old witch shook her head oracularly and said that "that young fellow has no fortune to tell;" and sure enough, when Adam's indentures had expired, a week later, he went straight to New Bedford, some thirty miles due east of Sylvia's hovel, where he sickened in a few days and died a fortnight later.

Thomas Robinson Hazard (1797–1886) was a Quaker, Yale dropout, shepherd, woolen-mill owner, abolitionist, and story-teller. He also communicated with spirits through dreams and seances. And he was a member of one of the oldest, wealthiest, and most eccentric families in South County ("a self-willed race of independent thinkers," he termed them), no mean feat in a place where independence and idiosyncrasy were, if not a way of life, then at least defining characteristics. The numerous isolated boulders left by receding glaciers in southern Rhode Island are called "eccentrics" by geologists, and the behavior of its inhabitants often matches the landscape.

A few days before interviewing Everett Peck, I drove down to South Kingstown to do some fieldwork and to interview a man whose father had known Sylvia Tory and many of the Hazards. Oliver Stedman's firsthand knowledge of South County was praised as unsurpassed. As a lifelong resident of Peace Dale, ninety-year-old Stedman had witnessed the village's rise to textile man-ufacturing prominence (reaching its peak of 1500 workers during World War II), its subsequent decline, and its settling in as a quiet, residential community adjacent to the more urbanized Wakefield. Under the leadership of the Hazard family, the village had grown from a cluster of small water-powered mills in the eighteenth century to South Kingstown's foremost manufacturing center, producing fine woolens, including the highly regarded Peace Dale shawl. The Hazards were responsible for many of the fine architectural treasures of the village, named for Rowland Hazard's wife, Mary Peace. Shepherd Tom was one of their nine children. Another son, Joseph Peace Hazard, also became a "spiritualist" and, in 1884, built "Druidsdream" (his family's seaside compound that, according to his diary, he had constructed after a Druid appeared to him in a dream, instructing him to build a stone house on that site). About the same time, he built the "Witches Altar" (a tomb and monument surrounded by eight granite pillars in a cemetery in the Narragansett Pier area).

Though I hadn't yet interviewed Everett Peck, I already had a sketchy impression of the Mercy Brown story. But vampires were not foremost on my mind in the Fall of 1981. While I was hoping that Stedman might fill in the partial picture of the vampire incident that I had read about, I anticipated that our interview would cover a fascinating range of topics, from local characters and places, to mysteries and murders. Since I was just embarking on a two-year project to document the folklife of South County, I was casting a wide net. The project focused on the three cultural groups—Yankees, Native Americans, and African-Americans—whose interactions had shaped the traditions of South County (comprising eight of Rhode Island's thirty-nine towns and cities: Exeter, North Kingstown, South Kingstown, Narragansett, Richmond, Charlestown, Hopkinton, and Westerly). I was accompanied by James Clements, my intern on leave from his job as archivist at the Rhode Island Black Heritage Society.

On the way to Peace Dale, we drove past the Austin Homestead Farm, located between Breakheart Hill and Nooseneck Hill Road in Exeter. Records show that about a hundred years earlier, John Austin had 13,000 boulders taken from the fields and added to the existing walls! Looking at these walls, I couldn't help but contemplate Robert Frost's poetic observation, in "Mending Wall," that "good fences make good neighbors." I always interpreted this as an allusion to the character of New Englanders: independent, isolated, even aloof. But an equally convincing reading transposes Frost's neighbors and fences. Historically, in New England, good neighbors made good fences. Dry walls were not only repositories for rocks removed from planting fields, they also served as property boundaries and animal enclosures. Able-bodied men were mustered to repair fences held in common, and fines were imposed on those who neglected their private fences. Early settlers placed high value on good fences.

We stopped at the home of Russell Spears, on Kings Factory Road in Charlestown. Spears is a Narragansett Indian stone mason in his midsixties. As he labored on a fieldstone facade on the front of his house, we asked questions and photographed him working. Spears comes from a long line of masons; he learned the craft as an apprentice to his uncles Paul, Tom, and Frank Babcock, who, in turn, had learned from their father, Charles. And Charles's father also had been a stonemason. How far back, who knows? The historical record shows that white colonists had paid Native Americans to build stone walls as early as 1653. One who had learned the mason's trade was "Stonewall" John, one of the unfortunate Narragansetts massacred by Connecticut militia in North Kingstown on July 3, 1676, at Queen's Fort—a Native American village John helped build for old Queen Matatunk. More than two-hundred years later, Joseph Peace Hazard employed another well-known Narragansett stonemason, John Noka (or "No Cake"), to lay out and construct the stone foundations for his visionary "Druidsdream" and "Witches Altar."

The Stedman interview began with a lively mix of history and legend, incorporating African–American and Native American, as well as Yankee, folklife. A little more than half an hour into the interview, there was a pause while I changed the audiotape. It seemed an opportune moment to broach the subject of Mercy Brown. I hoped to elicit the story without being too conspicuous. Stedman's demeanor and dress (he was wearing a tie and jacket while we interviewed him in his own parlor!), suggested that he might balk at a direct inquiry. I didn't want to prejudice his delivery by labeling it a "vampire" story. Although I wasn't quite successful at avoiding the term altogether, with some patience—and the timely intervention of my intern, James—I was able to draw out a reluctant and halting narration of the event.

Fumbling for words, I asked, "What about the . . . I'm trying to think of what it was called . . . it happened in Exeter . . . I guess, the . . . vampire story?"

"Ah, haaa! I don't want to talk about that one. That's too gruesome. That's too gruesome altogether. You go up and see, uh, Everett Peck on that one."

"Everett Peck? Where is he?"

"He's up in Exeter. It actually did happen. It actually did happen." Stedman laughed nervously. "Yup, they did. They dug 'em up . . . yeah. And that wasn't too long ago!"

"When was it?" I asked, hoping that my ignorance would persuade Stedman to continue.

"Well, I think that was the latter part of the, uh, long about eighteen hundred and eighty-five or ninety. It wasn't what I would consider way back in the Revolution days."

"You were a young boy then." I was marveling at the fact that I was sitting face-to-face with a man who was alive when Mercy's body was exhumed, and whose father had firsthand stories about Sylvia Tory, the fortune-teller who was born into slavery in the eighteenth century and lived to the age of one-hundred and four!

"Yes. I think what happened, you see, those people back up in Exeter then—you didn't get around same as we do now. It wasn't too much populated up there, so they got away with that all right. But, yeah, they really believed that."

"I guess it was a matter of fear, huh?" This was my feeble attempt to overcome his obvious reluctance to continue.

"Yeah."

"Being afraid?"

"And they . . . " Stedman sighed. "Yeah, that's quite a story. What's his name, this Peck, knows right where it happened and everything." He emitted a short burst of nervous laughter. I was thinking that he wouldn't go on, especially when he repeated Peck's authority on the topic.

"He can tell you the whole story, but I say it's just too gruesome." Stedman paused, as if thinking about what happened. "I can't, I can't imagine a thing like that, can you?" His voice began rising in both pitch and volume. "I can't, I can't imagine!"

His urge to tell was bumping up against his sense of decorum. Stedman loved to share his knowledge of the past. He had recently published a four-volume collection of columns he wrote for the local newspaper, *A Stroll Through Memory Lane*. It consisted mostly of his own recollections of South County and South Kingstown. He *wanted* to tell the story. Yet, at the same time, he was worried about propriety. Here was a man who graduated from Yale, served four years as a naval officer, then spent fifteen years as a town councilman, state representative, and state senator.

With perfect timing, James jumped in to push Stedman over the brink. "I never heard the story."

"Oh, you never heard, you never heard it? It's been written up." Turning to me, he asked, "You've heard it, you've heard the story, haven't you?"

As I nodded yes, Stedman said, "Yeah. Yup!" I wasn't sure if he was confirming his suspicions that I knew the story or reaffirming that it actually happened—or both.

Again, James stepped into the breach. "Does that have something to do with witch haven or something like that?" Perhaps James was referring to Hazard's "Witches Altar."

"No." Stedman sighed again, but this time his tone was one of resignation. I think we all realized right then that he was going to tell the story.

"These, this family, they had, uh, several deaths in the family."

There was a matter-of-fact expression in his voice, as if he was now just a conduit for the tale, with no emotional stake in it, as though he didn't want us to think that he was, in any way, connected to what he was about to relate.

"One right after the other, it seems so. They thought there was . . . " Stedman paused between each phrase, "something . . . about it . . . some . . . vampire." The word did not come easily, his discomfort obvious. He chuckled nervously, "they called. . . . "

More pausing and stammering. "I, I, . . . but then they, they did . . . after three or four of them had died . . . in the cemetery . . ." Now his words were coming out uncoupled, fragmented verbal images of a picture I supposed he was seeing in his mind. "And they, one night they got together, and they went over and they dug them up. . . . "

There was a moment of silence. When Stedman continued, his voice was solemn and matter-of-fact. "And they found, in one—this most recent one that had died—they [the following phrases were delivered one at a time, accentuated by their singularity] found . . . blood . . . in her heart. And they went and cut the heart out, and burned it, there. Well. Then they figured the whole thing was all over. It was all right. They'd, they'd fixed it. There'd be no more vampire."

Stedman returned to his regular speaking voice. "That's just a sketchy idea of it. That's about what the story was. You know. You read it." Both the volume and pitch of his voice rose sharply. "It's been printed. And it actually happened! No doubt!"

I asked about details, the procedures employed, hoping he would continue.

"I don't know how it was done, but, by God, I can't imagine anybody doing it, can you?" His voice rose again, strong, almost a laugh. "Ha, ha, haaa! Dear, I can't imagine anybody doing it, but, by any rights, it was done, I guess. Yeah. That's one, that's, that's quite a well-known story around, around South County, yeah. Yep."

After my interviews with Stedman and Peck, I made a list of questions. If those involved did not use the term "vampire," then on what grounds could outsiders justifiably use it? How widespread was this practice? Was it confined just to some quirky corner of Rhode Island? Did it actually extend throughout New England, and perhaps to other American regions? Where did the tradition come from? How did Rhode Island country folk learn about it? What are its underpinnings in folklore and history? How does it fit into larger systems of healing, belief, worldview, and religion? Why did this act seem to threaten certain groups of people, such as newspaper editorial writers? I realized that this pursuit of vampires would not be simple and direct. It would entail more than simply locating old documents and newspaper articles. Reconciling this "gruesome" practice with the prosaic life of Yankee farmers proved more of a struggle than I had imagined. Even the *Providence Journal* articles of 1892 raised more questions than they answered. The *Journal* introduced the vampire issue by rebuking their "local correspondent" for not correcting his informants' mistaken omission of the term:

All mention of "the vampire" is omitted from this account of the exhuming, but this signifies nothing. The correspondent simply failed to get to the bottom of the superstition. The files of the *Journal* when reference is made in them to the practice of the tradition in Rhode Island, without exception speak of the search of the graves in such cases as attempts to discover the vampire. The last illustration of the practice was six or seven years ago in the same county, and it was then so described. Previous accounts of the digging up of the bodies for the same purpose are also inspired by the vampire theory. Otherwise the analogy between this case and those which occurred in Europe in the 18th century is perfect, except in the terrible suggestion that the patient must take the ashes of the vampire internally to be cured. These ideas are not, so far as can be learned, based upon any form of the European tradition. The books and authorities of Europe do not connect the theory with consumption, nor, in its logical turn upon that application, with the victim's eating the vampire. This presentation of the theory must be of American or Rhode Island origin, and most likely it can be claimed as the exclusive possession of Rhode Island country people. It is horrible to contemplate, and the local correspondent can hardly be blamed for attributing it to the Indians. It seems very odd that South County people alone should ever had re-gendered and accepted such fancies.

The article corrected the correspondent's oversight by quoting the *Century Dictionary*'s definition of "vampire," citing Calmet's dissertation on the vampires of Hungary, and then offering an extended description of vampirism. The excerpt above suggests the practice was not uncommon in Rhode Island—was, perhaps, the "exclusive possession of Rhode Island country people." Yet, elsewhere the article claims that it was found in other parts of New England:

How the tradition got to Rhode Island and planted itself firmly here, cannot be said. It was in existence in Connecticut and Maine 50 and 100 years ago, and as far back in some cases as the beginning of the 18th century. The idea seems never to have been accepted in the northern part of the State, but every five or ten years it has cropped out in Coventry, West Greenwich, Exeter, Hopkinton, Richmond and the neighboring towns.

It was apparent that I would have to cobble together this story bit by bit. I thought of how Russell Spears, without mortar, built a coherent wall, functional yet beautiful, from a jumbled pile of fieldstones. How, without obvious effort, he eyeballed the rubble pile and selected the stone that fit with little or no trimming. I was told that, if chosen and arranged properly, the stones in the completed wall would sing to the builder. And I recalled another line from Frost's "Mending Wall": "We have to use a spell to make them balance." My search for answers began with the narrative equivalent of Spears' pile of stones: Stith Thompson's six-volume *Motif-Index of Folk Literature (1932-1936)*.

Motifs are the smallest fixed narrative elements that, when pieced together, create folktales, legends, ballads, myths, and other types of folk stories. In his pioneering work, Thompson used a decimal scheme to classify these recurring units, progressing from the mythological and supernatural toward the realistic and humorous. The letter E lists all motifs concerned with the dead. E250 incorporates bloodthirsty revenants (that is, those who return from the dead). E251 is vampire, a "corpse which comes from the grave at night and sucks blood." Included under this motif are numerous cross-references, showing that vampires appear in stories from Germany, England, Lithuania, Greece, the Slavic countries, Assyria, India, Indonesia, the West Indies, and Native cultures from both North and South America.

Two of Thompson's numerous cross-references caught my immediate attention since they related to New England. Although George Lyman Kittredge, in *Witchcraft in Old and New England*, did not mention Mercy Brown (or any other similar case in New England), he illustrated the diversified nature of vampire folklore and suggested some possible links between British and American traditions. It would take a few years—and the extraordinary archaeological discovery of an exhumed corpse along the Connecticut–Rhode Island border (which I describe in Chapter 8)—for me to appreciate the full significance of the following story:

> William Laudun, a brave English knight, came to Gilbert Foliot, then Bishop of Hereford (as he was from 1149 to 1162), and asked counsel: "A Welsh wizard (*maleficus*) recently died in my town. Four nights later he came back, and he keeps coming every night, calling by name certain of his former neighbors, who instantly fall sick and die within three days, so that but few of them are left." The bishop suggested that the evil angel of this dead villain had perhaps reanimated his body, and advised

the knight to have it dug up and beheaded, and then buried again after the grave had been sprinkled copiously with holy water. All this proved of no avail, and at length the name of Sir William himself was called. Seizing his sword, he pursued the demonic corpse to the churchyard, and, just as it was sinking into the grave, cleft its head to the neck. There was no further trouble. We have here, to all intents and purposes, a case of vampirism, and it is noteworthy that the vampire was a wizard in this life. Other instances of vampirism in the twelfth century are recorded by William of Newburgh.

I made a note to follow up the William of Newburgh reference and continued on to Kittredge's next indexed entry under "vampire," which was a discussion of the various creatures who get blamed when a cow stops giving milk. I knew that witches were commonly accused, and the inclusion of goblins, fairies, and imps was not startling. Such are the vagaries of folk tradition. But vampires? Kittredge's provocative link between milk and blood seemed to foreshadow recent oral-erotic, Freudian interpretations of the vampire:

> The German vampire who so impressed the imagination of Henry More, varied his ghoulish pranks by draining the cows dry. Witches may take away the milk of a nursing mother; they may even suck her breasts till the blood come—just as they can make cows give bloody milk. Sometimes, too, they suck the blood of infants. Such were the *striges* of antiquity, who were hags or demons in bird form.

Kittredge's connecting of striges, lamiae, witches, and other blood-sucking demons pointed me toward a resolution to my questions about the vampire figure in folklore and history.

Thompson's other reference was eye-catching, indeed. In

"The Animistic Vampire in New England" (*American Anthropologist*, 1896) George Stetson counted at least ten instances of vampirism in South County alone! Stetson wrote:

> In New England the vampire superstition is unknown by its proper name. It is believed that consumption is not a physical but a spiritual disease, obsession, or visitation; that as long as the body of a dead consumptive relative has blood in its heart it is proof that an occult influence steals from it for death and is at work draining the blood of the living into the heart of the dead and causing his rapid decline.

Stetson links Old and New World patterns, observing that in Turkey, Hungary, and Russia, "the vampire does not stop his unwelcome visits at a single member of a family, but extends his visits to the last member, which is the Rhode Island belief." I also saw a connection between Kittredge's "evil angel" that "perhaps reanimated" the Welshman's body and Stetson's observation that New Englanders regarded consumption as a spiritual visitation rather than physical disease. Stetson cites rural Rhode Island as a hotbed of the belief:

> By some mysterious survival, occult transmission, or remarkable atavism, this region, including within its radius the towns of Exeter, Foster, Kingstown, East Greenwich, and others, with their scattered hamlets and more pretentious villages, is distinguished by the prevalence of this remarkable superstition.

My excitement over finding evidence of the tradition's prevalence was tempered by Stetson's tactful use of blanks instead of family and place names. How would I fill in the blanks?:

> The first visit in this farming community of native-born New Englanders was made to _____ a small

seashore village possessing a summer hotel and a few cottages of summer residents not far from New-port—that Mecca of wealth, fashion, and nineteenth-century culture. The _____ family is among its well-to-do and most intelligent inhabitants. One member of this family had some years since lost children by consumption, and by common report claimed to have saved those surviving by exhumation and cremation of the dead.

In the same village resides Mr. _____, an intelligent man, by trade a mason, who is living witness of the superstition and of the efficacy of the treatment of the dead which it prescribes. He informed me that he had lost two brothers by consumption. Upon the attack of the second brother his father was advised by Mr. _____, the head of the family before mentioned, to take up the first body and burn its heart, but the brother attacked objected to the sacrilege and in consequence subsequently died. When he was attacked by the disease in his turn, _____'s advice prevailed, and the body of the brother last dead was accordingly exhumed, and, "living" blood being found in the heart and in circulation, it was cremated, and the sufferer began immediately to mend and stood before me a hale, hearty, and vigorous man of fifty years. When questioned as to his understanding of the miraculous influence, he could suggest nothing and did not recognize the superstition even by name. He remembered that the doctors did not believe in its efficacy, but he and many others did. His father saw the brother's body and the arterial blood. The attitude of several other persons in regard to the practice was agnostic, either from fear of public opinion or other reasons, and their replies to my inquiries were in the same temper of mind as that of the blind man in the Gospel of Saint John

(9:25), who did not dare to express his belief, but "answered and said, Whether he be a sinner or no, I know not; one thing I know, that whereas I was blind, now I see."

At _____, a small isolated village of scattered houses in a farming population, distant fifteen or twenty miles from Newport and eight or ten from Stuart's birthplace [Gilbert Stuart, whose portrait of George Washington appears on the one-dollar bill, was born in North Kingstown], there have been made within fifty years a half dozen or more exhumations. The most recent was made within two years, in the family of _____. The mother and four children had already succumbed to consumption, and the other child most recently deceased (within six months) was, in obedience to the superstition, exhumed and the heart burned. Dr. _____, who made the autopsy, stated that he found the body in the usual condition after an interment of that length of time. I learned that others of the family have since died, and one is now very low with the dreaded disease. The doctor remarked that he had consented to the autopsy only after the pressing solicitation of the surviving children, who were patients of his, the father at first objecting, but finally, under continued pressure, yielding. Dr. _____ declares the superstition to be prevalent in all the isolated districts of southern Rhode Island, and that many instances of its survival can be found in the large centers of population. In the village now being considered known exhumations have been made in five families, in the village previously named in three families, and in two adjoining villages in two families.

The latter case, with some discrepancies, seems to fit the Brown family. Chestnut Hill is about eight miles from Gilbert

Stuart's birthplace (now a museum) on Snuff Mill Road, in North Kingstown. The mother and two (not four) children had succumbed to consumption, and the body of Mercy, the "child most recently deceased" was exhumed and "the heart burned." The Dr. _____, "who made the autopsy" and found the body to be "in the usual condition" certainly could be Metcalf. Perhaps Stetson is referring to Eddie when he writes that he learned of the death of "others in the family." And the remark that the father at first objected and only later, under pressure, reluctantly assented to the procedure agrees with newspaper accounts.

Stetson left few footprints. Any published sources he might have used went unacknowledged. He seems to have gleaned his information about South County's "remarkable superstition" from interviews with people in the community, probably sometime around 1895. Stetson's article concurs with the *Providence Journal* article of March 21, 1892, in suggesting that the vampire tradition was not rare in the region, and that the locals "did not recognize the superstition even by name," nor did the doctors believe in its efficacy.

In the Fall of 1982, almost exactly one year after I interviewed Oliver Stedman and Everett Peck, I discovered the Arnold Collection in a neighborhood branch of the Providence Public Library. This fascinating and unindexed hodgepodge of old newspaper clippings and typed sheets was housed in numerous three-ring binders. A bookplate inside the first of the numbered binders read:

In memory of James Newell Arnold
born Aug. 3, 1844—died Sept. 18, 1927
A searcher of records
A careful historian
A lover of the past
Whose life was given to perpetuating its lesson

The binders have labels such as "Anecdotes of South County,

RI," "Town Notes," "Poems" (which include broadsides and ballads), and "Tombstone Records."

A yellowed newspaper clipping pasted into Scrapbook 7 grabbed my attention. The unattributed text was headlined, "The Vampire Tradition," with the date "December 23" just beneath. (The clipping's juxtaposition to other clippings describing events whose dates I could determine suggests that the article was probably published in a Rhode Island newspaper, though not the *Providence Journal*, in 1890 or 1891.) The anonymous author buoyed my spirits, providing yet further testimony that the practice of the vampire tradition in rural Rhode Island, as well as Rhode Islanders' knowledge of it, was much more widespread than official records would indicate. But that apparent fact also contained the seeds of looming frustration. As the author insinuated, the vampire trail consisted mostly of "stories told by old people" or written "allusions" and condensed "newspaper sketches." I could expect sanctioned records, such as "regular histories" and official documents, to be free of references to this tradition.

The author noted that, in every case he knew of, "the tradition has been that a deceased consumptive in a family has been possessed of a vampire that has fed on the living of such a household." He asserted that, "until a score of years ago," this "ghastly belief . . . was so firmly held in western Rhode Island that occasionally the dead was disinterred and the heart and associated parts of the cadaver removed, to be burned as the dwelling place and shape of the vampire." Because "nobody cared to spread the view that such an evil power had appeared in his family," then "the least noise made about the performance . . . the better." Besides, since "the burials were in family or remote country plots, the formalities necessary to secure disinterment were nil." The author argued that "the unaccountable, mystifying and weird vampire tradition" had as much claim as "the records of a scientifically historical past" to be included in any history of the state, since both had something to say about "the essential intellectual and spiritual fibre of the people of Rhode Island." To a growing list of "speculations as to the origin of the tradition," he added two more: "the French Huguenot settlers who lived at Frenchtown, below East Greenwich, in the early part of the eighteenth century" and the "very singular people [who] settled Rhode Island, and . . . brought out of Old England some of the oldest of its dark traditions." The author briefly described the last reported case, which he said occurred in 1888 or 1889, but did not provide the details that would have allowed me to undertake further investigation.

I checked the "regular histories" of Rhode Island as a matter of course and found, as predicted, no vampire references. The newspaper columnist James Earl Clauson kept me on the trail with two faint tracks. Most of his 1937 article entitled "Vampirism in Rhode Island" is a retelling of the Brown family incident. What a shame that he gave no clues to his sources. He wrote of Edwin Brown: "A photograph we've seen shows him a big, husky young man." What wouldn't I have given to see a likeness of Eddie Brown! Apparently Clauson was unaware of the 1892 *Journal* article, since he records that the hearts of all three exhumed bodies were burned. He does not know the date of the incident, writing that "the peculiar rite we have described occurred not longer ago than 1890." Clauson also makes reference to a case from Jewett City, Connecticut, and provides the following provocative tidbit: "The late Sidney S. Rider, historian and antiquarian, tells of a similar case in these plantations about the time of the outbreak of the Revolution. Unfortunately for record purposes he fails to locate it with any exactness."

Enter Alphonsus Joseph–Mary Augustus Montague Summers. A fascinating character, Montague Summers (1880–1948), after ordination as a deacon in 1908, left the Church of England to become a Roman Catholic curate. But it was his research and writing on a broad range of supernatural topics, including witchcraft, werewolves and vampires— combined with a curious blending of denunciation and belief in such matters—that earned him an enduring reputation. His thesis was that religious and governmental institutions were covering up actual cases of vampirism. In *The Vampire in Europe* (1929), his second book on the subject, Summers mentions two more new (to me, at any rate) cases and gives some particulars for the Jewett City case.

> During the year 1854 the *Norwich* [Connecticut] *Courier* (U.S.A.) reported some remarkable happenings which had taken place at Jewett, a neighbouring town. In 1846–7 a citizen of Griswold, Horace Ray, had died of consumption. Unfortunately two of his children, young men, developed the same disease and followed him to his grave, the younger and last of these passing away about 1852. It was found that yet a third son was a victim to the same fatal disease, whereupon it was resolved to exhume the bodies of the two brothers and cremate them because the dead were supposed to feed upon the living; and so long as the dead bodies in the grave remained entire the surviving members of the family must continue to furnish vital substance upon which these could feed. Wholly convinced that this was the case, the family and friends of the deceased on 8th June, 1854, proceeded to the burial ground, exhumed the bodies of the deceased brothers and having erected a great pyre, burned them there on the spot.

Summers offers a brief account of yet another incident in Rhode Island, then extends the range of vampirism in America to Chicago:

> *The Providence Journal* in 1874 recorded that in the village of Placedale, Rhode Island, a well-known inhabitant, Mr. William Rose, himself dug up the body of his own daughter and burned her

heart, acting under the belief that she was exhausting the vitality of the remaining members of the family. In the following year Dr. Dyer, one of the leading physicians of Chicago, reported a case which came under his own observation. The body of a woman who had died of consumption, was taken from the grave and burned, under the belief that she was attracting after her into the grave her surviving relatives.

There is no Placedale in Rhode Island, so I wondered if the reference might be to Peace Dale, located in the heart of South County.

A year on the vampire trail had uncovered the following: there were perhaps ten cases in Rhode Island alone, centered in South County, including the families of Brown (1892) and Rose (1874); the practice extended to nearby Connecticut (Jewett City is just across the state line from Exeter) with the Ray family (1854), and maybe well beyond to Maine and even Chicago; the time frame ranged from perhaps the early part of the eighteenth century up to 1892; the procedures employed varied from burning the heart (and sometimes "associated parts") to the entire corpse. Even though the amount of actual documentation was still meager, the results of my search were satisfying and the prospects encouraging.

CHAPTER 4
The Cause of Their Trouble
Lay There Before Them

A disembodied voice found its way through a wall of vegetation framed by laurel and swamp maples. "I can't see anything!" Standing on the edge of Mooresfield Road, I shouted, "Come on out!" Brian Hokeness, my intern in the Summer of 1994, emerged from the thick underbrush. He was dripping with sweat and had scratches on his bare arms. Honeysuckle was grabbing at his ankles. "Watch out," I cautioned, as I guided him toward the cleared shoulder of the road, away from the poison ivy poking through the narrow dirt-and-gravel apron that separated asphalt from wilderness.

If I believed in omens, I would conclude that we weren't supposed to find the remains of Ruth Ellen Rose, or even South Kingstown Historical Cemetery #11, and let it go at that. But, having no history of supernatural experiences, and being somewhat stubborn, I said, "I'll try again in the Fall, when some of the brush has died and the visibility's better. Clippers would be a big help." It was hard to believe it had been twelve years since I discovered that the Rose family had a vampire problem, and I still hadn't found the grave. I'd learned patience. So many trails I've followed have led to dense wilderness or, worse, dead ends.

I'm not the only one this has happened to. In February, 1975, Raymond McNally was in Rhode Island to address a University of Rhode Island honors colloquium on aging, dying and death. Three years before, McNally and Radu Florescu had coauthored *In Search of Dracula*, a description of their search for the historical Dracula, Vlad Tepes, after whom they claimed Bram Stoker modelled his fictional vampire. This connection is not universally accepted. In *Dracula: Sense & Nonsense*, Elizabeth Miller writes: "Count Dracula and Vlad the Impaler. Never has so much been written by so many about so little." Then, in 1974, McNally wrote *A Clutch of Vampires*, a cursory treatment of a variety of vampire cases, including Mercy Brown, drawn from the *Providence Journal* account of 1892, and William Rose. While in South County, McNally and *Providence Journal-Bulletin* staff writer Fritz Koch went in search of the Rose family vampire, presumably interred about seven miles south of Mercy's gravesite. Koch described their quest in the newspaper.

And in Peace Dale, William Rose disinterred the body of his daughter in 1874, cut out the heart and burned it to prevent further attacks from her grave on the living family members. . . .

A hired hand at a handsome old estate on Rose Hill Road said he knew where the Rose family burial ground was and, sure, he'd be glad to take us there himself. After he joined the expedition, he was politely informed that our "interest in local history" had to do with vampires. But, proving a bit of an occultist himself, he said he, too, had heard of the incident. He guided the party up Rose Hill Road several hundred yards to a cemetery, set off in the woods and surrounded by a chest-high stone wall. The sound of a gate latch snapping shut startled, but did not deter, the searchers.

"I've got it," McNally cried suddenly, rushing forward to a large gray stone marked "William Rose" and pointing to engravings that indicated the man would have been just about the right age in 1874 to dig up his daughter's grave.

A thorough search of the graveyard, however,

failed to turn up the resting place of the daughter. The group beat a hasty retreat, delivering the professor to the University just in time to deliver his 4 p.m. lecture.

More than a month before we were thrashing about in the swamp maples, I had asked Brian to write to McNally in the hope that he could fill in some of the information hinted at in the *Journal-Bulletin* article. McNally included the following in his reply:

> I know that William Rose dug up the body of his daughter in 1874 and burned the heart of the corpse, because he thought she was a vampire. I visited the Rose family graveyard; there I was told that rumor had it that William Rose was involved in Druid rituals. I was even shown what was purported to be an altar on which he performed sacrifices.

The mention of Druid rituals and altars triggered my memory— but it didn't connect with William Rose. It was, rather, Joseph P. Hazard's "Druidsdream" (built about 1884) and "Witches Altar" (built in the late 1800s). Obviously, this was a matter that begged for further investigation.

Brian and I began our ill-fated attempt to locate the grave of William Rose's daughter in the cemetery book at the South Kingstown Town Hall. We noted the four cemeteries that seemed promising and set out with list and map, full of hope. We found no Roses, but I did spot the gravestone of William E. Peckham (1860–1884). After photographing the headstone, I told Brian that I had heard from students at the University of Rhode Island (located in the village of Kingston about two miles east of the cemetery), who said that Will Peckham's ghost was seen wandering about the campus. Much of the land on which the university campus is built was part of the Oliver Watson Farm, not the Peckham Farm as the campus newspaper erroneously claimed. But Jeremiah G. Peckham (1826–1908, buried in the Peckham Lot; William's father?), a banker and farmer, was one of the trio of South Kingstown figures who established, in 1888, what became the University of Rhode Island in 1892. According to the legend, William Peckham killed his wife, Nancy, because he thought that she was being unfaithful. He was found guilty and sentenced to be hanged on July 11, 1884, the date on his tombstone. About a year after his execution, evidence came to light that he was innocent.

The haunting and subsequent legend apparently began after a seance was held in the cemetery by members of the Chi Phi fraternity. According to the campus newspaper, the fraternity brothers, unaware of any details of Will Peckham's life, went to the cemetery in 1962:

> It was a warm summer night, but the wind was still blowing strongly. They had brought a candle with them and were using it during the seance and the calling up of the spirit. It was lit on the tombstone of Peckham, but despite the strength of the wind, the flame did not flicker at all.
>
> During the seance one of the participants in a voice not his own, called out the name 'Nancy', and began crying violently. Later, when questioned, the individual didn't remember anything about the incident except arriving at the Peckham family [burial] plot earlier in the evening.
>
> In the ensuing weeks there were several incidents involving loud noises, moving furniture and disappearing items reappearing in unusual places.

In 1965, two additional seances were held in the fraternity house for the purpose of banishing Peckham's ghost:

> ". . . all power in the house was cut off, the candle went out and the room became extremely cold. The same individual became possessed and this time

cried out in a voice not his own, 'no, no, no, . . not
any more!' "

I told Brian that there were some problems with this story, the
major one being that Will Peckham could not have been executed in 1884. The last person executed in Rhode Island was
John Gordon, fifteen years before William Peckham was born!
(Some years later I searched the Rhode Island Historical
Cemeteries Database and found no Nancy Peckham that would
fit the time frame.)

The stories of Will Peckham and John Gordon show some
interesting similarities, including the hanging of an innocent
man and subsequent seance by college students, that suggest
they may have mingled in the legend conduit. Amasa Sprague,
a businessman and manufacturer from a politically powerful
family, left his stately Cranston home one day in December,
1843, to travel to Johnston. The following morning, his bludg-
eoned body was found beside the road, almost within sight of
his mansion. Gordon, an Irish immigrant and employee at the
mansion, had been seen arguing with Sprague the day he was
killed. Gordon was tried, found guilty of murder on the basis
of circumstantial evidence, and hanged in 1845. Evidence later
came to light that proved his innocence. Public indignation
following John Gordon's execution led to legislation abolishing
capital punishment in Rhode Island. The actual killer was
never found.

For many years, Sprague Mansion, now the home of the
Cranston Historical Society, has been reputed to be haunted.
Visitors report seeing an astral presence. The apparition is most
often observed descending the main staircase or is felt as a
passing breath of icy air in the wine cellar. Likely candidates are
plentiful. Until several years ago, many believed that the ghost
was that of John Gordon. Besides Gordon and Amasa Sprague,
himself, other suggestions have included Lucy Chase Sprague,
who lost a fortune, her reputation, and her beauty; William
Sprague, who died after a bone lodged in his throat during a

family breakfast; or the son of Governor William Sprague, 2nd, who committed suicide in 1890. But a seance held by students from Brown University, in Providence, to determine the ghost's identity, revealed the agitated spirit of a subsequent owner's butler, who had expected—but not received—an inheritance. The seance was hastily concluded when the Ouija began to move violently, spelling, "My land! My land! My land!" Finding William Peckham's gravestone—instructive and interesting, as it was—did not move us closer to resolving our immediate problem. Oddly enough, although I did not know it at the time, the Sprague family does enter into the vampire picture in a most unexpected place. But that's a connection I would not discover for several years.

Brian and I crossed the dirt road to the "Old Fernwood Cemetery," where we found some Rose family graves, but none that matched our needs. Finally, in the "Rose Lot," we located and photographed the graves of William G. Rose and his second wife, Mary G. Rose. The grave of his daughter, Ruth Ellen, was not there. In October, 1982, I had interviewed Jeanne Bradley, a local historian from North Kingstown. She knew the Rose family story and told me that "the vampire's grave" was in the cemetery across from Rose Hill on Moorsefield Road. Reviewing the audiotape from that interview, I concluded that she was referring to the cemetery Brian and I had been seeking, the "Rose-Watson Lot." The test of that hypothesis was thwarted, at least temporarily, by the thick growth that Brian and I had been trying to penetrate.

Perhaps I should have counted myself fortunate to have gotten as far as I had with the Rose event, given the paltry and often inaccurate record. Working back from Montague Summers' report yielded the following description, in 1879, in Moncure Daniel Conway's *Demonology and Devil-Lore*: "In 1874, according to the *Providence Journal*, in the village of Peacedale [sic], Rhode Island, U.S., Mr. William Rose dug up the body of his own daughter, and burned her heart, under the belief that she was wasting away the lives of other members of his family." Conway's misspelling of Peace Dale as Peacedale was picked up by subsequent authors and, after more than a hundred years and half a dozen citations in the vampire literature, Peace Dale had become Placedale. The printed versions of this case are as vague as the few I have collected from current oral tradition. A newspaper article from 1977 hinted at a family story of the incident:

> William C. [sic] Rose of Peace Dale feared an attack by vampires in 1874 because of his daughter's recent death. The then 53-year-old man exhumed his daughter's body in Rose Hill Cemetery just outside of Kingston on Route 138 and "burned her heart" to avoid even the possibility of vampirism, according to a living descendent of Rose.
>
> The graves of Rose and his wife Mary A. [sic] stand out prominently in the graveyard just inside the iron gates but the daughter's grave cannot be found. A search through birth, marriage and death certificates in South Kingstown Town hall showed no record of the family.

Evidence from genealogy and gravestones was corroborated by information in the newspaper article. It seemed likely that the girl's father was William G. Rose, who was born in 1821 in Exeter, died on January 19, 1911, and was buried in the family plot of Rose Hill Cemetery. Rose seems never to have lived in Peace Dale, the nearest village of any size. The daughter whose body was exhumed probably was Ruth Ellen Rose, born in 1859 to William and his first wife (who died in 1863). The gravestones of both Rose and his second wife, Mary G. Tillinghast, are in a South Kingstown cemetery. But the grave of Ruth Ellen, who died on May 12, 1874 (according to her obituary in the Narragansett Times) has never been found.

My primary purpose in searching through genealogical and

town records was to verify that these events actually happened. I did not expect to find a "smoking gun," such as permission granted to exhume bodies or perform autopsies, in official records. Yet, if I could discover that the families described were real people, I would have a foothold in history. The more evidence, the firmer that foothold. So, I sought out family trees, obituaries, cemetery and burial records, organizational membership lists, and other social registers. If I had to take a leap of faith, I wanted the chasm of uncertainty to be as narrow as possible. Occasionally, the tedium paid off. I was enthralled by the rare and unanticipated connections that transformed a list of names and places into a scene so palpable that I could envision people talking among themselves.

I finally located the source of the vampire incident dating from the time of the American Revolution cited by James Earl Clauson in his 1937 article. The following story appeared, in 1888, in Sidney S. Rider's "The Belief in Vampires in Rhode Island":

> At the breaking out of the Revolution there dwelt in one of the remoter Rhode Island towns a young man whom we will call Stukeley. He married an excellent woman and settled down in life as a farmer. Industrious, prudent, thrifty, he accumulated a handsome property for a man in his station in life, and comparable to his surroundings. In his family he had likewise prospered, for Mrs. Stukeley meantime had not been idle, having presented her worthy spouse with fourteen children. Numerous and happy were the Stukeley family, and proud was the sire as he rode about the town on his excellent horse, and attired in his homespun jacket of butternut brown, a species of garment which he much affected. So much, indeed, did he affect it that a sobriquet was given him by the townspeople. It grew out of the brown color of his coats. Snuffy Stuke they called him, and by that name he lived, and by it died.

For many years all things worked well with Snuffy Stuke. His sons and daughters developed finely until some of them had reached the age of man or woman-hood. The eldest was a comely daughter, Sarah. One night Snuffy Stuke dreamed a dream, which, when he remembered in the morning, gave him no end of worriment. He dreamed that he possessed a fine orchard, as in truth he did, and that exactly half the trees in it died. The occult meaning hidden in this revelation was beyond the comprehension of Snuffy Stuke, and that was what gave worry to him. Events, however, developed rapidly, and Snuffy Stuke was not kept long in suspense as to the meaning of his sin-gular dream. Sarah, the eldest child, sickened, and her malady, developing into a quick consumption, hurried her into her grave. Sarah was laid away in the family burying ground, and quiet came again to the Stukeley family. But quiet came not to Stukeley. His apprehensions were not buried in the grave of Sarah.

His unquiet quiet was but of short duration, for soon a second daughter was taken ill precisely as Sarah had been, and as quickly was hurried to the grave. But in the second case there was one symptom or complaint of a startling character, and which was not present in the first case. This was the continual complaint that Sarah came every night and sat upon some portion of the body, causing great pain and misery. So it went on. One after another sickened and died until six were dead, and the seventh, a son, was taken ill. The mother also now complained of these nightly visits of Sarah. These same characteristics were present in every case after the first one.

Consternation confronted the stricken household. Evidently something must be done, and that, too, right quickly, to save the remnant of this family. A consultation was called with the most learned people, and it was resolved to exhume the bodies of the six dead children. Their hearts were then to be cut from their bodies and burned upon a rock in front of the house. The neighbors were called in to assist in the lugubrious enterprise. There were the Wilcoxes, the Reynoldses, the Whitfords, the Mooneys, the Gardners, and others. With pick and spade the graves were soon opened, and the six bodies were found to be far advanced in the stages of decomposition. These were the last of the children who had died. But the first, the body of Sarah, was found to be in a very remarkable condition. The eyes were opened and fixed. The hair and nails had grown, and the heart and the arteries were filled with fresh red blood. It was clear at once to these astonished people that the cause of their trouble lay there before them. All the conditions of the vampire were present in the corpse of Sarah, the first that had died, and against whom all the others had so bitterly complained. So her heart was removed and carried to the designated rock, and there solemnly burned. This being done, the mutilated bodies were returned to their respective graves and covered. Peace then came to this afflicted family, but not, however, until a seventh victim had been demanded. Thus was the dream of Stukeley fulfilled. No longer did the nightly visits of Sarah afflict his wife, who soon regained her health. The seventh victim was a son, a promising young farmer, who had married and lived upon a farm adjoining. He was too far gone when the burning of Sarah's heart took place to recover.

Sarah returns from the grave at night to bother her living family members? Now there's a motif I did not expect to find applied to a New England case by a nineteenth-century historian.

What do I make of Sarah's night visits? Sarah, more monster than scapegoat, was a snug fit with the vampire of Gothic literature, but a figure ill-suited to what I knew of Mercy Brown. Mercy's was the most recent death in her family, yet she was singled out as responsible for . . . what? Her brother's illness? Then, what about Mercy's mother and sister? They *preceded* her in death. Was Mercy the culprit? How was that possible? The way out of this dilemma was to acknowledge the differences between Mercy Brown and Count Dracula as played by Bela Lugosi. A wide expanse separates the vampires of folklore from those of literature and mass media. In New England tradition, the unnamed evil resided in the grave, perhaps locating itself within the corpse of a deceased family member. The term "vampire" was used by outsiders, never by those in the community. Once that term was applied, the familiar vampire caricature, well-formed even before Stoker's *Dracula*, crept out of its coffin and into the story.

Rider followed established precedent by introducing his tale with an image drawn from Europe and well-known to the reading public. "Vampires," he wrote, are a "comparatively modern delusion" that originated in the "lower Danubian provinces." These "unseen beings, which, though dead, nevertheless possess some attributes of a living existence . . . wander at night sucking the blood of living human victims." A vampire "developed from a human being who had died. During the day this unquiet spirit would lie quietly in the grave in which it was buried, but at night it would assume the form of some animal or insect, and wander forth, seeking and sucking the warm blood of its sleeping victim." Rider commented that this "superstition . . . seems to have been prevalent at one time here in Rhode Island. In fact, it may even at this day be held in her remote regions." He found it "strange, even incredible" that "anybody should believe in such absurd superstitions. It is true, nevertheless. There were, and there are now, those who do believe them, and the purpose of this paper is to narrate a case which took place here in Rhode Island at no very remote period. It was of a genuine vampire."

The dream in Rider's story is another one of those folk motifs that can be found in Stith Thompson's *Motif-Index*. In folk narratives of all sorts, the prophetic, allegorical dream plays a significant role in foreshadowing the future and perplexing protagonists. Its roots are ancient. Pharoah's dream, described in the Old Testament (Genesis 41), parallels that of Snuffy, and was equally puzzling until interpreted by Joseph. Armed with foreknowledge, Pharoah was able to store enough food during seven years of plenty to stave off starvation during the seven years of famine that followed. In folklore, death and misfortune are the usual conditions heralded by dreams. An English superstition specifies that "to dream that a tree is uprooted in your garden is regarded as a death warning to the owner."

How did I interpret Snuffy's prophetic dream? Combined with Sarah's actual return from the dead, it suggested that someone (Rider's source? Rider himself?) had "improved" the narrative (assuming for the moment that it was, indeed, based on an actual event). The existence of such folk motifs in a narrative did not mean that it is a complete fabrication, of course. People do have dreams that seem to predict the future. Stepdaughters sometimes are exploited by wicked stepmothers and abused by jealous stepsisters. Young boys, sent out by their single mothers to do a man's work, have been swindled by unscrupulous traders. Though fictional, folktales (and written literature, as well) include real social relationships and cultural contexts. While the line between fantasy and reality may not be hard and fast, it does exist. When pumpkins transform into carriages and beanstalks ascend into a land of giants, that line is breached. Revenants and prophetic dreams are not so unequivocal. This shadowy region between the possible and impossible, the known and unknown, the natural and supernatural is precisely the domain of legend. Was the story circulating orally for some time, long enough to attract traditional motifs, before Rider encountered it? Everett Peck's tale, told to me in 1981, seemed to be headed in the same direction, with Mercy turning over in the grave and an eerie blue light appearing above her tombstone. If Rider himself embellished the narrative, he may have been employing a literary convention, not imitating folk tradition. In both oral and written literature, a dream can perform a dual function. Near the beginning, it is a symbolic foreshadowing of events; at the end, it is a device of closure. The uncertainty introduced by Snuffy's dream is resolved when he finally understands its terrible meaning: half of his orchard, half of his children, perish. Sarah's return from the grave also may be a literary device rather than a reporting of fact. In the Gothic literature of Rider's day (or today, for that matter), how else would a vampire behave?

The following comments by Rider raised other questions:

> The conditions here narrated are precisely similar to those alleged to have taken place in the Danubian provinces and the remedy applied the same. But in those countries certain religious rites were observed, and occasionally, instead of burning a part or the whole of a body, a nail was driven through the centre of the forehead. At the period when this event took place, religious rites were things but little known to the actors in the scene, and fire in their hands was quite as effective an agent as an iron nail. Those from whom these facts were obtained little suspected the foreign character of the origin of the extraordinary circumstances which they described; but extraordinary as they are, there are nevertheless those still living who religiously believe in them.

What does Rider mean by "religious rites were things but little known to the actors in the scene"? Is he characterizing Snuffy and his community as unbelievers? Ungodly? Something worse?

In Rider's published account, every kind of clue that might lead to further documentation or corroboration of his story, such as time, place, and person, is vague to the point of being useless: "At the breaking out of the Revolution there dwelt in one of the remoter Rhode Island towns a young man whom we will call Stukeley." Besides the daughter's name, Sarah, we have only the surnames of neighbors who assisted: Wilcox, Reynolds, Whitford, Mooney, and Gardner. Rider is equally vague concerning his sources: "those from whom these facts were obtained." That's it. End of trail?

I believed so, until January 5, 1983, when I came across a promising lead as I was checking the card catalogue for other publications by Rider at Brown University's Rockefeller Library. Brown's archives of special collections, the John Hay Library, contained something called "The Rider Collection." I hurried across the street to the John Hay without even bothering to put on my jacket. The Rider Collection did, indeed, include a great deal of material compiled by Sidney S. Rider, some of it indexed and some not. I requested the material labelled "Exeter Notes" and was ushered into the hushed, high-ceilinged reading room. This "room" was actually the center portion of space that was divided into thirds by dark wood bookcases ascending perhaps a third of the way to the forty-foot ceiling. On three sides of the huge neoclassical space were generous windows. At each of the long wooden tables, one had a choice of chair styles: comfortable, stuffed or, for those who needed the feel of a hard surface to stay attentive, unadorned wood. I selected wood. The librarian brought Box 300, which I eagerly opened. My heart sank when I saw a thin brown notebook. How much information could there be in a notebook measuring five-by-three inches? Two short lines seemed positively bountiful: "Story of Stukeley Tillinghast & his digging up of his six dead children—Snuffy Stuke." A surname was all I needed for a genealogical search that yielded a Stukeley Tillinghast, father of fourteen children, residing in the town of Exeter. On the basis of newspaper clippings pasted into the notebook, I concluded that Rider probably made this entry about 1888, not long before publishing the story in his *Book Notes*.

As I anticipated, I found no mention of an exhumation in the Exeter Town Records. But I did locate three sources, including the Town Records, that, with minor discrepancies, substantiated the existence of the family described by Rider. Stukeley (with various spellings) Tillinghast of Exeter, son of Pardon Tillinghast of West Greenwich, was born in Warwick on November 24, 1741, and died in West Greenwich in 1826. He was married to Honor (or Honour) Hopkins, the daughter of Samuel Hopkins of West Greenwich, on November 22, 1762; she was born in West Greenwich on January 6, 1745, and died in West Greenwich on December 3, 1831. Stukeley and Honor produced fourteen children (see APPENDIX B: CHILDREN OF STUKELEY AND HONOR TILLINGHAST for names and dates).

The nickname "Snuffy" rings true to an established South County tradition, and probably was not an intrusion into the story or an invention by Rider. The names Pardon and Stukeley (of Saxon derivation, meaning "stiff clay") were so common among the Tillinghasts that unique sobriquets had to be applied to distinguish one from the other. Snuffy's great-grandfather, one of the many Pardons, acquired his nickname after building a wharf trading in two of the three commodities of the "notorious triangle"—the thriving, and to many, unconscionable, trade in slaves, molasses, and rum that linked Africa, the West Indies, and Rhode Island. An historian wrote that Pardon Tillinghast's "lucrative business in rum and molasses gave him not only a fair estate, but a sobriquet which proved as lasting, and to his death he was known as 'Molasses Pardon.'" The Hazard family took this practice to perhaps an extreme degree. There were thirty-two "Tom Hazards" living at one time. These included not only Shepherd Tom (author of *The Jonny-Cake Papers*), but also College Tom, Barley Tom, Little-Neck Tom, Fiddle-Head Tom, Pistol Tom, Nailer Tom, and Tailor Tom.

Despite the many agreements between Rider's narrative and other sources, there are discrepancies. First, the event seems to have occurred in the year 1799, some twenty-three years after "the breaking out of the Revolution." Also, half of Snuffy's four-teen children did not die in close proximity, though four of his five youngest children, beginning with Sarah (b. 1777), did die of consumption in 1799. Sarah was not the first child born, as Rider wrote, but the tenth. Rider also wrote that the last to die was a son, "a promising young farmer, who had married and lived upon a farm adjoining." None of Stukeley's six sons seems to match Rider's description. Four of them lived beyond their seventies and another died at age forty-seven, thirty-three years after Sarah's death. Evidence regarding James, the youngest child, is conflicting. One genealogy lists James as dying of consumption in 1799. If this is true, he was only thirteen—young, even at that time, to be married and living on his own. But in June of 1995, a Tillinghast descendent living in Connecticut wrote to me that he had discovered a will of the same James Tillinghast. The will was dated 14 August 1810, which suggests that James lived well beyond Sarah's exhumation. Actually, it is a daughter who most closely matches Rider's description. Hannah Tillinghast married Joseph Hoxsie in 1797 and died three years later. Since Joseph Hoxsie resided in a village located less than a mile south of Pine Hill, it is very likely that the Hoxies lived in close proximity to the Tillinghasts.

More than a year after I found a surname for Snuffy, after examining several hundred gravestones in four Tillinghast lots in West Greenwich and Exeter, I finally located a Tillinghast family cemetery that contained at least some of Snuffy's family. On a cool, sunny day in April, 1984, I found the small, neglected family plot on a rock-strewn hillside. Stukeley's wife, Honor (d. 1831), was apparently the first to be buried in this plot. The most recent burial seems to have been Frank Tillinghast (1852–1919). Honor's stone reads: "She was the mother of 14 children and all lived to grow up." Either James or Andris was the youngest to die. In an era before the invention of "teenagers," one who had attained the age of thirteen no doubt would have been consid-ered grown-up. Other marked and legible gravestones included that of Stutley (Stukeley, Jr.) (d. 1848) and Clark (d. 1832), and several of Stukeley and Honor's grandchildren and in-laws, including, perhaps, the Whitfords mentioned by Rider. Two adjacent stones are inscribed simply B.W. and A.W., which might be Benjamin Whitford and Snuffy's daughter, Amay Tillinghast Whitford, who married Benjamin in 1794. There were five uninscribed, upright field stones in a row, perhaps marking other graves. One of Rider's statements made me wonder if the Tillinghast house was located next to the cemetery: "Their hearts were then to be cut from their bodies and burned upon a rock in front of the house." When I found the cemetery, there was no evidence of a nearby house (which, of course, could have been destroyed long ago).

Rider's statement that "religious rites were things but little known to the actors in the scene" seems at least untrue, if not disingenuous, in light of the Tillinghast family genealogy. It may be difficult to find a consistently more religious family, at least if measured by those who became members of the clergy—a trend that continues into the present. Stukeley Tillinghast married Honor Hopkins, daughter of Samuel Hopkins and Honor (nee Brown) Hopkins. Sarah's maternal grandfather, pastor of the First Congregational Church in Newport from 1770 to 1803, has been called "one of the leading antislavery reformers in revolutionary America and later a heroic figure to many antislavery reformers in the nineteenth century." Samuel Hopkins was born in Waterbury, Connecticut, in 1721, graduated from Yale, and studied, in Northampton, Massachusetts, under the evangelical theologian Jonathan Edwards, whose hellfire sermons exhorted sinners to repent and convert. Prior to settling in Newport, Hopkins served a parish in Great Barrington, the backcountry of western Massachusetts. Hopkins' opposition to slavery was inflamed by his firsthand exposure to the slave trade in Newport, after which he worked closely in the antislavery movement with the Quaker Moses Brown of Providence, who often was opposed by his brother, John, a slave trader. Theologically, Hopkins advocated "disinterested benevolence," described as "a Christ-like, sacrificial love of God and mankind. . . . a life of self-denial, avoiding not only the selfish pursuit of worldly things but also the selfish pursuit of his own salvation."

I recently corresponded with a descendent of Stukeley, Rev. Harold "Bud" Tillinghast. He sent me an article he had written for the newsletter of the family's American branch, *Pardon's Progeny*, which included the observation that their "first ancestor in America was named Pardon and he had been associated with the Baptist Church in Providence, Rhode Island." Researching the family history in England, Bud found that "the Rev. John Tillinghast, graduate of Caius (pronounced "keys") College, Cambridge 1585, and Rector of the Parish of Streat, Sussex, in Queen Elizabeth's time was related to Pardon." And later, "So I found nearly 20 recordings of baptisms of Tillinghast (a half-dozen marriages and about a dozen burials), some later than John's term as rector but recorded by another Rev. John Tillinghast who proved to be his son." The Tillinghast family appears to have had more than a casual awareness of religious rites.

Rider wrote that "another similar case in Wakefield, Rhode Island" came to his attention after he had completed his narrative, and that "still another now is in contemplation in a family of respectable surroundings, several of the members of which have recently died." True to form, he left me to guess the identity of these unnamed families.

The procedures used by desperate families to stop consumption were not disembodied ideas floating in the air, just waiting for the right moment to materialize. This knowledge was transmitted via the folklore process, an ancient, intimate way of communicating that has remained vigorous over the centuries, even in the face of technologies such as print, the telephone, and the Internet. As we interact with close acquaintances during the normal course of daily life, we make observations, give opinions, discuss our lives, share our burdens, seek—and give—advice, and convey other expressions that we deem important enough to pass along. This organic process is educational, informative, entertaining, affirmative. Just think about how much of this information exchange is in the form of personal narrative! In his article on vampirism in New England, Stetson makes it plain that eyewitness accounts were the primary means of spreading the awareness of the practice and validating its effectiveness. The observation in the *Providence Journal* that "the people of South County say they got it from their ancestors" hints at a long-standing oral tradition for the vampire practice. Social networks of relatives, friends, and neighbors must have been the medium through which these alternative approaches to disease control were transmitted. In his scrutiny of folklore processes, Lauri Honko has found that decisions regarding supernatural occurrences, including even their perception as such, often are communal activities: "A person who has experienced a supernatural event by no means always makes the interpretation himself; the social group that surrounds him may also participate in the interpretation. In their midst may be spirit belief specialists, influential authorities, whose opinion, by virtue of their social prestige, becomes decisive."

Was William G. Rose one of these "influential authorities" who urged George Brown to exhume the bodies of his family in 1892? Rose was elected Worthy Master of the Exeter Grange in 1890, and he also was a member of the Exeter Town Council during that period. Brown was a respected farmer in this town of fewer than one thousand residents and, according to his obituary, a member of the Exeter Grange. I can visualize the scene following a meeting of the Grange or town council: Rose takes Brown aside and, after exchanging the usual pleasantries and small talk, conveys his sympathy over the recent deaths and illness in Brown's family. Rose tells Brown that he, himself, had the same problem some years earlier. As Rose reveals the procedures he followed to save his family after the medical establishment conceded defeat, he becomes, as it were, a "spirit belief specialist." Because of his standing in the community, and his own experiences in the matter, he is an authority whose opinion is decisive. We know from accounts in contemporary newspapers that Brown, reluctant to interpret his misfortune as a supernatural event, was "besieged on all sides by a number of people, who expressed implicit faith in the old theory." In the family story related by Everett Peck, the decision to exhume the bodies came from "twelve men . . . of the family" who "got together and . . . took a vote, what to do." This is a crucial moment, when the supernatural nature of the problem is acknowledged, at least tacitly, and the exhumations can proceed. We don't know if personal-experience narratives or family stories were brought to bear on this decision, but the circumstantial evidence in their favor is compelling.

We can add the Tillinghast family to the Exeter social network that was in place for interpreting vampire incidents. William Rose's second wife was Mary G. Tillinghast, a great-granddaughter of Stukeley Tillinghast, Sarah's father. Could Mary, who was about twenty-six when her grandfather Amos died, have listened to his stories of how, when he was a young man in his thirties, the bodies of his younger brothers and sisters had to be exhumed to stop a deadly epidemic? Could she have played the role of belief specialist in 1874 by providing her husband, William, with a family story that offered a solution to their own consumption epidemic? I know from my own experiences that children crave such family stories, and they are not soon forgotten.

The stories told by my own grandmother, Nana, fit squarely into this genre. Rather than the impersonal narration of timeless folktales, she told me—or, more accurately, acted out—only personal experience stories. And, my God, what experiences she'd had! Younger than my grandfather by some fifteen years, she was singing and dancing on the stage or traveling with the carnival while Grandpa, a career Marine, was in some foreign port of call. When the Second World War broke out, she was one of the first women to join the WACs.

Her performances were dramatic. Sitting in a chair, Nana would begin calmly with the necessary background of who, when, and where. Soon she would rise, possessed by her narrative, and pace around the room, throwing her arms about as she advanced the plot through a combination of description and dialogue. Her voice, low and throaty, would purr when she talked about a person whom she loved deeply, such as her father, George Peirce, killed by lightning in 1923 at Coal Hill, Arkansas. She would sigh, and actually cry. Often, she would look directly at me, take my arm in her hand and say my name, pulling me deeper into her story, making me feel that this performance was for me, and me alone. When I heard, "And, Mike, honey . . . " I felt the thrill of some impending twist. She had a good ear and well-developed visual sense. The real characters in Nana's stories interacted in real spaces, all painted in rich detail. Her tales included incidents that didn't seem to have rational explanations. Although Nana wasn't religious in any conventional sense (I don't remember her going to church), she was profoundly spiritual. She described portents, premonitions, signs, and omens— spirits returned from the dead.

Above all others, one of her stories has occupied a seminal position, spanning four generations in our family. I think one reason that Everett Peck's story of Mercy Brown struck me so solidly was that it somehow connected with Nana's story of her father, George Peirce, which I needed to hear again and again. After beginning my folklore studies, I recorded the story several times from both Nana and my father. In 1975, three years before she died at the age of 82, Nana gave me her last performance of "The Spirit on the Staircase." Sitting in her small apartment in Louisville, she set the scene for me, my wife, and our very young daughter.

In the Summer of 1924, Florence (Nana) arrived at the combination home and antique store of her mother, Minnie, in North Little Rock, Arkansas, after having been away traveling with the carnival. Her ten-year-old son, Lester, my father, was being cared for by Minnie. Nana had been summoned by Minnie, who feared that her new husband, Richard, was "out of his mind" and would kill her and Lester.

"Hell, I took the next train. . . . Well, I got there and I went upstairs and cleaned up. Now, they slept downstairs, like in an old-fashioned drugstore. You walked in through old double doors, right in off of the pavement onto a little porch. Right down the middle was all that furniture, antique furniture. On one side was glass and clocks—Oh, God, she had the glass!—and all the antiques on shelves. When you got to the back there was a kind of hallway and a stairway that went upstairs. Across from the stairs was the bedroom downstairs and across from that was the kitchen and the dining room."

"So, I said, 'I'm going upstairs to take a nap. If you need me, call me, even if I'm asleep.' "

"Well, I was awakened out of a sound sleep. Mom and Les were crying and Mom was screaming and hollering, 'Don't, please don't, don't.' "

Here's where Nana, still a handsome woman and amazingly agile, got up and began to enact the various roles, gesturing as she flitted around the room.

"He didn't know I was in the place, and I got right up and went down. The table's there and he was over that way and they were on the other side of the table hugging each other and he had a chair and was going to come around with it and hit them with the chair."

"I said, 'PUT IT DOWN! I mean put it down!' He knew. He put it down."

"I said, 'Come on out of there Mom, Les.' "

"They walked out into the hall and Mom says, 'Don't worry' to Les. Richard set the chair down and stayed back in there where we couldn't see him. He didn't say a word. He just stood there."

"So, Mom walks out, and I took Les and we walked over to right where the glass started on the shelves."

Nana was in full-acting mode now.

"And here's what Mom did. She walked over there. She faced the shelves some way or other and she put her hands up and touched one of the shelves, like to lean. I didn't know what she was doing, what she went over there for, whether she was going to look for something or what, the way she was doing with her hands."

"She says, 'Dear God, please send the spirit of George Peirce back to help us.' "

"Lester, he'll tell you himself, he heard it, Mom heard it and

I heard it, and Richard heard it. We heard my father coming down them stairs. It's daylight now. It is daylight, late in the afternoon in the summertime, still light. And he walked, and walked down the stairs, and he walked toward the dining room. About then that guy, Richard, come rushing out. The footsteps stopped. Nothing else happened. And that bird, he ran all the way to that corner. He got a wheelbarrow, brought it back in, grabbed all his clothes and everything, put them in the wheelbarrow, and piled all his hats on top of his head. We looked out and saw him with that wheelbarrow, and those hats on his head, going down the road, and we haven't seen him from that day to this."

I've told this family story many times. Everett often repeats his family story of Mercy Brown. Of the several themes common to family stories, supernatural occurrences are the most compelling. They challenge natural boundaries, stretch the limits of our understanding, force us to reexamine our view of the world. Supernatural stories are remarkable no matter how many times we hear them. If Mary Tillinghast Rose had not heard, and repeated, the story of Sarah Tillinghast, it would have been an extraordinary exception to our understanding of how the folklore process works.

Separated by nearly one-hundred years, these three vampire incidents involved families—the Tillinghasts, Roses, and Browns— who were linked through descent, marriage, and other personal ties. In small, close-knit communities, such as Exeter, social networks begin with kinship. Genealogy reveals more than simply who begot whom; it also charts the channels for the transmission of folk knowledge. George Stetson, James Earl Clauson, and Sidney Rider turned to European examples and literary images to make sense of events that left them bewildered. In my search for answers, I looked closer to home. What is vital in a community is recorded in the mundane features that exist at eye level. Building a narrative out of gravestones, town records, family trees, and family stories is a make-do process. Like constructing a wall from the rubble pile, you may have to "use a spell to make them balance." If you do it well, they may sing.

CHAPTER 5
I am Waiting and Watching For You

I Am Waiting and Watching For You

This inscription—provocative to some, conventional to others—appears at the bottom of a gravestone that *was* located in the cemetery behind the Plain Meeting House Baptist Church in West Greenwich, Rhode Island. Incised above the inscription, the following information seems mundane by anyone's standards:

Nellie L.
Daughter of George B. & Ellen Vaughn
Died Mar. 31, 1889,
in the 19 year of her age

Why—and where—Nellie's stone has gone makes sense if we follow Nellie's odyssey—a strange journey that began long after her death. To answer the question of whether Nellie Vaughn was a vampire requires an entirely different approach from that employed when asking the same question about Mercy Brown. Yet, Nellie and Mercy are stubbornly, perhaps inextricably, intertwined.

The first published reference to Nellie Vaughn does not appear until 1977.

Another tale of vampirism involves Nellie L.

Vaughn of Coventry [sic] who died in 1889 at 19. Her grave in Rhode Island Historical Cemetery No. 2 is the only sunken grave in the cemetery and continues to sink into the earth. "No vegetation or lichen will grow on the grave," reports a local university professor despite numerous attempts by grave tenders and the curious. Along the bottom of the headstone are inscribed the words, "I am waiting and watching for you."

By the time this story was printed in the *Westerly* (Rhode Island) *Sun*, the tale of Nellie the vampire already had the characteristics of a well-established legend. The blossoming belief that Nellie was a vampire brought a plague of vandalism to the cemetery where Nellie was buried and to the adjacent Plain Meeting House Baptist Church in West Greenwich (*not* in the adjoining town of Coventry, as reported in the article).

In 1982, the *Providence Journal-Bulletin* ran an article on the occasion of the church's semiannual service (in itself, a fascinating custom) that contained what was becoming the accepted explanation for how, through a combination of misunderstanding, coincidence, and imagination, this legend began:

But the biggest irritant, members say, has been the constant vandalism to the church and its property, which they attribute not only to their church's remote location but to a persistent rumor that there is a vampire buried in the church cemetery.

What was that about a vampire?

"As far as we can determine, it started 15 years ago when a teacher at Coventry High School told his students that there was a vampire buried in a cemetery off [state route] 102," reports church historian Evelyn Smith. "The teacher never mentioned the name of the cemetery, but the students tried to find where the vampire was. They stopped here and came across a tombstone for Nellie Vaughn. She died in 1889, and her stone reads, 'I am watching and waiting for you.' [sic]

"The kids assumed that she must have been the vampire, and the story has just spread ever since. What we want to do now is set the record straight. There is an alleged vampire, but her name is Mercy Brown and she's buried at Chestnut Hill Cemetery, not here. People have got the wrong cemetery and the wrong person."

Mrs. Smith wants people to know that Nellie Vaughn was not a vampire. "There is a man in our congregation who is 100 years old who knew Nellie personally. He says there was no talk of her being a vampire while she was living or after her death."

Nonetheless, the story about Nellie persists, she says. And hardly a day goes by without people showing up at the cemetery to look at the woman's grave. Tombstones have been overturned. There even appears to have been an attempt to dig up the coffin.

Some town residents believe that legend trips by vandals explain why Nellie's grave "continues to sink into the earth" and "no vegetation or lichen will grow on the grave."

Just over a year after this article appeared, I drove out to the West Greenwich Town Hall to see what I could find out about Nellie Vaughn. I arrived during a time of transition, as Mary Ann Brunette had just succeeded Cora Lamoureux as Town Clerk. Cora was a tough act to follow. She was, perhaps, the oldest town clerk in New England when she retired at age 87, with twenty-seven years in the post. And her uncle was Town Clerk for the thirty-four years before Cora's tenure! Mary Ann was conversing about this and that with two middle-aged women and an older man—nothing that seemed like pressing town business. Good! I introduced myself and explained that I was interested in stories passed around town by word-of-mouth. It didn't seem wise to jump right into the Nellie Vaughn issue. I was more than aware of the local resentment over Nellie's—and the town's—apparently unwarranted notoriety.

I asked about how the nearby Nooseneck Hill got its name. Surely there must be an interesting story behind such a name (pronounced "newsneck" by locals). I was offered two different explanations: it was an area where local Native Americans set nooses for capturing deer or, alternately, it was named after the bend in the river or, perhaps, the road. The storytelling session was now underway, and I was told several urban legends that were circulating at the time. Of course, they were told as true, having happened to some FOAF (friend of a friend) of the narrators. In "The Hatchet in the Handbag" (or "The Hairy-Armed Hitchhiker"), a man is dressed as a woman and hiding, with his hatchet, in the backseat of a car. I was told this happened at the Warwick Mall. I heard two versions of "The Dead Cat in the Package." In one, a woman hits a cat with her car, and, feeling sad, places it in a paper bag and slips the bag under her car while she goes into the mall. Another person sees her hide the bag and, thinking it must contain something valuable, takes it into Newport Creamery (a local restaurant chain), opens it, and faints. In the other version, the bag is placed on the passenger side of the car seat and is taken to a Chinese restaurant near the Warwick Mall. Finally, I was told about a woman shopping at Ann & Hope (a local discount department store—an institution, actually—that recently had to shut its doors forever) who lost track of her little girl. When she reported to the manager that she couldn't find her daughter anywhere in the store, the doors were locked and a search undertaken. The girl was found in the men's room with a man who was still holding the scissors that he had used to cut her hair very short. The woman who told this story, known as "The Attempted Abduction" to folklorists, said that she had heard it from a grandparent of the little girl.

Having established my genuine interest in legends, I broached the subject of Nellie Vaughn, and was grateful when the new Town Clerk checked the records instead of telling me to mind my own business. According to the death certificate and other records on file, Ellen ("Nellie") Louise Vaughn died of pneumonia at the age of eighteen on March 31, 1889. None of the records mentions heart-burning or any other practices associated with the vampire tradition. According to those present, Cora Lamoureux believed that Nellie had first been buried on the family farm (still a common practice at the time) on Robin Hollow Road and then moved to her current resting place, one of the first public cemeteries in the area. The records showed that Nellie's mother was given permission, on October 26, 1889, to remove the remains of her daughter to the "Plain or Washington Cemetery." Another woman at the town hall suggested that Nellie's story might have begun when her body was moved, an act which would have required exhumation. That intriguing possibility was enhanced when I came across a general superstition stating that "to exhume a body and rebury it in another grave makes the spirit restless forever." A third woman seemed to bolster the latter's opinion when she asserted that she had heard the story "for a long time," which, she said, meant "longer than ten or twelve years," the approximate time frame suggested by those who attribute the story to a Coventry teacher. She told me that her husband was the workman who had done the plastering for the crypt situated next to Nellie's grave. He told her that Nellie's stone was "too modern for 1889" and must have been a replacement. He said that the inscription was probably copied exactly from the old stone. I left the West Greenwich Town Hall still believing that, in all likelihood, Nellie's reputation as a vampire was unwarranted. But I was open to contradictary evidence.

At the suggestion of the town-hall folks, I arranged an interview with Cora Lamoureux, esteemed for her encyclopedic knowledge of the town, and Blanche Albro, known in the community as the town historian and genealogy expert. If these two couldn't set the record straight regarding Nellie Vaughn, I doubted that anyone could.

I pulled up to a small red cape on Weaver Hill Road, just south of the Coventry town line. In the front yard, white and purple crocus were winning their annual struggle against gravity, while the old farm buildings across the road appeared ready to give up after a century or so. Inside the parlor, Cora and Blanche talked a little while about their upbringing and their ties to the community. Cora joked that she was a newcomer to West Greenwich, having lived in the town for only about fifty years. She was born on a large farm in rural southwestern Cranston, but had long-standing family ties in West Greenwich. She and Blanche are related through several lines.

Cora said that Blanche "knows all about Nellie Vaughn. She's the town historian. And my father would have been related to Nellie Vaughn if he had been alive at the time."

Blanche seemed both plaintive and annoyed when she interjected, "We can't understand why they keep bringing it up. We lived here all our lives and never . . . it was a schoolteacher in Coventry that started that rumor. And that's the first time. And we tell and tell everybody it's not true, but it doesn't amount to anything."

I tried to soften Blanche's indignation by suggesting how, from a folklorist's point of view, a rumor can become a legend and then continue of its own accord, whether or not it's based on fact. "I think once a story starts, it's very difficult to stop it."

I brought out a map so that Blanche could show me where the Vaughn family had lived. She verified what I had learned earlier, that the family farm was located on Robin Hollow Road. I mentioned that there were other verified cases of the vampire practice in Rhode Island, including several in Exeter.

"Yeah," Blanche responded, "but we never had one 'til this kooky teacher. And the only reason she started it, 'cause it says, 'watching and waiting for you' on her stone in the cemetery . . . She told the story in high school, Coventry High School, and my nephew was there. And from then on, all they've done is dig that grave up. If I ever told you the things that have been done in that cemetery . . . because these kooky people think they're going to dig Nellie Vaughn up. They have tried it."

Cora jumped in. "Blanche, do you think that the monument that's up at Plain [Cemetery] is the one that used to be on the farm? Or is it a new one."

Drawing out her first word and speaking deliberately, Blanche seemed unsure. "I . . . think . . . I don't know. But I think, maybe, it was a newer one because, usually, back there, then, when she died, they were white marble. And this is like a gray granite, with a polished surface. I haven't been up there in a couple of years."

Cora added, "But that inscription . . . I've been to Plymouth—you know, the old cemetery there—many times. It's on an awful lot of stones there. I mean, there's nothing unusual about it."

I began fishing for a possible alternate explanation for the story's genesis, independent of the teacher from Coventry. "I talked to one woman at the Town Hall last Fall and she said maybe the story got started because they moved her grave. . . . Probably from the farm out to the church."

Blanche responded, "You know when they moved her grave? Six months after she died. And I think they moved it because . . . Plain Meeting House Cemetery had been built, and was a big cemetery. And you can find in the records where loads of people took their dead out of these little individual farm cemeteries. They moved them there. When Ellen Vaughn asked, . . . she got permission to move that girl's body."

I asked how long ago the teacher had told the story. Blanche replied in her slow, deliberate fashion: "I would say between ten and fifteen years ago, because my . . . "

I interrupted to ask, "Do you remember her name?
"No."

"Because I would like to contact her and find out why she told the story."

"I don't know. From what my nephew said, it was just because the stone said 'watching and waiting for you.' " Blanche became emphatic. "We had never, never, in this town, we had never heard there was a vampire in this town. And I don't believe . . . "

Cora interjected, "It's all a new thing."

"It's all a new thing," Blanche echoed. "We have asked people not to publish the story because the minute it comes out in the paper they go up there by the hundreds."

"It's been in the newspaper," I observed.

"It has been, loads of time[s]," Blanche said. "And they just vandalize the cemetery. They drive right over the graves, and all such things. . . . I'm sure it's fiction, because I have read all of the West Greenwich Town Council meetings, from the time the town started. And if you know about old town-council meetings, they tell everything that went on. Somebody wanted a divorce, the town talked it over. I have never found anything about this Nellie Vaughn and vampires."

"It would probably turn up in print somewhere," I said, indirectly reinforcing Blanche's conclusion. "Nellie Vaughn died of pneumonia, anyway, and not consumption, which usually . . . was the disease that was related most to that practice." I thought for a moment, and added, "Actually, the people involved didn't call it vampirism, anyway. It was a way to prevent consumption. It was a medical practice."

Cora said, "We were talking about it today, my niece and I, what they used to do if you were sick. They'd bleed you. No wonder you died, after they took half your blood out of you!"

Blanche said that she had no idea who the schoolteacher was, and reiterated her belief that the whole story is fiction.

"Besides," I said, "there were no other members of her family who . . . "

Blanche interrupted, "She had half brothers and sisters, but they're all dead."

"I know. But were they getting sick at the same time she died?" I wanted to know.

Blanche answered, "No. The father died four years later." Then she consulted some notes she had with her and said, "I can tell you. Her father died in 1902, so he didn't catch nothing from her, did he? She had one sister that had died twenty years before, half-sister, eleven years old. Another sister, half-sister, she was the only child by his second wife—George Vaughn's second wife. I don't know when she died. Cora would. Another half-sister was Georgiana Vaughn . . . and she died in 1933. So, she didn't get nothing from her."

We discussed these family connections and agreed that the usual vampire circumstances did not exist.

Blanche continued her genealogical report. "And her mother died . . . her mother was Ellen Knight Vaughn. She was the second wife. She died in 1926. So, usually, like you say," she turned to me, "when they say a vampire, two or three sisters had died at the same time, and they say, 'Oh, the vampire . . . come out . . . and sucked their blood' and all this foolishness. Well, her brothers and sisters didn't."

Cora brought up the Brown case in Exeter, and Blanche broke in. "But, this one, we never heard about it. And it irritates you to think some foolish remark would've started what they have done to that cemetery. That's what irks me, is when I go up there, and. . . . At one time—I'll give you a laugh—they'd go up there at night, and there's dope and beer and all this, and they'd have their party. I used to keep check on 'em because my husband has got family that's buried up there. They would take all the bouquets off of the other graves and put them on Nellie Vaughn's. Then they had a spell that they left money on Nellie Vaughn's grave. It would only be change."

Cora asked, apparently astonished, "Did they really?"

Blanche's voice raised an octave when she responded, "Yes they did. And I could tell you the fella that went everyday and picked up the change and put it in his pocket. And he'd say, 'If they're . . . damn fool enough to leave that change,' he said, 'I'll be dumb enough to pick it up.' He said, 'Let 'em think Nellie Vaughn's come out and gone somewhere.' "

Which may be exactly what they want to believe, I thought. The man who picks up the change may be reinforcing, inadvertently, Nellie's legend by providing legend trippers additional evidence that she leaves her grave at night and roams the countryside.

Cora began to laugh as Blanche continued. "And he'd go two or three days later and pick up all the change. Now, you know, that gets disgusting after a while."

Cora, still laughing, said "Isn't that crazy! I never heard that."

Blanche continued, "I knew a lot of the people that live in that vicinity, that they were like us. We'd hear about 'em being up there and tipping over stones. So the next day, my husband would say—his grandfather and grandmother were buried up there—he'd say, 'We'll go up and see if they've knocked over my grandfather's and grandmother's grave, because we'll have to have it put back up again.' Well, we'd get up there and we'd meet some of these other people that were doing the same thing that we were doing—to see if their family's stones were . . . " She paused, then exclaimed loudly, "They're still doing it! Last Halloween we had to drive them out of there. They're worse at Halloween."

Cora elaborated, "And Blanche, all of our police department, with three or four cops, have to spend the whole night there because so many people get up there. The street will get so crowded that you'd have to walk a mile or two to get there, right? Because they're parked all along the road."

"Where do they come from?" I wondered.

Blanche answered, "They come from Coventry, they come from North Kingstown, all the high schools! All high school kids."

Blanche summarized, "Well, I hope it does you some good, but like I say, I don't think she was a vampire. I know she was never called a vampire. My husband has died and his people all lived and grew up around that cemetery, and they had never heard it."

"That's convincing," I said.

"Yeah, it stops you," Blanche responded. "You know, when they started telling it and they went up there and, of course, you know how they keep adding to it. And it's just not true."

Thinking out loud, I said, "Yeah, that's the process of legend formation."

Blanche persisted. "To me, it's not true. I don't see how it can be true. Everything I've looked for and found—I can't find nothing."

Blanche said West Greenwich had an appreciably larger population at one time. Later, when I checked the record, I was surprised to see that the town's population peaked at 2,054 in 1790.

"For some reason," she said, "in the late seventeen hundreds and early eighteen hundreds, whole families moved right out, and went to, like, New York, New Hampshire, and Vermont. Because, for one thing, they were giving them property, especially Vermont and New Hampshire. Well, now, of course, genealogy is a big thing. So, people in Vermont or, I'll say, New York, they can trace back four or five generations. They find out that their great, great, great grandfather come from West Greenwich. So, they'll write. Well, I find what I can in West Greenwich. A lot of times they'll send me a whole big pamphlet. With what I add, and what they've got, it will bring 'em right down. Well, I think that some day— not now, 'cause I use 'em—I will put them in the West Greenwich library. In years to come, if somebody else is looking up that same family, they will have that all together, you know." When I asked, Blanche told me that the West Greenwich town council records go back to 1741, when West Greenwich was divided from East Greenwich.

I thought about how the narrators I had interviewed laid the foundation for their stories with family connections and sprinkled their discussions with genealogy. Who is related to whom, and through what line, has an obvious import to these people, rooted, as they are, in their communities. And, following their lead in this matter, I was finding that genealogy pointed toward how the vampire practice had spread in the region.

The topic shifted to records and accessibility to information. Cora and Blanche agreed that, prior to about 1850, there were no medical records, and that, even after that, death records were just entered in the town hall. Blanche said that she believes that, in many instances, people "just didn't bother" to keep records.

To illustrate her point, she discussed her experiences with death entries in the town records. "When I was going through the town council records . . . in the early 1800s, somebody would die—and evidently they died suddenly—I'll just say drunk, and they were found in a field or something. So, the town council would appoint a committee of three men—and I knew by the names they weren't doctors, they were just men, probably the neighbors—to investigate that person's death. That's all you'd see! There wouldn't be anything in the next meeting. The man was dead, that was all. They never mentioned it again."

Cora concurred, "There was no report, or anything."

Blanche continued, "So, then I'd go get the book—because we have the death records after 1850. By then, you were supposed to record the deaths. They had passed a law in Rhode Island. Before that, you did it if you wanted to. . . . I'd go look in the death records—nothing!"

Cora asked, "Didn't they bury them, sometimes, right off on their own farm, anyway? Nobody knew about it. And not always in one place on that farm."

Blanche came right back with an illustrative story. "My father told, when he was a young boy, maybe ten years old . . . I could tell the names, but I forgot." She lowered her voice to almost a whisper and repeated, "I could tell the names." Her tone of voice led me to conclude that perhaps she hadn't quite forgotten.

She continued. "There was this young man and another one, and they were drunk. . . . And they could come from Nooseneck into this section with, I call 'em woods paths—they were just paths, like in back of my father's house there was a wood path that would take you right over into the village. . . . And these two people lived on Fish Hill, which would have been over there [pointing]. They'd come through my father's property. Then there's another wood path that goes over onto Fish Hill. And he'd say they were always drunk, anyway. So, this day, one of 'em come runnin'! And he said, 'So-and-so is dead. He's in a puddle. He's dead.' My father said he didn't believe him. And his father said to him, 'You run out there and pull him out of the puddle.' And my father said when he went out there, he *was* dead! He fell facedown in the puddle, and the other one was so drunk, you know, he didn't know enough to help him out."

Cora interjected, "And he was too drunk to get out himself!"

Blanche agreed. "Yeah. And he was too drunk. And he died. And he's buried down Maple Road. 'Cause one time, my father took me down there and he said, 'This is where so-and-so's buried.... That's the one that fell in the puddle,' he said, 'and I was about thirteen, ... and when I went out and pulled him out of the puddle,' he said, 'so-and-so was right! .. He was dead.' ... And I don't think that death was ever recorded."

Cora again concurred. "Oh, no, sometimes they didn't record them right away. They didn't have to. And they'd come in and record five or six at a time, sometimes. I suppose they did that in all the old towns."

Blanche picked up the thread. "The family would come in and write down the whole list, and then sometimes on the bottom of the page, it says, 'recorded such a year' and sometimes it don't say nothin'. But if you look at it close, you can tell it's all the same handwriting and same pen and everything."

Their discussion of the casual approach taken to record keeping, at least prior to the latter part of the nineteenth century, reinforced my hunch that it would be very difficult to find the smoking gun—a recording in the town council or other official records of permission to exhume a body.

The interview with Cora and Blanche left me feeling like an unwelcome guest in town. They were pleasant and friendly, yet I sensed that they really would prefer that I—and everyone else who was interested in Nellie Vaughn—would just disappear, forever. While both were steeped in local history, neither put much stock in local legends. I was unable to win over Cora and Blanche, even though I tried several times to communicate that my concerns as a folklorist were not predicated on Nellie being a vampire, and that the legend process, the actual focus of my interest, would continue whether or not Nellie was, in truth, a vampire.

Two weeks before Halloween in 1995, I received a phone call from Evelyn Arnold, formerly Evelyn Smith, the church historian mentioned in the *Providence Journal-Bulletin* article of 1982 who deplored the vandalism to the Plain Meeting House Church and cemetery by Nellie Vaughn legend trippers. Still the caretaker of the church and cemetery, she was irate over a recently published article in a local periodical that recounted the story of Nellie

Vaughn as a vampire. The author had credited me with providing him information for his article, which I did in the form of newspaper articles and other references he could pursue. In effect, Evelyn asked why I would tell people that Nellie was a vampire. The continued publicity, she said, leads to ongoing vandalism at the church and cemetery. She gave some examples, including the preceding Friday (which happened to be October 13th!) when thirty cars, including the entire high school soccer team from a nearby town, converged on the cemetery.

I assured Evelyn that I did not tell people that Nellie was a vampire, that I always made a point of stressing the likelihood that it is a case of mistaken identity. I told her that, even though I share with the public the materials I have collected as a public-sector scholar, I have no control over how people, including the press, interpret the materials I supply. I avowed that, as an academically trained folklorist, I attempt to sort out history from legend, fact from fiction. Unfortunately, I said, many others do not take this approach. I also told her that, when I speak to the press or the public directly, I make a plea that people respect both the families and sites that have been incorporated into local legends.

Since I had not seen the article she was referring to, I asked her to send me a copy. A few days later I received both the article and her letter of response to the newspaper. Following are excerpts from the article, which appeared in the *North Kingstown Villager*:

> Many in [North Kingstown] know the story of Mercy Brown, the vampire of Exeter, who was exhumed and whose heart was burned to ash on a stone near her grave. She was blamed for the failing health of her brother Edwin, and for the deaths of her sister and mother. The ritual, supposed to rid the corpse of the vampire spirit, failed to save Edwin Brown. Many now believe that the family died of consumption, the 19th century name for tuberculosis.
>
> But the stories of Rhode Island vampires do not

end with Mercy Brown. Just a few miles to the north, in the town of West Greenwich, lies the body of Nelly [sic] Vaughn, who died in 1889 at the age of nineteen. Etched in her headstone is the inscription, "I am waiting and watching for you."

Nelly Vaughn was thought to be a vampire at the time of her death. To this day it is claimed that nothing will grow near her grave, in spite of many attempts to plant there. Now for the frightening part: At least 12 people have reported seeing, hearing or feeling the presence of Nelly Vaughn while visiting her gravesite. Her ghost has often been heard to say, "I am perfectly pleasant," but it has also been known to scratch the face of those who may not agree. One [woman] mistook the spectre for an insane person before the spirit vanished.

. . . These stories are purported to be true, but like many such stories, they can be explained away by facts or are examples of superstitions and folklore carried from generation to generation. Some curious individuals who have wished to test the validity of these stories and/or just to frighten themselves have been the cause of the desecration of several historic cemeteries. Please remember that while the folklore is a matter of public record, the people which the lore surrounds are very precious and private.

Special thanks to Michael Bell, Rhode Island State Folklorist, for his help in unearthing these haunting tales.

I was not pleased to see my name attached to the article, particularly because the author wrote that Nellie "was thought to be a vampire at the time of her death." I remembered telling him that the opposite was probably true. At least he passed along, indirectly, my appeal for would-be legend trippers to show proper respect for the places they visit.

The text of Mrs. Arnold's undated letter to the editor follows:

> I am writing to dispute Chris Carroll's story, Local Haunts in the October 1995 issue. The story of Nellie Vaughn is not true. In the early 1970's a high school teacher told his students about a 19 year old girl [whose] body was exhumed. Her family thought she was a vampire . . . The teacher was talking about Mercy Brown. When the students found Nellie Vaughn, they were sure that they had found the grave. The students were wrong, but the rumor continues.
>
> Before the mistake in identity, grass always grew on the grave. When grass is constantly being trampled, and dug it will not grow. Nellie's stone has been broken into chunks, and stolen. Now that no one can find the grave, the grass grows. No grass has ever been planted there. I have gone to this cemetery all my life, and have witnessed this myself.
>
> A man who died at the age of 101, in the 1980's, knew Nellie when he was a child, before or after her death. This man told me himself. Much vandalism has been caused because of this mistake.

Evelyn Arnold told me that Chris Carroll got most of the information for his story from the 1994 book, *The New England Ghost Files,* by Charles Turek Robinson, which includes eye-witness accounts by people who have reported supernatural occurrences while visiting Nellie's gravesite. Robinson's entry for Nellie Vaughn recounts the belief that no grass will grow on her grave, then launches into personal experience stories. Several people, including two "former town officials," have reported seeing a young woman dressed in Victorian attire in the cemetery, especially around Nellie's tombstone. When approached, the specter disappears. But, according to Robinson, "the most common manifestations have been auditory. A number of people claim to have heard the disembodied voice of a young woman speaking out in the vicinity of the grave. In all instances, the faint voice was heard to be repeating the curious phrase, 'I am perfectly pleasant.' "

The bulk of Robinson's narrative recounts the experiences of Marlene, a woman from Coventry who visited the site several times in 1993. On her first visit, Marlene was attempting to obtain a rubbing of Nellie's gravestone, but her paper kept showing moisture stains even though the stone was completely dry. Adding to the mystery, her charcoal stick disappeared. She gave up on making a rubbing of the stone and took some photographs of Nellie's stone and several others in the cemetery. When she got the photos back from the developer, all of the gravestones were normal except Nellie's. In every photo of her stone, the letters appeared backwards. Marlene returned to the cemetery with a friend a few weeks later. In front of Nellie's grave, her friend could feel, but not see, someone poking her arm. But it was Marlene's husband, during a subsequent visit, who first heard the female voice in front of Nellie's tombstone say, "I am perfectly pleasant." He also felt something "invisibly scratch him across the left side of his face." And, according to his wife, "he had several red marks to prove it." He never returned to the cemetery.

Marlene went back alone several days later, where she encountered an attractive young woman. As they walked among the gravestones, chatting, the woman said that she was a member of some historical society. They stopped at Nellie's stone and Marlene asked the woman what she thought about the vampire legend. The woman said that she thought the legend was silly because Nellie had not been a vampire. At that point, the woman's behavior changed, and she began to repeat, "Nelly [sic] is not a vampire." Marlene, alarmed, returned to her car. As she glanced back at the cemetery, she was "astonished to see that the strange young woman was no longer there." On reflection, Marlene came up with the following theory to explain Nellie's haunting of the cemetery:

> ... Nelly is trying to vindicate herself. From the time of her death—perhaps because of the strange inscription on her tombstone—local folklore has mistakenly designated her a vampire. Marlene thinks that the young woman cannot rest with such a black slur on her name. For this reason, her apparition often appears troubled, and the ghost is sometimes heard to be saying "I am perfectly pleasant." [sic] as if to counter the notion that she is somehow evil.

Now, as these recent accounts of encounters with Nellie enter oral tradition, particularly the "I am pleasant" incident, a new legend appears to be forming. In this updated version, Nellie is longer a vampire; she is a ghost attempting to clear her name. Currently, then, there are three distinct Nellie Vaughn legends:

Legend 1. Nellie is a vampire;

Legend 2. Nellie is not now, nor has she ever has been, a vampire;

Legend 3. Nellie is a ghost on a mission to let people know she was never a vampire.

Legend 3 relies on legends 1 and 2; it is, in fact, a combining of them that acknowledges the existence of the "Nellie is a vampire" legend but accepts the truth of the "Nellie was never a vampire legend" to explain why Nellie's ghost haunts the Plain Meeting House cemetery.

All of the elements necessary for the marriage of a legend with the legend tripping custom exist in the first legend:

- The story is set in a specified locale that is relatively isolated yet readily accessible by automobile;
- the core of the legend involves some sort of supernatural crisis;
- the supernatural crisis has never been resolved; therefore,
- there is a threatening presence at the legend's locale; so,
- something spooky, mysterious, and even dangerous, might occur there.

A legend trip transforms a mere *story* into an *event*. Visitors to a legend's site become more than a passive audience as they literally step into the tale and become actively engaged in its incidents. They are, themselves, shapers of the tale. Any experiences that seem out of place or inexplicable, such as strange noises or creepy feelings, are likely to become incorporated into the legend, as these weird events are reported to friends and classmates. Legend tripping provides not only a *setting* for storytelling, but also the *experiences* that feed back into the legend and continually re-create it.

It is, no doubt, this process that accounts for the elements that have been incorporated into the legend of Nellie as a vampire. And, not surprisingly, most of them have a documented existence in folklore. After all, our underlying wellspring of folklore informs us about the nature of the supernatural world, guiding our interpretations. What is the meaning of no grass growing on Nellie's grave? There might be an explanation that does not have to resort to the supernatural. Some spoilsport, like Dr. Killjoy Rational III, might attribute the lack of vegetation to the tramping feet of legend trippers. A more satisfying solution—one that sustains, rather than undercuts, the legend—is found in numerous folk narratives: Grass does not grow on a murderer's grave. A vampire, of course, is a special genre of murderer.

Nellie's sinking grave also has rational explanations—legend trippers walking on, and even attempting to excavate, her grave, for instance—that can be ignored in favor of more ominous, but reinforcing, folk connections. A widespread American superstition states: "If one's grave sinks very much, another member of the family will die soon." In this form, the belief makes no explicit connection between the corpse in the grave and any subsequent deaths; the sinking grave is merely a sign, not a cause, of an impending death. But, in some European examples, the causative link is clearly stated. An early nineteenth-century Serbian schoolbook warns, "If the grave is sunk in, if the cross has taken a crooked position, and [if there are] other indications of this sort, [they] suggest that the deceased has transformed himself into a vampire."

Leaving money on Nellie's grave also relates at least indirectly to a variety of folk customs. The practice of supplying the dead with money (or some other form of exchange) to assist them in their journey to the otherworld is so ancient and widespread that it hardly needs discussion. Whether seen as a form of bribery or simply as a way to move the dead out of this world and into another, the outcome is the same: the dead will not return to bother the living. Ancient Greeks paid the ferryman to deliver them to the otherworld. African-American voodoo practitioners leave money on a grave to "pay the spirit" for taking his grave-yard dirt for ritual use. In Romania, the corpse is given a coin, candle, or towel to prevent it from becoming a vampire. The following account, recorded in Illinois in the 1930s, shows that this ancient custom was carried into twentieth-century America: "Another thing my mother did if anyone died, she always put some money under their pillow so they could have money to travel on. She did this to my brother forty years ago, put two silver dollars under the pillow in his coffin so he would have money on his way."

The folk motifs that have been incorporated into the legend of Nellie the vampire—no grass growing, the sinking grave, and the disappearing money—provide legend trippers with the tangible evidence they need for believing that the door to the supernatural realm remains open. That some Dr. Rational might interpret these phenomena without resorting to the supernatural does not lessen their impact for those disposed to believe. After all, one can point to alternative explanations that are widespread and long-established in folklore. Could so many people in so many places be wrong for so long?

For a very long time I never considered the second legend of Nellie a legend at all; it was, simply, THE TRUTH. I changed my mind after some reflection stimulated by a recent experience.

In November of 2000, I gave a talk at a meeting of the Western Rhode Island Civic and Historical Association. It took some patience and ingenuity to set up my slide projector and tape recorder in the cellar of the organization's seventeenth-century house in Coventry, since the electrical outlets were added long after the house was built but well before the advent of grounded plugs. As my wife searched for a three-pronged adapter and I struggled to remove a hot lightbulb from an overhead fixture so that I could replace it with a primitive screw-in outlet, I made small talk with arriving members. Actually, what most people think of as small talk often is, for me, fieldwork, part of a process for learning, firsthand, about local folklore. I was not surprised when told that the house was haunted. Any house that is more than three-hundred years old *has* to be haunted, if it has any character at all.

The towns of West Greenwich and Coventry were well-represented, so I raised the topic of Nellie Vaughn. Naturally, the origin of the legend was discussed. A woman from Coventry said that she did, indeed, know the identity of the teacher who started the whole thing. When I pressed for specifics, such as an actual name, I was told that, well, she would have to track it down—but she promised to get back to me with all of the information I requested. As weeks became months, I contemplated the elusive quarry. Then it struck me, not slowly, in logical increments, but in a single, unified flash. The TFC (teacher from Coventry) is a FOAF (friend of a friend). How many times had I heard the explanatory story? Countless. From how many people? Ditto. Had anyone ever given me a name? Never. Moreover, the teacher has been both a "he" and a "she."

By calling the story a legend, I'm neither asserting nor assuming that it's untrue—just merely acknowledging what I finally recognized: it has all of the defining characteristics of a legend. The story is set in the real world of historical time, with authentic places and credible characters. Although it is told as true, and the realistic setting with ordinary people in everyday situations provides an air of veracity, its truth is open to question. It is essentially a conversational story, loose and shifting in narrative form, revolving around the stable idea of mistaken identity. The actual words change, but the core of the story is always remembered and repeated: Nellie Vaughn is not a vampire. The story circulates primarily by word of mouth, communicated face-to-face, from one person to the next, although occasionally it is printed in a local newspaper. No one knows who first told the story. It has become a community's story, providing the insider's view of the issue, balancing (some hope, canceling) the outsider's story that continues to attract legend-trippers.

The story, though unverified, appeals to my rational instincts. Sometime in the late 1960s or early 1970s, a teacher at Coventry High School told his or her students about a vampire, probably Mercy Brown. Did *she* forget Mercy's name? Or did *he* omit Mercy's name purposefully because he didn't want his students to visit and vandalize the cemetery? Perhaps the teacher said that the vampire was a young woman who died sometime around 1890, and was buried in a cemetery behind a Baptist church south of Coventry, located off Victory Highway. Of course, one dark Friday or Saturday night, some of the students, armed with their limited knowledge, set out on Victory Highway in search of the vampire's grave.

Victory Highway (Route 102) is the main artery connecting Rhode Island's western towns that border Connecticut. This two-lane blacktop, which begins in the small mill village of Slatersville, near the Massachusetts border, meanders south through the towns of Burrillville, Glocester, Scituate, Foster, and Coventry. In West Greenwich, it arcs gently toward the southeast until it junctions with Ten Rod Road in Exeter. At that point, it makes a beeline due east to its terminus in North Kingstown at Wickford Cove on Narragansett Bay. Victory Highway's fifty miles traverse the most isolated, desolate areas of the state. Two vampires, Mercy Brown and Sarah Tillinghast, are buried within sight of the highway in Exeter. Sarah Tillinghast is likely interred in an unmarked grave in her family's small cemetery about two hundred meters north of Victory Highway, just east of its junction with Ten Rod Road. But, until I discovered the family name and located the cemetery in 1984, no one would have known who Sarah was or where she was buried. Not three miles down the highway toward Wickford is the Exeter Grange and Chestnut

Hill Baptist Church, behind which is the grave of Mercy Brown, Rhode Island's most notorious vampire.

As the legend goes, the students came upon the Plain Meeting House Baptist Church and cemetery in West Greenwich, the town located between Coventry and Exeter. They never made it as far as the Chestnut Hill Baptist Church. As they pulled up to the diminutive Plain Meeting House, with its windows ominously shuttered, they could see, dimly lit by the headlights, the beckoning stone pillars of the cemetery's entrance. It didn't take long for the flashlight beam to hit upon the gravestone that was just to the right of the dirt road, only a few meters in from the entrance. The students let out a spontaneous gasp/scream when the light fixed on the inscription at the bottom of the gravestone. As they read aloud, "I Am Waiting and Watching For You," poor Nellie's fate was sealed through mistaken identity.

One glitch in this reasonable scenario is that the Plain Meeting House is not at all visible from Victory Highway. One must travel west on Plain Meeting House Road for about four miles, with many curves and sharp turns. Maybe some of the students already knew about the church and cemetery and decided it was a likely place to search? Another question: What does the inscription on Nellie's gravestone mean? If you're thinking about some undead creature entombed under the stone, surely it has a threatening aura. But, take a step back, adopt the persona of Dr. Killjoy Rational, and ask some follow-up questions: Who would have chosen that inscription? Traditionally, it would have been Nellie's parents. Why would they have chosen this seemingly ambiguous statement? Viewed in the context of conventional tombstone inscriptions, it is neither threatening nor ambiguous. This phrase is found on the stones of family members who died while in the flower of youth. In heaven before fulfilling their earthly promise, they await a reunion with loved ones left behind. But, even if Nellie's body had been exhumed as part of a healing ritual, why would it be necessary to post a public warning? Dr. Rational answers: procedure finished, vampire laid to rest, end of threat, mission accomplished.

The stable core of this legend—that Nellie's vampire reputation is the result of mistaking her for Mercy Brown—has been borne out over the years as people continue to confuse the two. Take, for example, the *Providence Journal* article by reporter Kevin Sullivan, "A Journey through Old Rhode Island: Quietly But in Vain, The Rural Areas Try to Fend off Modernity," which appeared in May 1990:

> . . . just before dark, we arrive at West Greenwich Center, which is the center of absolutely nothing in West Greenwich. There's an old boarded-up church and a graveyard, and when we arrive, a pickup truck.
>
> In the graveyard, three high school aged boys are looking at gravestones. They say they are looking for the grave of Mercy Brown, the vampire.
>
> . . . Her gravesite has become a Halloween favorite among vandals and spook-seekers. But these lads, all high school sophomores, are not interested in vandalism or history, or even vampires and the occult.
>
> Explains Erik Johnson: "We want to bring girls down here and freak them out."
>
> Mercy Brown is buried in Exeter, at least 10 miles away.

Freaked out is precisely what several adult legend-trippers were on Halloween of 1993, as they poked around the Plain Meeting House cemetery. Two days later, the following account appeared in the *Providence Journal*:

> Two couples out for pre-Halloween fun in a historical cemetery Friday night made a macabre discovery that has police baffled—a newly opened grave, with a body in an opened casket beside it.
>
> State police say they don't know who dug up the

casket or what the motive was. They said nothing
was missing from the casket.

. . . Theresa Safford, one of the four who found
the casket, said the group had intended to visit a
staged haunted house attraction in Coventry but
arrived just after it closed.

Then they decided to visit the historical cemetery
to look for the grave of someone, who, according to
local legend, was a vampire.

As they were walking through the cemetery,
under Friday night's full moon, they stumbled upon
the opened grave.

It shouldn't take a police detective to figure out why the
casket was dug up. Someone must have been looking for
Nellie's grave, which is unmarked. In the words of one of the
legend trippers, "I was ready to pass out and die. It was a new
grave. I started to hyperventilate." Just the sort of thrill that
legend trippers crave. I have no doubt that they have
recounted their experiences to everyone they know, and that
the sprouting variants of Nellie's legend will bolster her supernatural status and add to the mystery of the Plain Meeting
House Cemetery.

After reading about this incident, I contacted the State
Police, requesting more information. I was told that someone
would get back to me. (Perhaps that someone who never
returned my call was engaged in conferring with the people
who know the TFC—"teacher from Coventry.") I asked an
acquaintance who is a member of the West Greenwich fire and
rescue department if he knew anything about the exhumation.
He told me that the corpse had been buried only a few days
before, and that the deceased had been an older man; my friend
referred to him as a "town character." He said that, given the
coffin's weight, it must have been dug up by several rather
strong individuals.

Almost exactly two years after this illicit exhumation, I

finally did receive some information from the State Police—but it was entirely accidental. I was in the Tillinghast family cemetery with a production crew from the *Sightings* television series for an on-location interview. Midnight was approaching, bright lights were illuminating the old gravestones, and a gasoline-driven generator used to power the lights, cameras, and—I hesitate to admit—fog machine, was humming, a bit too loudly for nearby neighbors. When a car with two state troopers pulled up, the producer suggested that I fill them in on what we were doing. I stifled the urge to ask, "Why me?" and approached the officers. After they were satisfied that we weren't ghouls, cultists, or even just legend trippers, they relaxed. One of the troopers explained that they were being extra vigilant because someone had actually dug up a body a couple of Halloweens before in West Greenwich.

"Yes," I said. "I read about it in the newspaper, and called the State Police and asked for more information. But no one would tell me anything."

Somewhat apologetically, he said that they don't like to publicize that kind of activity because of the "copycat" phenomenon. He told me that he was one of the officers called to the scene. The corpse was that of a local character, he said, and when they found him, he had a can of beer in one hand and a pack of cigarettes in the other. Then he added, "It was really weird. He had all this long hair and a beard. He looked like a werewolf."

Under my breath, I muttered, "Oh, jeez." I should have known that it was only a matter of time before a werewolf joined our local vampire.

American legend trippers looking for vampires are not limited to American cemeteries. Some U.S. soldiers in Kitzingen, Germany, became attracted to a cemetery because one of the gravestones is decorated with bats and skulls, the functional equivalent of the "I Am Waiting and Watching For You" inscription on Nellie's grave. And, like the legend trippers at Nellie's gravesite, the soldiers of the 3rd Infantry Division would not be deterred from their midnight vigil, even when confronted with rational thought. Despite the fact that Transylvania was seven hundred miles away, the American soldiers continued to gather at the site, waiting for Count Dracula to rise from the grave in search of his victims. One of the nontripping soldiers commented, "I don't know if they really think they'll see him, but when somebody is convinced, perhaps they can make it happen." Like the local folks in West Greenwich, the mayor of Kitzingen realized his impotency in the face of belief: "You can't stop these young fellows from believing what they want," he said. Garlic may stop a vampire dead in its tracks, but nothing seems to ward off spellbound legend trippers.

Unrelenting vandalism is often the price paid by a cemetery that attains to legendary status. Gravestones are defaced, broken, and even stolen. While Everett Peck remained steadfast in his vigilant protection of Mercy Brown's gravestone in the Chestnut Hill cemetery around Halloween, he was caught off guard in mid August in 1996. As the newspaper reported, "In 1892, they took her heart. In 1996, they've taken her gravestone." It wasn't the first time. For many years, the stone was unattached to its base, the separation a result of earlier vandalism. In this recent theft, the town offered a $50 reward for information leading to the recovery of the stone. Less than a week later, the gravestone was reported recovered (with no other details released to the public). Everett said, "There's no damage to it. The recovery made my night. I slept for the first time in a long time." Now, Mercy's stone has a thick iron collar connecting it to its base.

Over the years, Nellie Vaughn's gravestone has been knocked over, broken in two, then chipped away, piece-by-piece. Some have even attempted to excavate her grave. As a last-resort attempt to stem the vandalism, community members moved what remained of her gravestone to a safe, but publicly unrevealed, location. Naturally, the "disappearance" of Nellie's gravestone has served only to heighten the mystery and reinforce her supernatural status.

Perhaps it's time we—all of us, scholars, commentators, and legend trippers, alike—let Nellie Vaughn rest in peace. But I can't leave this case without offering a tantalizing scrap of genealogy. While it does nothing to resolve Nellie's status as a vampire, it does suggest that her community had access to firsthand knowledge of the tradition. From 1840 to 1878, the pastor of the Plain Meeting House Church was Reverend John Tillinghast, a second cousin of Stukeley Tillinghast, the father of Sarah, the vampire. The Tillinghast family is woven into the tapestry of New England vampire practice.

CHAPTER 6
I Thought For Sure They Were Coming After Me

T he day was tailor-made for a trip to the grave of a vampire. A cold, steady drizzle made it seem more like March, without the wind, than early May. Mary-Lou, my administrative assistant, and I packed up the cameras, film, tape recorder, audiotape, and spare batteries, and headed straight west from Providence on Route 6. We had interviewed Jennie Boldan and her husband, David, some six months before, just a week after a Halloween article about their family ghost (whom they call "Frank") appeared in the *Providence Journal*. But they had never mentioned the vampire that was interred in their town of Foster, a dozen miles west of Providence, on the Connecticut border.

Mary-Lou was acquainted with them through the Second Rhode Island Regiment and the Glocester Light Infantry, two of Rhode Island's several colonial militia units. She told me that she and Jennie were "camp followers." Mary-Lou must have noticed the puzzled expression on my face, so she explained that camp followers were the unofficial, nonmilitary personnel, mostly the wives and children of soldiers, that accompanied military units. At the time of the American Revolution, the expression did not have the same negative connotations that it had acquired by the Civil War, when the phrase "camp follower" was practically synonymous with prostitute. Being a member of the colonial militia in New England is ... well, somewhere between a hobby and a way of life; exactly where varies from individual to individual. In February, Jennie had stopped by the office to talk about colonial militia activities over lunch with Mary-Lou. She mentioned, in casual conversation, something about "vampires in an old family cemetery in Foster." Ordinarily, I'm not an eavesdropper, but certain words seem to transform my normally placid ears into vibrating antennas. The three of us made a date to meet in the spring so that Jennie could take us out to the cemetery, where we would take photographs, and, of course, she would tell us the story.

Though long accustomed to the scale of Rhode Island, I'm still amazed at how quickly one can go from city to country. Rhode Island has all of the zones that most states now have—urban, suburban, open country, sprawl, new cookie-cutter cul-de-sacs wrapped up in themselves—but each is highly compressed. On the way to Jennie's early nineteenth-century house in Foster, the following transitions occur in about twenty minutes of driving time: for its three-mile Providence stretch, Route 6 is a four-lane, divided highway through long-established neighborhoods (coalesced mill villages) and suburbs. Entering the town of Johnston, the road travels past scattered nineteenth-century farm houses connected by the unrelenting sprawl of strip malls, convenience stores, gas stations, fast food, and the occasional church and liquor store. This mercifully short three miles ends abruptly at Famous Pizza, the last outpost before open country and the Scituate town line. Traversing Scituate one literally takes a breath of fresh air driving the five, gently rolling miles to Foster.

Jennie lives in the northeast corner of the town and the cemetery is in the far southwestern corner, a distance of about eight miles for a crow but considerably farther on winding roads the likes of Cucumber Hill and Plain Woods. There would be plenty of time for Jennie, riding shotgun and acting as navigator and narrator (with a small microphone clipped to her jacket), to fill us in on what we were about to encounter. She is flaky, in an appealing way, bubbly and forthcoming, an attractive woman who looks too young to have two teenagers (a son and a daughter) in addition to two younger sons. The slap of windshield wipers provided a rhythmic accompaniment to her tale; her words seemed to get in synch with them and stay there. The "thump ... thump ... thump" kept even the pauses linked to the tale. Jennie began by describing her last trip to this cemetery with Mary, her legend-tripping companion, about three years earlier.

"You know, I've gotta tell you something. You won't believe this, I know you won't. But, about three years ago, Mary and I decided to venture over to this place. And the first time we went ... it wasn't dusk or anything like that. ... It was a nice Spring day, and ... we did a little studying of the gravestones, and the whole thing. Couple of weeks went by and I said to Mary, 'Let's go back there.' And she said, 'I was going to ask *you* if you wanted to go back.' It's almost like a drawing feeling. So we decided to go back again and I had, oh, maybe about three glasses of wine at her house, you know, just to get myself ready for this! Here we go back a second time, looking for trouble, right?"

Pause. Thump ... thump ... thump. Jennie dropped her voice to nearly a whisper. "It was just before dusk." Then she increased the volume dramatically, "You oughta see us book in there and try to book out of there before the sun was droppin'!"

She laughed at the memory, then continued, matter-of-factly. "I had picked jack-in-the-pulpit, right? I had gotten all of the names on the gravestones embedded into my mind—I didn't think to take a pencil and pad with me—but, anyways, I remembered them. One was Sarah, one was, ohh. ... "

"What was their last name?" I asked.

"Last name. It wasn't King. Jinks. Jenks? Maybe it's Jenks."

Jennie was momentarily sidetracked by my question, then decided to forget trying to remember the family name and, for-tunately, continued with her narrative. "Ah, but anyways, I picked the jack-in-the-pulpit and I put it into a little tiny vase on my bureau."

Jennie chuckled as she said, "You're not going to believe this when I tell you. You know, I had a dream that night ... " Drawing out the word "dream" for emphasis, she paused. " ... about that family. And it was almost like I could see them and who they were. And they were talking amongst themselves. An argument broke out. And there was all kinds of problems going on. I woke up in an awful sweat. You know, my jack-in-the-pulpit was dead the next day on the bureau."

She practically screamed the following words, almost laughing, "And I'm going, 'I'll never go back there again!' And here I am! Look at this!"

Everyone laughed. Looking through the windshield at what had become a steady rain, I said, "And it's a nice day, too."

"Yeah." More laughter.

Jennie continued to describe her dream. Her voice was puzzled, quizzical. "This real crazy dream that I had, though, they were dressed in their long dresses and . . . ." Her voice just trailed off. She seemed momentarily lost in the memory of her dream. Thump . . . thump . . . thump.

I broke the spell with a question. "How long ago was it?"

"That was about three years ago. I haven't been back there since."

I tried again, clarifying my question. "How long ago did they die?" I was pushing to get specifics—the family's name, the dates. Dr. Rational was annoyed by Jennie's incessant returning to her dream. Looking back, I'm embarrased by my impatience. I should have allowed Jennie to elaborate on her dream. Instead, I missed a fascinating opportunity.

Jennie gave me the best answer she could. "1800s."

"You can tell me the background as we're going out there . . ." I suggested, " . . . because I don't know the particulars." I was understandably excited about what we might find. I couldn't wait for the information to come rolling in. As a folklorist, I have an innate appetite for information. But why did I assume that Jennie cared about details such as names and dates? In retrospect, I find my lack of empathy disturbing. I'm forced to listen to myself as I log and transcribe hundreds of interviews. Perhaps this is appropriate punishment for asking questions that I should have known could not be answered—and should not have asked. Why not let people tell me what *they* know, instead of attempting to pry out what *I* want to know? How many times I've wanted to shout to myself, "Oh, shut up!" Of course, it's just wishful thinking, because every time I listen to the tape, I say the same things. Thankfully, in the years since 1983, those moments have diminished. I've learned how to listen, if for no other reason than to avoid hearing my voice, over and over. Listening, truly listening, is difficult and exhausting, much more so than most people imagine. Try it for a two- or-three hour stretch.

Jennie didn't know anything factual about the family in the cemetery, nor did she care much. Her focus was on the spiritual and mystical aspects surrounding them. The two of us were on entirely different wavelengths, but Jennie was trying to accommodate my insensitive probing.

"Well, the family was, uh, somebody was supposed to have taken ill. . . . I think it was one of the older children that was supposed to have taken ill, and they buried her, right? And, I guess a couple of days went by and they went back to the grave, to do something, and when they got back to the grave, the grave was empty. So, then it started, the dream. They thought they were having dreams. You know, she would come into the house and, little by little, I guess she killed off the family. And you'll see all the dates. The dates are the weirdest damn thing! They're all in sequence, like one died May 20th, then you look again, one died May 26th—right down the line! It's unbelievable!"

The unfolding story reminded me more of Sarah Tillinghast than Mercy Brown, with the vampire actually leaving the grave to come back at night and kill her family, one by one.

"And all the gravestones that have these dates on them are tilted like this." Jennie demonstrated with her hand that the stones were tilted sideways rather than front-to-back.

"And according to an old legend, I guess it is, when a gravestone . . . becomes tilted, the devil flies up out of the grave. And that's what makes the gravestone tilt. And in front of that gravestone you can see something had scraped completely across all them graves. You'll see it when you get there. Did you bring the camera?"

Mary-Lou and I began to chuckle. "Yeah, I brought the camera," I said. I was laughing at the thought of photographing the devil flying out of the grave, but I think Jennie interpreted our laughter as sarcasm. As if we were saying, "Oh, sure, Jennie, something's waiting to get us in the cemetery!"

"Wait!" She implored us not to be hasty in our judgments. She's not the only one who's had those feelings, so maybe there's something wrong with us, not her. "I don't know. Maybe you don't get these kind of feelings. But I'm very psychic and can pick up feelings. Other people have gone there. There's been two, three other people in Foster that have been there, and they say they get the same kind of feelings I have. So I can't be crazy. And when I go to this place I get the leeriest darn feeling."

"What kind of feeling?" Mary-Lou asked.

"Leery. Leery inside. Really haunting-like. . . . And there's an old rusty iron gate to the graveyard, and. . . . " Jennie began to chuckle, nervously. "Ooohhh," she squeaked. "It's almost like I'm invading on private property. Like they're actually saying, 'You don't belong here. Get out of here.' You know?" Jennie paused and began laughing again. "And look at the weather we're going in!"

Still probing, I asked, "Where did you first hear about that? You heard about it before you even went out there?"

"Yeah, I had heard about it a couple of years before. It took me a couple of years to get there, you know, because I was doing other things. But . . . it was very strange, because it just kept popping up in my mind. . . . And I don't know if one of the girls was born May 20th, which is my birthday, or died May 20th. But I got the leeriest feeling when I saw that on the gravestone. I just went, 'Aaughhh.' "

Jennie began preparing us for what to expect. "Now, you're going to walk through the woods to get there. The gravesite is not seen from the road. . . . It's a little family plot. Some little family plot! They're all in order. They're all down the line. All neatly in there, and ooohhh!"

Jennie continued her inventory of the things about the cemetery that give her those "leery" feelings. "I wasn't sure whether I was seeing things correctly or not, but the first time I went I had

checked the grounds and, you know, they were OK. The second time I went, it looked like one of the graves had like slid in or something, like it was sinking. . . . I'm going, 'Mary, that's impossible. In this short length of time they don't sink in that way!' "
Now she was screaming softly, almost like a pretend weeping. "I said, 'See, it's gonna come after us 'cause we're out here nosin' around.' And she says, 'Let's stay after dusk.' And I goes, 'Well, you do it! Not me!' "

Jennie obviously was really enjoying this experience. And the closer we got to the cemetery, the more excited she became. She was like an athlete getting psyched for the big game, visualizing what lies ahead. It was contagious, but my adrenaline rush was in anticipation of discovering a new vampire family.

Jennie directed me to turn left onto Cucumber Hill Road. We fell silent. The windshield wipers were squeaking, not thumping. The rain had eased, and everyone seemed to calm down. Jennie, without prompting, began talking in her normal speaking voice, describing an appetite for legend tripping that she shares with her friend, Mary.

"In the beginning, when we first went, we were very excited about it. Because she and I usually do these kind of things together. We hear about something, and then we go looking for it. . . . I decided that this was the trip that I *really* wanted to take . . . and we decided to do it. And when we went out there, I was feeling very good. . . . And the second time we went I didn't feel so hot about it. I kept drawing back. I kept saying, 'I don't really want to go, Mary.' And she'd say, 'Well, I don't either, but let's go. Curiosity will kill us.' "

"How do you feel this time?" I asked. "This is the third time."

"Like I'm invading." Jennie chuckled. "Again! I don't know what they're going to do to me. 'Oh, it's her again! And look what she brought! *More*, with her! Next time, you know, we'll have the whole country here. Can't rest in peace at all.' "

I asked what finally happened to the one suspected of being a vampire and Jennie replied, "They think she still roams the countryside."

"No one ever dug her up and tried anything, like burning her heart?"

When Jennie replied, "Nope," I was puzzled. This vampire story didn't seem to fit the New England pattern. In every case I knew of, some sort of measures were taken to restore balance in the family and community; to kill the evil and cure the sick. That nothing was done, and that this vampire is still at large, struck me as more Hollywood than history.

Jennie continued, "From what I understand, this family was a family that was . . . I'm trying to look for the word. When people don't like them. It's a word they used back then. . . . It's a Yankee term. That they don't bother with you. They put you aside."

Mary-Lou offered "shun."

"Shunned upon! Yeah, that's it. It was a family that was shunned upon. It was a family that was not recognized . . . . in this town, as far as I know. . . . I've inquired, asked questions. And they go, 'Oh, that family!' You know, 'We don't talk about that family. A lot of weird things happened in that family.' "

Jennie directed me to take a right. Then she continued her discussion of slanted gravestones, telling us that, if they tip to the front or back, that's OK. But, if they're tilted sideways, "It's usually that they're flowing right out of the ground."

I told Jennie that I'd never heard that before.

"Well, when I was a small child . . . my grandmother used to tell me . . . 'Don't go in a graveyard that most of the stones were slanted this way [Jennie demonstrated with her hands that the stones slants sideways] because that's where the devil has flown up out of the grave, that evil spirit has come out of that person.' "

Relaxed, almost yawning, Jennie said with theatrical understatement, "I really don't think I'd care to have that demonstrated."

Mary-Lou and I laughingly agreed. We all discussed why the family didn't take any measures against "Sarah" when she started coming back. Jennie speculated that maybe she worked too fast and killed them off before they could do anything to stop her. I stated that, typically, a vampire will keep going after it finishes with the family.

"Maybe it was revenge on the family, or something," Jennie suggested.

"A loving family," Mary-Lou observed dryly.

We were having fun now, joking about vampires. But I wasn't sure if Jennie's trepidation over the impending site visit was actual, feigned, or a mixture of both. When we passed "Hidden Hollow Farm," we were about as isolated as you can get in Rhode Island. I asked Jennie if she knew the people living out here. She said she knew most of them.

"Some of them like to talk about different things like that, and others, they're not the least bit interested because they get too ..." Jennie searched for the right term or phrase, and finally said, with an exaggerated Yankee dialect, "Not logical." Then, in her own, enthusiastic voice, "But any time an old-timer mentions anything like that about the town of Foster, I'm like, 'Let's go!' "

At the junction of Moosup Valley Road and Plain Woods Road, Jennie pointed to the right, toward Plain Woods and Connecticut. With obvious relief that we weren't lost, she said, "There you go."

After a short distance, the road bent left onto Jenks Road. I wondered if the road was named for the family (recalling that Jennie thought their name was something like Jenks or Jinks). Jennie ordered me to slow down because we were getting close. "Go past this driveway. . . . Go up the hill. . . . It's on the other side of these trees. . . . Told you, it's in the woods. . . . OK, go ahead up. There's an open space you can park in."

Jennie switched to her frightened stage laughter and voice, "OK, guys, I'll see you later. You're on your own! . . . Well, it was nice knowin' you guys. Have a good time."

Mary-Lou and Jennie were giggling, as I deadpanned, "OK, you want me to leave the keys in the car and the engine running, right?"

"You oughta see me book out of this place the last time I was here. *I thought for sure they were comin' after me!*"

We parked on the side of the dirt road and began walking through mucky sod toward the cemetery, which was hidden in the woods perhaps two or three hundred meters to the west. We speculated that the cemetery might actually be in Connecticut. We were that close to the border. Along the way, we had to climb over several rubble walls surrounding smallish areas of dense brush and trees. The three of us, who had spent considerable time dwelling in the past, laughed at an insider's joke when Mary-Lou asked in mocked astonishment, "Hey, what are all of these stone walls doing out here in the middle of nowhere?" It's a question heard often from newcomers who don't know that most of the "nowheres" in this region of western Rhode Island and eastern Connecticut once were "somewheres": relatively isolated, self-sufficient family farms with planted fields, orchards, and grazing pastures, though perhaps considered small in comparison with farms elsewhere. Certainly they did not rival the plantations of South County, a mere ten miles away. This "nowhere" of 1983 is becoming, once again, a "somewhere," though of a much different character. When I went looking for this cemetery again, in early 1996, I was completely disoriented (and not because, like Jennie, I had fortified myself with three glasses of wine!). Jenks Road had a number of new houses. I couldn't find the cemetery, though it hadn't moved. I guessed that it was hidden behind someone's aboveground swimming pool. In 2001, I looked again and was successful. It was just behind a newer house, and the young owners said that they had heard that there was "some sort of witch" buried in the cemetery.

At the cemetery, we examined each gravestone, reading aloud from the inscriptions, noting the dates of death. The family name turned out to be Young, not Jenks. Jennie pointed out the slanted gravestones that she said one must take care to avoid. The rain continued to fall, but somewhere in the white pines that embraced the Youngs' neglected last home, a lone cardinal was singing. The melancholy of reading about consumption wiping out entire families does not approach the feeling of standing amid the tumbledown headstones of young adults who perished before their parents, too soon. Perhaps Jennie was nervous, frightened, and thrilled. I was immensely saddened.

Jennie picked up the thread of her story:

"One of those girls—check the earliest date—one of those girls died, and then she came back. From the story I understand, the first time they saw her, they saw her face in the window. And then after that she came into the house, at night, you know. They thought they were dreaming."

I prodded for more. "And she would come back?"

Jennie continued, "And keep coming back, and coming back. I guess she took her whole family." In a rational, serious voice, she wondered aloud, "You know, years ago, the stories . . . they probably all died of consumption, or whatever it is."

Mary-Lou interjected, "But they're all so young . . . "

"That's it. It doesn't click," Jennie responded.

"Yeah, but consumption is contagious," I said.

In the car while returning to Jennie's house, she shared other supernatural stories of Foster. She said that she had gone down to Dolly Cole Pond, near her house, and looked for "the woman who cries for her baby," drowned in the pond. Then there was the suicide (or was it murder?) of mill owner "Peg Leg" Walker. (His name was actually Peleg, which probably was altered to make sense of such an unusual first name.) He told his partners after an argument that, one morning, when they tried to open the mill door, they would have to take the keys from a dead man's pocket. Sure enough, one morning the villagers awoke to the sound of the mill bell and, hurrying to investigate, found Walker hanging from the bell rope. After that, the bell would ring on its own. When Walkers' co-owners finally removed the bell and its rope, the mill wheel began to turn backwards. Jennie has gone to Hopkins Mill and listened for the toll of the bell that is no longer there, and watched for the wheel to reverse its course. I did some research later and found this interesting detail:

> William Potter purchased the sawmill in Hopkins
> Mills in 1790 and by 1799 had also built a fulling mill,
> to process and clean home-spun wool. . . . In 1813
> William Potter, Peleg Walker, and several partners

acquired a site a half mile south of the Hopkins Mills. They subsequently expanded operations to include the mechanized spinning and weaving of woolen cloth, hence the names Foster Woolen Factory and the colloquial Ram Tail Mill. William Potter's sons, William and Herbert, in partnership with Peleg Walker, ran the mill; but Walker committed suicide and rumors arose thereafter that the mill was haunted. The mill was abandoned, partly burned in 1873, and was listed as "haunted" in the 1885 census.

When I asked what other vampire stories she knew, Jennie said, "The one in East Greenwich. I've heard of that one." I wondered if she was thinking of Nellie Vaughn in West Greenwich, or if she meant Mercy Brown in Exeter. But when she said that the vampire's body was dug up and burned, I was confused. I told her about Mercy Brown's *heart* (not her entire corpse) being burned to ashes, which were then given as medicine to her brother. Jennie was surprised (and delighted). Then she wondered if the faces of the people who were considered vampires "protruded back" as they were dying, thereby presenting a fanged appearance. I offered my view on how late-stage consumptives begin to take on the wasted appearance, like the walking dead, that is associated with vampires.

Then, in my Dr. Rational persona, I explained that the people involved didn't use the "vampire" word. Jennie then brought up the topic of premature burial as a possible explanation for the vampire belief. "An old guy that was a friend of my father-in-law used to tell me about that. He used to work down in Providence in the grave sites, and they had to move one whole cemetery, right? . . . And he said the caskets that he dug up and opened up, that had claw marks, were unbelievable. . . . He worked for years in the cemeteries down there." Jennie answered my question about why they opened up the caskets with, "Just curiosity, to see who's in it."

Jennie spoke about many supernatural beliefs and practices,

from divination at the crossroads to making pacts with the devil and practicing witchcraft. Then she began to talk about Frank, her family's ghost. A local televison show had recently visited Jennie's "haunted" house.

"This is what they wanted me to do in my house. They wanted me to keep a tape recorder . . . going to see if we can pick up anything. You . . . can hear him, you know he's there. . . . It really thrills me to the bone at night when you're laying there and you're dead to a sleep, and all of a sudden, you get this [Jennie waved her hand in front of her face] and that's just how it feels, you know. And I go, 'That's the wrong side, David's not sleeping on that side. Get your hands off me!' "

When I asked if Frank hears what people say, Jennie answered matter-of-factly, "Of course, he does. He makes noises now and then. Occasionally he's done things to David and the boys. Well, he slammed the door in young David's face, almost took his fingers right off. He didn't want him in that room and he was determined he was not going to have him in that room. You know, there are certain times he just gets upset."

"How do your children feel about having something like that?" I asked.

"Uh, they accept it, but at times they're very nervous. Especially when they know he's around." By now, I had noticed that, when Jennie was talking about Frank, her speech lacked the playful bantering that characterizes her discussion of vampires and other locally haunted sites. Legend-tripping is fun. You go out to a cemetery or old mill building, experience the heart-pumping chill of fright, then go home. But when a ghost *lives* in your house, and assaults your children, the game turns serious.

We arrived at Jennie's Greek Revival house, on Danielson Pike (Route 6) and continued our discussion inside. Since the day that a descendent of an early Foster family, the Hopkins, stopped by and shared some history of the house, Jennie has deemed that its haunting makes sense. She was told that the house, built about 1840 and in the Hopkins family from 1870 (until purchased by the Boldans in 1971), was used as a temporary morgue during the winter, and that the bodies were displayed in the parlor. Frank may have been one (perhaps even more than one) of them.

Jennie described her daughter's first face-to-face encounter with Frank. "She was, maybe, fifteen, sixteen years old. . . . It was in the evening. She went upstairs . . . to fix her hair in my bedroom. If you look into my mirror, you could see the whole length of the hallway and right into the boys' room, which is across the hall. So, she was standing there . . . combing her hair. And as she looked up into the mirror, she could see this figure coming out of the bedroom, and she . . . got quite nervous about the whole situation. She booked it on out of there real fast, came downstairs and said, 'I just saw him! . . . I saw Frank.' She said he was all in black—full length of him was black—and a white face, very, very white. But you couldn't make out what he looked like. And he disappeared just as fast as he came." Jennie snapped her fingers as she said "disappeared" and continued. "When she told *PM Magazine* this, you ought to see the guy that was taping that. . . . His hair was standing on his head. He really didn't want to stay here." Jennie laughed for the first time since we had entered her house, tempering the serious tone that pervaded all discussion of Frank.

As the talk shifted away from Frank, the atmosphere lightened. Jennie began to talk about the "ghost lot," located on Tucker Hollow Road in the far northeastern corner of Foster. "It's about a witch. Now, I know several police officers, and in order to be a police officer you have to go through a psychological test, and if you don't pass the psychological test you don't get to be a police officer. So these police officers are pretty well with it, you know, and, two or three of them have seen this bright light that shows in the woods. . . . Maybe it's a bluish white light. But I know that my husband had seen it and had mentioned it to me. And then the sergeant of the police team up here came to the house one night, and he says, 'Is David here?' I says, 'Yeah.' He says, 'I want David to come with me and see something.' I said, 'OK.' So David and him went up there, right? A little while went by and they come back and he came in the house and he says, 'I think I need a cup of coffee.' Like that, right? I says, 'Why, what's the matter?' He says, 'I just saw the light.' I says, 'You saw the light, did ya?' "

Everyone laughed. The atmosphere definitely had returned to what it was in the car on the way to the cemetery.

"And he says, 'Yeah, it's like a ball just bouncing around in the woods there.' And I said, 'Well, isn't that nice! Why don't you come right in?' "

Jennie gave us the background story for the strange lights at the ghost lot. "She was a witch, this woman that lived there. . . . I don't know if they went up and burnt her out, or she started a fire and caught herself on fire, or what the story was. But they claim that her ghost remains there. And this is what that bluish white light is that bounces around in the woods."

"And she died in the fire?" I asked.

"Yes, she died in the fire. You know, I went looking for it one night with my husband, and we sat up there, and sat up there, and sat up there. I didn't see anything. . . . But they claim that there's been several police officers that have gone up there just, just to go down the road to make sure everything's OK . . . and they saw it."

Mary-Lou asked, "Could it have been a flashlight or something?"

"I don't think so. . . . You see, Foster is a really strange town. I have often put forth the theory that Foster has a cloud around it. Because if you live in Foster, and you go out of Foster, you feel completely different. And as you're approaching to come into Foster, you start getting that *heavy feeling* again."

I asked if she had that feeling when she went to the Young family cemetery. "Well, I had never really gotten that feeling until I had . . . approached it the first time. I had never gotten that feeling anywhere else I'd been, in search of things. I usually get . . . very excited. . . . Let's go, let's get there, you know. And once I get there, I'm all excited and I want to stay there. And when I went this first time, it was like, you know, there was a wall up. 'What are you doing here?' . . . I just got the strangest feeling out of it. I just didn't like it."

When Jennie and her friend Mary made their trips to the Young family cemetery, "It was very strange! Like I said, I had very strange feelings. We got out of the car and I said, 'I don't see any *grave* sites,' you know, like that. And I'm looking, and looking, and looking. And I said, 'Well, maybe it's way back in the woods.' And I started walking through the woods. And she was behind me, you know. She was, like, away from me, and I go, 'Oh, come, hurry up and catch up to me,' you know. I say, I'm not going to go in by myself. I say, 'If I'm going to do this you're going to go in with me.' We kept walking, and walking, and walking. And then finally I said, 'It's in front of us. I can see it now.' You know. And it was almost like a suction cup." Jennie imitated a suction noise. "I was drawn to it, but once I got there it was the leeriest feeling, you know, like I didn't belong there. But then the second time I went in, it was even heavier. . . . I kept watching the sun going down and Mary, of course, she wanted to take pictures, and she wanted to . . . get the grave rubbings and names, and the whole thing." Jennie's tone turned sarcastic when she described what Mary wanted.

"Right. Did she get the grave rubbings?"

"Yeah, she started to. And I said to her, 'Mary, the sun is going down. Will you get out of here? They're gonna fly right up and out of here. Let's go.' "

In a deliberately theatrical voice, rising in both pitch and volume, Jennie said, "Pretty soon you are going to see these people that you don't want to see, you know." She imitated the sound of vampires lapping up blood, and everyone laughed. "Dripping blood. I says, 'Let's get out of here.' And when I was coming out of those woods, the sun was down. I could almost feel . . . the pressure . . . building. You know, like I didn't belong there. . . . If you are an intruder . . . you're threatening them, and they will destroy you."

We had some fun bouncing around the common stock of vampire images. We did not share knowledge of local folklore—such as the Ghost Lot, Dolly Cole Pond, or the Young family vampire—but we all knew that vampires leave their graves at night, suck blood, and must return before cock crow and first light. The vampire of popular culture gave us common ground. But I couldn't help wondering if Dracula's shadow had fallen over Jennie's story of the Foster vampire. Consider the motifs that are prominent in the rather disjointed narrative that she delivered in the car and at the cemetery: the family discovers, soon after her interment, that the grave of the first child to die (nineteen-year-old Nancy, as we learned in the cemetery) is empty; then she begins to haunt the family at night; at first, they believe they are dreaming, but as they begin to die, one-by-one, the truth becomes obvious; as far as Jennie knows, Nancy's body was not exhumed and no remedial measures were taken; so, in Jennie's words, "she still roams the countryside."

Jennie had passed the tale of the Foster vampire along to her children. To complete the last link of this legend chain, Mary-Lou and I paid another visit to the Boldans in the fall. Sitting around the table in the kitchen, which was heated by a wood stove, were Jennie, her teenaged son, Paul, and two younger sons, David, Jr. and William.

Mary-Lou asked if any of the kids had been to the cemetery. Paul replied that he and a friend had recently gone there. Remembering that we had forgotten to close the iron gate to the cemetery, I asked Paul if it was still open when they visited. He replied that they had found it hanging from a tree branch. That news elicted a collective combination of laughter and ooohhhs.

Paul said they had a difficult time locating the cemetery but, following his mother's directions, they finally found it on their second visit. When they stopped and asked people in the area, no one seemed to know anything about it. Jennie agreed, saying she had made inquiries, too, and each time, had "come to a dead end."

"Well, how did you hear about it?" I asked.

"Ronnie Jackson," Jennie and Paul replied in unison.

"Yeah, he's a cop," Paul said.

"Does he still live around here?" Mary-Lou wanted to know.

Paul answered, "Yeah, he lives right next to it. Right down the road from it. . . . He lives in a red house on the right-hand side, just before you get to the cemetery."

"Wow," I said, "we should probably go talk to him."

Jennie and Mary-Lou got up to make tea, and I continued questioning Paul. He said that his mother had told his friend Jim the story before they went to the cemetery. Then he asked, "You know the cemetery down in Exeter? That's what brought it up, because he went down there with a bunch of his friends. Then he brought it up and was telling Mom about it, and Mom told him about that one and we had to go over there the next day."

William started to ask a question, "What about that one that he saw—"

"Oh, yeah," Paul interrupted. "Do you know the church down there?"

"Where? In Exeter?" I asked.

Paul responded, "One of them. I think there's two graves. There's one in East Greenwich, too, I think?"

"One in East Greenwich?" I asked increduously.

"Yeah." Then, turning to Jennie who was over at the stove, he asked, "Mom, which is the one with the church in it? The one that's all boarded up?"

"Oh," I interposed. "That's West Greenwich."

Meanwhile, in the background, Jennie was repeating, "I would not go there!"

"Yeah, that's the one," Paul affirmed. He said he and Jim ripped one of the boards off the windows to look inside.

When I suggested that vandalism was an ongoing problem there, both Paul and his mother began talking excitedly at the same time, telling me "it's a church that worships the Devil."

"That's a *Baptist* church," I protested.

"No," Jennie said. "This one's all abandonned. . . . It's all boarded up and you can't even see into it."

Paul continued to describe his visit to the church with Jim. "So, he went up and he ripped one of the boards off the window to see what it was like inside the church. . . . And he saw this picture hanging on the wall. And it wasn't Jesus or God or anything like that."

"It was a figure of a man," Jennie said.

On that score, both were correct. The painting that hangs on the wall in the modest interior of this unpretentious church, erected about 1822, is a portrait of its most esteemed pastor, who served from 1840 to 1878: Reverend John Tillinghast.

Paul went on. "You know the star with the symbols around it?"

"The pentagram, or something like that," Jennie said.

"So, that's what was hanging inside the church," Paul concluded.

"Now, I heard," Jennie said, "that somebody else, a long, long time ago—and I'm trying to think of the person's name—but, we were talking about ghosts and stories and stuff like that, and this person turned around and said to me, 'Jennie, if you ever want to see anything that makes your hair stand on end, there is a church on the West Greenwich–Exeter line. . . . ' And these people went down there one time and observed what was going on. And they said there was a whole group of men and women that went into that church. And they were doing all kinds of things."

"Like what?" I snapped. "Singing songs and praying?" Thinking of the semiannual service held at the Plain Meeting House in West Greenwich, and the continual vandalism suffered by the church, I couldn't mask my disapproval.

"No," Jennie protested. "It was really strange. . . . They were chanting and they came outside and . . . did some kind of rituals and. . . ."

"It was at night?" I asked.

"Yeah, at night," Jennie said.

"I tried to contact the church historian at the Plainfield Baptist Church, there in West Greenwich," I said in my most even, rational voice. "And the letter was returned. . . . It was stamped 'addressee unknown.' "

There was a collective, "Whoa!" and lots of laughter.

I didn't offer that information as a testament to supernatural goings on. I explained that I wanted to talk to the Church historian because, in a newspaper article, she had said that she was acquainted with a hundred-year-old man who had known Nellie Vaughn and knew that she wasn't a vampire. I wanted to talk to this man.

Jennie continued. "But I had heard this story from other people, that there are people that belong to that church and they go there at certain times. . . . "

"Are they Devil worshoppers?" Mary-Lou asked. I thought that Jennie really didn't need that kind of prompting.

"Yes, they are Devil worshippers," Jennie answered matter-of-factly. She said that when she first moved up to Foster, she "caught drifts of an organized group . . . that does worship the Devil." Jennie continued describing this cult of Devil worshippers and their *Book of Shadows*. I concluded that she was referring to Gerald Gardner (1884–1964), the father of modern witchcraft. "He's the one that wrote the satanic bible," Jennie intoned gravely. She went on to present a hodgepodge view of witchcraft gleaned from casual reading and hearsay—her main informant was a local woman who was "up to be a high priestess."

After several minutes of listening to Jennie's accounts of initiation rites and torture, Mary-Lou asked, "This is all done at that church, on the West Greenwich–Exeter line?"

Jennie didn't answer the question directly. Instead, she said, "I understand, in Foster, that there is a witches' cult, and there are thirteen witches."

"In Foster?" Mary-Lou was incredulous.

Jennie began citing her various sources, including people "who were on the school committee at one time." She mentioned a cemetery in town that she had been unsuccessful in locating. Inside this cemetery, there is "a section where there are thirteen stones, in a complete round circle, and they're completely flat, all thirteen stones. And on those stones, stand the witches."

Jennie continued. "Margery Mathews came here one day . . . I do grave rubbings . . . and she said, 'It's a nice afternoon. Would you like to go grave-hopping?' And I said, 'Sure!' "

Jennie explained how Margery, who was head of the Preservation Society in Foster, was helping to record gravestone inscriptions in town cemeteries. "So, anyway, we started bounding from cemetery to cemetery. We came across this cemetery. Now, Lord knows where it is. I've never been able to find it again. There's so many dirt roads in Foster, how do you know? So, the cemetery was off the dirt road. I was, like, prowling around—let's put it that way. I got sick and tired. I did all my grave rubbings and she was still on the ground taking all kinds of people's names and numbers and so on and so forth. And I started, like, walking in the back, right? And she says to me, 'Oh, Jennie, there's nothing back there.' And I said, 'What do you mean there's nothing back here? What's all those stones back there?' I said, 'Gee, the grass is so low.' It was all cut and everything, all nice and neat. And we walked back there and she said, 'This is where the original witches of Foster met.' And I said, 'Oh! That's nice. What do they do here?' And she said, 'Oh, I imagine that they carried on their ceremonies.' I never found the place again!"

Jennie paused, then continued with a description of a subsequent encounter with Margery. "And I approached her one day. She was at a school committee meeting. And at the end of the school committee meeting we were all coming outside and I approached her and I said, 'Margery, it's been . . . months, and I have looked for that place you took me to. . . . ' And she said, 'What place?' And I said, 'That place where all the stones, the witches' stones, were.' And she said, 'I don't remember any place like that.' "

"That was really strange!" Jennie squealed. "I came home and I said to David, 'She's telling me she don't remember any place like that!' "

Mary-Lou suggested that perhaps Margery didn't want to say anything in front of other people because "they might think that she was into witch stuff."

After this diversion to witches, I managed to get the conversation back to vampires. David, Jr. and Paul said that Ronnie Jackson had told them lots of stories, and that their father had heard the vampire story from Ronnie and then passed it on to their mother.

I mentioned how odd it was that Nancy's body had not been exhumed.

Paul said, "They did stab the thing in her heart."

His younger brother disagreed, saying, "They took out her heart and burned it."

"Are you thinking of Mercy Brown?" Mary-Lou asked.

"No, no," Paul protested. "You see, all the people in this area were dying."

David, Jr. was attempting to talk at the same time. Trying to restore order, I said, "OK, let's hear Paul's version of the story."

David, Jr. would not desist. "One of the stories, they burnt her heart, then they burned—"

"Will you shut your face!" Paul shouted.

"—her on a pole," David, Jr. resolutely persisted.

In a kindergarten teacher's firm but patient voice, Mary-Lou said, "No one can talk at the same time. Speak distinctly, Paul."

"Everybody in the family was dying." Paul began talking faster, as if he were trying to squeeze in his story before his younger brother had an opportunity to intrude again. "Did you see how the dates keep on going? Supposedly, to stop everybody from dying, they dug up her body, right? And it still was there, nothing had rotted or anything. So they took her, and they put her on a . . . thing."

"What?" I asked.

"Yeah," Paul said, "they burned . . . at the stake . . . stake."

Paul obviously was having trouble remembering the procedures involved. "And they took . . . a . . . thingumajiggy . . . and pounded it. And the spirit came out of her. And that's why the stones are all pushed back."

"This is Nancy Young?" Mary-Lou asked.

"This is the one over here," Paul answered.

I looked at Jennie and said, "You didn't know that part. You didn't tell me that part." It came off sounding like an accusation, which was not my intention.

"I knew that the spirit came out and moved all the stones like that," Jennie answered.

"That's why," Paul explained, "because they pounded it right through her heart."

"The stake?" I asked for clarification.

"Yeah, through her heart," Paul said.

As if on cue, Jennie's husband, David, walked through the door at the climax of Paul's story. We started talking about local stories and, again, Ronnie Jackson's name came up. I asked if he was an older man. Everybody said, "No, he's young." They guessed he was in his early thirties. We began discussing various Foster legends.

David said that the house of the man hanged from the bell rope at the mill, Peleg Walker (like Jennie, David also called him "Peg Leg"), was just up the road—and it is haunted: "My daughter used to baby-sit up there. And, just going in the front room . . . you start to get chills running through you. It's just an eerie type feeling. Your hair gets pulled. And this happened to a number of people . . . at night time, when it starts to get dark. . . . "

Jennie added, "You're pinched, slapped."

David said, "Now, Sandra, she baby-sat there twice, and she'd never go back again. She said she could hear chains dragging in the basement. And also upstairs, she could hear them walking and making all kinds of noise."

Jennie said that the Walker family, who lived there before the current occupants, "had so much trouble in the house that she [Mrs. Walker] had several priests from the neighboring communities come up and do exorcisms on the house. I went into the house with her—she invited me in one day—and they had big crosses all over the wall. And she said, literally, at night, those crosses would spin around like this." Jennie twirled her index finger in the air.

Jennie and David began describing the ongoing supernatural encounters in their own house, which ranged from disembodied voices and strange noises to furniture and other objects moving without being touched. After Jennie completed this inventory, she launched into stories of yet-another-haunted house, the Barnet Hopkins House (c. 1810) up on Old Danielson Pike.

Mary-Lou mentioned that the last time we visited, Jennie had told us about the Ghost Lot and strange lights. David said, "Oh, yeah, that's up here. I've seen that many a time."

"That's not the place where the witch's house was burned, is it?" I asked.

"No," David answered, "just below it. And the thing of it is, we had almost the same type of light right out in the backyard."

Mary-Lou and I asked what kind of light.

"It's a phosphorous light," David responded. "It's a white light, but it's very hard to explain. . . . You know, the neon lights when the first come on, they have that flickering glow. And then, as they warm up, they get brighter and brighter. But it stays in a small round ball, about the size of a softball."

We ended this session by making a date to return and check out the mysterious lights.

On the way back to Providence, I told Mary-Lou about the blue-tinted light that Everett had seen near Mercy Brown's grave when he was in his teens (football- rather than softball-sized). My limited research informed me that these "corpse lights" often appear over buried bodies and are interpreted, at least in folklore, as representing the soul, spirit, or ghost of the deceased. Sometimes their presence indicates that the corpse is restless; perhaps the light is a mute request that the living do whatever is necessary to help the dead rest in peace. We agreed that an opportunity to experience this phenomenon firsthand would be worth a return to Foster.

We spent most of the ride discussing the vampire story. In both Jennie's and Paul's versions, Nancy returned from the grave to kill her family, and the slanted gravestones acted as a passageway for whatever evil resided within the grave. But Paul said that Nancy *sucked the blood* of her brothers and sisters. He also said that her body had been exhumed and a stake was driven through it, the kind of closure that one expects of a vampire narrative in a movie, short story, or novel. Jennie told us that *no* actions were taken to dispatch the vampire, so it is still at large. Mary-Lou and I agreed that Jennie's open-ended tale was perfect for legend trippers.

The next order of business was to track down the source of the legend.

CHAPTER 7
Don't Be a Rational Adult

What is scarier than a vampire? A ghost? A poltergeist? For someone on the trail of a legend, it would be a FOAF. Just as the worst nightmare for an inquiring citizen is the bureaucratic buck passed in perpetual motion, it is the "friend of a friend" that strikes terror in the heart of a folklorist. Following the chain of a story's transmission back toward the dawn of its existence typically ends well before one reaches the source. With Nellie Vaughn, I finally gave up on the TFC (teacher from Coventry). But, with Nancy Young, I got lucky. I had actual names to pursue.

Jennie told me that she first heard the story from her husband, David. It had been told to David by a colleague on the Foster police force, Ronnie Jackson, who lived on Jenks Road very near the Young family cemetery. Ronnie had learned it while enrolled in a class that was taught by Margery Matthews. I arranged an interview with Ronnie, but he called in sick. After another failed appointment, he admitted that he just didn't want to be interviewed. So I moved on to Margery.

Margery was a teacher, librarian, historian, genealogist, author, and the voice of historic preservation in Foster. She was elected to the Foster Town Council, and then became the first woman to serve as its president. Although I was acquainted with this remarkable woman, it was more than ten months before I was able to visit Margery in her home on Cucumber Hill Road, less than five miles from the Young cemetery. On this visit, I was

134

accompanied by Joe Carroll, an anthropology student from Rhode Island College who had just begun a year-long internship with me. I hoped that getting to the source would prove worth the wait.

As I set up the tape recorder and we engaged in some small talk, I noticed that the handsome grandfather clock in the room kept a nice, very audible, cadence. Ordinarily, such background noise is avoided when making a sound recording. Yet I was pleased that the "tick . . . tock . . . tick . . . tock," instead of the thumping, squeaking windshield wipers underneath Jennie's stories, would serve as the rhythmic accompaniment to Margery's version of the tale.

Two people more different than Margery and Jennie would be hard to find. Margery's reasoned and logical approach to the vampire story brought into high relief Jennie's spooky legend tripping. Margery began by referring me to a published account of the Young family incident that appeared in James Earl Clauson's newspaper column in 1936. I remarked that in one of his weekly columns the next year, Clauson had mentioned three other vampire incidents. Margery obviously had an historian's reverence for published documentation, for when I told her that the reference she had just given me was the first printed version I had encountered, she absolutely beamed. Until now, I said, I knew about the Foster vampire only through the oral stories of local residents. I told her that I understood that they got the story, at least indirectly, from her.

"Yes, they did," Margery confirmed, "because they were students over at Ponagansett High School [which serves the adjoining towns of Foster and Glocester] when I was a librarian with a course in local history. And that's where they picked it up."

Margery told me that she is a tenth-generation descendent, through her mother, of John Harrington, a settler of Foster. She is related to the Young family through that line, and she recalled hearing the story from both her mother and grandmother during her childhood on the family dairy farm in Moosup Valley, situated between Cucumber Hill and Barbs Hill, very close to the Young family cemetery. Margery certainly seemed to have her facts in order. She said, "My mother's family grew up on an adjoining farm, across the river. The farm was partly in Connecticut . . . and partly in Rhode Island. So it was right close to the Young residence. . . . There were two houses on the farm, and the line went through them. I never quite figured out how it got through both of them, but it did. . . . The house that was in Rhode Island and Connecticut—my Aunt Myrtie was born in Rhode Island, my mother was born in Connecticut, because the line went through the house, and my grandmother changed bedrooms!"

Margery said that the birth certificates reflected the two states. When I asked if her family had to pay taxes in both states, she said they did. The children went to school in the state where their father registered to vote. When I asked how he decided that, she responded, "Well, if it was my grandfather, it was whatever town he was getting along with best at the time!"

As Margery began looking through her notes, she said that her grandmother "wrote down some of these legends. . . . Some of them she copied from her father-in-law."

Margery continued going through her notes. After several moments of silence, strung together by the clock, she explained, "Of course, some of the Youngs lived. They didn't all die of consumption. And a man named Casey Tyler wrote the story. Basically the same as Clauson has."

Another published version! "Was it printed somewhere," I asked.

"Uh, yes."

"Um," I uttered with an air of nonchalance, hoping that she had the source and would share it.

"In the *Pawtuxet Valley Gleaner*. Well, one date is April 27th, 1892. That's the reprint. There's an earlier one, and I don't have the date of the early one."

While Margery got up to answer the doorbell, Joe and I discussed where we might locate Tyler's article. Margery returned and introduced Gladys and Charles. She had invited them over to participate in some legend-telling after I requested this interview. I had told her about Joe's legend internship, so this session was to cover more than simply the Foster vampire. After introductions, I told Gladys and Charles that Margery had been sharing her story of the Young family vampire.

"Over around the Dorrance neighborhood on Jenks Road," Margery specified. "I don't know whether you know that story or not, Charles."

"No," is all Charles said.

Margery continued, "Well, Casey Tyler's version is basically the same. He mentions that, at the time he wrote this, there was one daughter, Sarah. . . . Some of the family survives, but they don't live around here. I don't think that they would . . . have any versions of the story."

"It would be interesting if that story was kept alive in the family," I said, "down through several generations." You could say I was hoping out loud.

Margery said, "I doubt if it is. Aunt Berta's son is too far away, I think, to have been very familiar with it." She thought for a moment, then added, "And I don't think any of Casey Tyler's family now living would know it. . . . And Casey wrote, well, maybe the 1880s—I don't know when he first wrote these articles. But this one is 1892. He was still living at that time."

We discussed the problems of looking for these cases in newspapers and other published sources. Margery made an observation that was, by now, painfully obvious to me. "Well, the problem is, these were oral traditions and they didn't think it was important to cite the source." She paused and added another telling insight. "Or perhaps the person didn't want it known."

I asked Margery if she would tell her grandmother's version of the Young family story.

Margery kept looking through her notes as she said, "I'm trying to find her notes on it. I think they're in here." After a few moments of searching, she said, "I may be wrong about their being in here." The clock ticked relentlessly in the background as Margery continued to look. "I can find other things, but not that."

Joe and I discussed the dates on the gravestones as Margery kept going through her notes.

Gladys asked, "How long after she died did she start being a vampire?"

"I don't know," I responded.

Margery looked up from her notes to address the question. "Well, . . . Nancy died and then several of the others died in the succeeding years. And—after they had tried all kinds of medical help—they felt as though maybe Nancy was a vampire. So she was the one that was dug up." She looked at me and said, "Maybe you could determine that from some of the other dates. I don't know. And you know her stone is tipped. . . . So perhaps when her grave was dug up it wasn't set back in firmly."

I made a mental note of this contrast between Margery's story and Jennie's.

Gladys asked, "And what year was it dug up?"

Margery replied, "Well, that's what I, we don't know."

Finally, Margery said, "I don't see that. I thought I had something in here that she wrote, but I don't find it."

More tick-tocking. "I wonder if that took care of the problem?" I asked. "As far as they were concerned?"

"No," Margery responded, "because some more died after that, according to the belief, according to the story."

Joe asked, "Well, what did they do after they dug her up—according to the story?"

"Well, according to Clauson's version, they burned the body," Margery said. "According to my mother's version, they cut out her heart and burned it."

Gladys responded, "It seems as though I had read in the paper somewhere where they had just burned the heart."

Joe asked if they did anything with the ashes, and Margery answered, "Oh, they scattered them around I believe. They did something with them."

Margery continued looking over newspaper clippings. Then she began to read from Clauson's article, " 'The belief being that the smoke would cure the sick and render the others immune.'

But it doesn't say what happened to the ashes. And I can remember my mother saying something about the ashes, but I don't remember what that was."

I was beginning to see, on the one hand, similarities between Margery's family story and that of Everett Peck—exhuming the body, burning the heart, and doing "something" not remembered with the ashes—and, on the other hand, striking contrasts with Jennie's tale.

I responded to Margery's uncertainty about the ashes. "In some cases they fed them to someone in the family who was sick."

"Uh huh," Margery agreed, "I've heard that."

Charles seemed surprised (and maybe disgusted) when he interjected, "Is that right?"

"In water," I continued, "or ... "

"Some medicine, or something," Joe completed my thought.

Things were moving very slowly. In an attempt to draw out memories and get some discussion going, I said, "I have no idea where the belief would come from, though. It's not strong in the English tradition. That's what's odd. It's more like what you find in Romania."

Margery now began to read from Tyler's article, " 'In the summer of 1827, the neighbors and friends at Mr. Young's request, came together and exhumed the remains of Nancy, and had her body burned while all the members of the family gathered around and inhaled the smoke from the burning remains, feeling confident, no doubt, that it would restore them to health and prevent any more of them falling prey to that dread disease.' "

"What dread disease?" I asked.

"Consumption," Margery answered. "This article names consumption." More silence. "The daughter Sarah lived for many years. She was dead when this article was written. And then this author mentions Albert Young, and I don't know whether he's the son or not. But Albert was the father of William, who married my grandmother's sister. And then there was a Susan, who married Holly Kennedy, who lived down on Moosup Valley Road."

Charles asked, "Were they any relation to the Youngs who were up on South Killingly [Road] there? Hollis Young, Comer Young."

"I don't know, Charles," Margery said. "This is Levi Young, and I've never tried to trace him. There were some Youngs that bought property down in that southwest corner."

Charles began to name some of the Youngs he knew about.

I asked, "Would the records for that family be in Rhode Island, or Connecticut?"

"This Levi Young family?" Margery asked.

"Yeah," I answered. "You know, the cemetery itself seems to be in Connecticut. Right? Was the farm off of Jenks Road in Rhode Island, or was it—"

Margery jumped in with, "The farm was actually in Rhode Island. I'm not quite sure whether it's the one where the Jacksons live now. I think it was a little further down where there's an old foundation. I've never looked up the records. The deeds would be over in Foster. But whether there's anything in the vital records, I don't think so, because I've looked up Youngs. There might be something in Sterling [Connecticut]. A lot of the deaths weren't recorded at that time."

Joe asked, "Why was that?"

Margery answered, "It wasn't required. Transportation was difficult. And you might depend on, perhaps, the minister to do it. And perhaps he never did it. Or the doctor, and he didn't get around to recording it."

Joe asked, "Was there a doctor present at this incident?"

Margery answered, "It doesn't say that there was. It says that they called in physicians to, uh, try and stop the spread of the disease. But it doesn't say that there was a doctor present. I wouldn't think that a doctor would attend."

"But he did at Mercy Brown's, though," I observed. Margery was surprised when I told her the medical examiner for the town was at the scene.

Thinking out loud, I asked, "I wonder what pinpointed Nancy Young? According to the gravestones—if they did it in the summer of 1827—she died in April of that year. It would be a couple of months later, but the next death I can find in the cemetery, in the family, is 1828, August. So, it would be the next year. Perhaps they were sick at that time."

Joe asked, "She was the first one to die?"

"Yeah," I answered. "That's what it looks like."

Gladys seemed surprised. "Oh, and her body was dug up before any of the rest of them died?"

"If you go by the gravestones," I said.

Margery said, "Well, Casey Tyler says another one died before Nancy. That's what Casey said."

"Oh." Now, I *was* surprised. "I didn't find it."

Margery said, "The grave might not be there, or Casey might not be right."

I said, "There were some small ones that I assumed were infants, and they had no inscriptions."

"Yeah," Margery agreed. "There are some fieldstones, plain fieldstones, in there."

Joe asked, "Did the article call it vampirism?"

"Clauson does," Margery responded. Looking through her notes, she wondered aloud, "What does Casey say? No, he doesn't mention a vampire." Then she read from Tyler's article, " 'There seemed to be a curious idea prevailing at that time in some localities, that by cremating or burning the remains of a departed friend or relative while the living relatives stood around and inhaled the smoke from the burning remains, that it would eradicate the disease from the systems of the living and restore them to health.' "

I said, "That's a new theory of the belief. The one I've encountered, it's the ashes, not the smoke."

Margery added, "The smoke is in Clauson."

Gladys asked, "Did they mix the ashes with water, for the people to drink it?"

"Yes," I answered, "for the ones who were sick, in the family. It was supposed to be a cure."

Margery handed me a reprint of Casey Tyler's article. The excerpts below fill in some of the details not mentioned by Margery:

Sixty years ago or more Capt. Levi Young of Sterling, Conn., who married Annie Perkins, bought the extreme southern portion of the original "Dorrance purchase" and erected a house thereon which is now the southwest corner house in the town of Foster and commenced life as a farmer. His oldest daughter, Nancy, a very bright and intelligent girl, at an early age became feeble in health and died of consumption on April 6th, 1827, aged 19 years. Previous to the death of Nancy, the second daughter, Almira, a very sprightly girl commenced a rapid decline in health with sure indications that she must soon follow her sister. The best skill of the most eminent physicians seemed to be all in vain. There was a large family of children and several of them were declining in the same manner. Mr. Young was a very worthy and pious man and wished to do everything possible to benefit his family, and he had the sympathy of all his friends and neighbors.

. . . A short time after the decease of Nancy, in the summer of 1827, the neighbors and friends at Mr. Young's request, came together and exhumed the remains of Nancy, and had her body burned while all the members of the family gathered around and inhaled the smoke from the burning remains, feeling confident, no doubt, that it would restore them to health and prevent any more of them falling a prey to that dread disease, consumption.

But it would seem that it was no benefit to them, as Almira died August 19, 1828, aged 17 years. Olney, a son, died December 12, 1831, aged 29 years. Huldah died August 1836, aged 23 years. Caleb died May 8, 1843, aged 26 years. Hiram died February 17, 1854, aged 35 years. Two other sons lived to be older but are now dead. The youngest daughter Sarah, is the only one now living of the family. She seems as yet to escape the disease of consumption. Some scientific persons thought perhaps the water in the well contained impurities which caused the disease as the whole family were of exemplary habits and very much respected; but it seems to have not been so as no disease of that kind has visited the people who have since occupied the same premises.

The following notations by Tyler were added to the article when it was reprinted:

Possibly this is the only instance of cremation in Rhode Island for the purpose of curing or preventing disease.

Sarah is now dead but lived many years after removing from the old place.

Dwight B. Jenks now owns and occupies the farm and has done so for years with a healthy family and no death in the house to the knowledge of the writer since the Young family passed away.

It now seemed apparent why the names "Sarah" and "Jenks" were in Jennie's memory.

Later, my search of state Historical Preservation Commission reports indicated that the house built by Captain Levi Young, in about 1810, still stood and, in fact, *was* owned by the Jackson family (which served only to increase my disappointment that Ronnie Jackson did not want to talk about the story). Sarah Young is listed as the owner from 1851 to 1862, when D. Jencks took possession. The house, a modest, one-and-a-half-story frame house of the Federal style, was in his name until it was sold to Ralph H. Jackson in 1971. Citing Tyler's article, the statewide preservation survey form (completed in 1969) includes the following note: "Mysterious disease said to have wasted the family."

The discussion turned to how this practice might have come to Rhode Island. Margery thought it was strange because the people were of English origin. She said, "Most of these happened in the more isolated parts of the state, too, where there wasn't much communication" with outsiders.

I asked, "In your versions of the Nancy Young story, did she come back to the family?"

"No," Margery answered.

"One person told me that was part of the story here," I said, referring to Jennie's version.

"No," Margery said, "I think that's a recent addition. . . . I never heard that before. Perhaps the person who told you that read some of the other versions."

Margery expanded the scope of our discussion. "Our preservation society is taking schoolchildren on tours of places around Foster. And sometimes in talking with them afterwards . . . we'll hear stories that they've been told. You'd be surprised how many houses in Foster are haunted. There are a lot of ghosts roaming around!" Driving around Foster with Jennie had left me with the same impression.

I mentioned hearing about a recent exorcism in Foster. No one knew about that case, but Margery offered another account of a recent haunting. "Well, there was a story about some people in Foster over on Route 6 that were having trouble with poltergeists and various other mysterious happenings. I didn't hear whether they had an exorcism or not."

Margery turned to Charles and said, pointedly, "You know who I mean."

Charles demurred, and Margery persisted, "Yes, you do. Going up Dolly Cole Hill."

"Oh, yeah," Charles said.

Gladys also knew. "That wasn't too long ago. Around Halloween, I think, it was in the paper."

"Oh, yeah," I said. Then, as if I were guessing, "probably the Boldans."

In a whispered shout, Margery hissed, "Yes!" She laughed. "A few years ago she took me all through the house. I heard everything about ghosts."

Margery's icy tone and crooked smile clearly conveyed her attitude about Jennie and her haunted house. It was a dramatic reminder of how words get all of the credit when it is often the *texture* of language that points toward intention, opening a path into another person's meaning.

As Gladys muttered, "No," I said, "I've been out there. . . . It is an interesting house." Both my tone of voice and choice of words were noncommittal. Then, fishing for more information, "She said at one time it was used as a funeral parlor. . . . I don't know if that's true or not."

Margery asked Charles if he knew. He said, "Eva Hopkins would know more than [Jennie] would. She's probably guessin' at it. But, unless you get it from the horse's mouth . . . Eva is still alive. I think she would know. And Jane Hopkins, she's still alive."

Gladys said, "That was . . . a Hopkins that had the funeral parlor there, wasn't it?"

Charles replied, "I couldn't tell ya."

"It was a Hopkins house at one time," Margery said.

"Oh, yeah," Charles shot back. "Yeah. It *was* a Hopkins house. Yeah. . . . William Henry. Yeah."

"His son was Nathaniel, I think," Margery added. "John Lester Brown called him 'Than'l Bill', I think. They had wonderful combinations of nicknames to designate people, when a name was repeated. And I think that one was 'Than'l Bill', which was Bill's Nathaniel."

"That's a real Rhode Island tradition," I agreed. "You find it in South County, too."

"Then there's another nickname that I think is really nice," Margery said. "Otis Hopkins was the son of Abel Hopkins, and he was referred to as 'Oat Abel'."

Joe steered the conversation back to vampires by asking, "What about the Nancy Young story? Do people still tell that?"

"No." Margery thought for a moment, then added, "Except for the . . . that was revived when we talked about it over in Ponagansett. And people have talked about it since that time. But in between, it hadn't been passed down. People hadn't talked about it."

(In the years since this interview, I've sometimes wondered if Margery was the teacher from Coventry. Perhaps it was students from Ponagansett High School looking for Nancy Young, not Coventry High School students in search of Mercy Brown. The timing is right. Ronnie Jackson would have been high school age in the late 1960s, and Victory Highway also traverses Foster. But, the Young family cemetery is isolated, even more distant from the highway than Nellie's grave. I've always ended the speculation with, "No, it's too much of a stretch.")

Joe continued to question Margery. "Did you get this from your mother, this story?"

"Yes," Margery answered.

Charles and Gladys began to share some folk remedies that their families had used, including skunk oil for muscle aches and pine tar or cobwebs to stop bleeding. The conversation then veered to stories about interesting places and names in the town. Margery, Charles, and Gladys offered different versions of the "Ghost Lot" story. Margery's was the most detailed, probably because she had some notes and a newspaper clipping from the *Providence Bulletin*. She related the following: "Aunt Lonnie Davis lived on Tucker Hollow Road, and she said she'd haunt her house after she was dead as long as there was one board nailed to another. She breathed on the backs of people's necks. The neighbors pulled the house down, and the site is called the ghost lot. . . . I was always going to look up Lonnie Davis in the vital records, but I haven't done it."

For clarification, I asked, "So people who lived in the house could feel her breath on their necks, after she died?"

Margery answered, "Yes. So they pulled the house down."

Margery mentioned that Witch Hill was up in that vicinity, too. She said, "Martha Hopkins lived on Route 101, more or less across from Maple Rock Road, and some people say that's how Witch Hill got its name. But I think the name goes back before Martha Hopkins. . . . "

Charles agreed. Both remembered that Martha Hopkins lived in the early 1900s.

Then Gladys contributed: "My father said she was very eccentric. She never married. And, I don't know if she couldn't get anybody to cut wood for her, but she used to burn, like, four foot lengths, right in the stove. And as it burned out, she just pushed it in. And that's how her house burned."

It dawned on me that several elements from these stories by Margery, Charles, and Gladys appeared in Jennie's tale of the Ghost Lot, where an unnamed witch, a hybrid of Aunt Lonnie Davis and Martha Hopkins, is put into a combined Ghost Lot/Witch Hill to account for the eerie "bluish white light that bounces around in the woods."

At the very end of the interview session, all three of the Foster natives recalled a murder in the early 1900s. Two local brothers, drunk, poured kerosine on poor Sadie Mathewson and set her on fire, then hit her with an ax until she died. It was Gladys's tag to the story that caught my attention: "Somebody had told me that where her body laid on the ground, where they had thrown the kerosene on it to burn her, that, years and years later, grass never grew on that spot—that it was the shape of a woman's body laying there, with no grass growing." I thought of Nellie Vaughn's grave.

Joe and I had ample opportunity to talk about how the story of the Young family changed from its beginning with Margery Matthews to its culmination with Jennie and Paul. Nancy Young was transformed into the vampire that we all know and love (to hate): undead, she leaves her grave at night to return to her family and suck their blood; to kill her, a stake is driven through her heart; yet she still roams the country-side, looking for victims. In the time it took to pass through four storytellers, Nancy Young had become the consummate popular-culture vampire.

Jennie's version also reinterpreted the meaning of the slanted gravestones. Where Margery suggested that Nancy's stone may have been out of kilter because of the exhumation, Jennie, not timid about combining separate but similar traditions, linked it to a belief she had heard as a child from her Swedish grand-mother. There is, indeed, a European folk belief stipulating that a crooked cross on a grave indicates that "the deceased has trans-formed himself into a vampire." But this belief does not appear in general American folklore, nor have I found it associated with any other case in the New England tradition.

How do we explain the changes? Perhaps the key is the inter-action among tradition, community, and personality. A well-documented phenomenon of the storytelling process is the magnetic effect of a local legend, particularly one that is based on a certain place, such as a cemetery, house, or bridge. Over time, stories of these places become the center of attraction for various elements drawn from modern horror stories. Storytellers tend to shape their tales to fit the experiences and expectations of their audiences. So it is not surprising that stories told many times drift towards a shared tradition. Often, the recounting of a supernatural experience tells, not what actually happened, but what *should have* occurred. For Jennie and Paul, Nancy should behave like the vampires they know, the vampires from recent fiction and film.

Jennie is attracted to the supernatural and has made an effort to seek out local people who know about places and events con-sidered unusual, mysterious, spooky. She remembers enough about these accounts to share them, eagerly, with listeners. When Jennie recounts such events, she is willing to fill in any "missing" details. These motifs may be absent because she has forgotten them or because they were not included in the story as she received it—but should have been. Jennie's familiarity with supernatural topics provides her with an extensive stock of material that she can insert into her tales where she supposes they belong. Her interpretations also gravitate towards the super-natural. During my several visits to her home, she had described a variety of events that she conceived to be mysterious or inex-plicable in rational terms. These events included objects thrown through the air and pieces of furniture that appeared to move by themselves. Her explanation was that her house was haunted by a spirit dubbed "Frank" by the family. Others might have first sought alternate, rational explanations.

Unlike Jennie, Margery has a strong commitment to empirical methodology. As a teacher, librarian, historian, and genealogist, she demonstrates an obvious respect for the received text, whether printed or oral. When questioned about the details of the Nancy Young story, she (as did Everett Peck) frequently turned to the printed sources, using them as points of comparison and contrast with the story as she heard it in her family. (This act, incidentally, challenges the notion that oral tradition and print media are mutually exclusive; I have found that people often combine the two when telling their stories.) Margery's fidelity to fact prevents her from deliberately passing along anything she might regard as misinformation. She takes an historian's approach to interpreting the Nancy Young account. She accepts the differences between her family story and that recorded by Casey Tyler, so—without further documentation, and not knowing Tyler's source—the question of which version is factual remains open.

The differences between Margery's story and that of Jennie's highlight the distinction between history and legend. Historians are guided by the proposition that reality—what actually happened—must be one's guiding principle. Legend tellers often owe their allegiance to the traditional ideas, beliefs, and models of a certain group. In her tale of Nancy Young, Jennie's obligation is to the widespread, collective tradition of the pop-culture vampire, which, on a more general level, rests on the realm of supernaturalism as it is presented in print and broadcast media. In a local newspaper article about Mercy Brown that was published in 1979, for example, the author manages to bring in parapsychology, mysticism, dream interpretation, astrology, graphology, ESP, UFOs, biorhythms, the Bermuda Triangle, and—whew!—psychokinesis. These phenomena represent, for many people, areas of abundant uncertainty, shadows of doubt in a world driven by science and fact. Without ambiguity, rumors die and legends fade. A legend trip feeds on it, demanding a lurking mysterious threat, poised to strike at any moment. An open door invites active, visceral, participation; a closed door offers only intellectual engagement.

A foray into the legendary "Ghost Lot," to seek the strange lights, brought these abstractions down to earth. On a cool October night in 1983, Joe, Mary-Lou, and I joined Jennie and her son, Paul, for a trek to the ghost lot. To prepare for this event, I researched the appearance of mysterious lights. A number of variations appear in folk narratives. There are ghost-like lights, luminous ghosts and luminous spirits, souls as lights, and illusory lights. In British ballads, the blood of the slain is transformed into a miraculous light that burns over their corpses. Sometimes the light appears only over the graves of murder victims. Other European traditions relate how a corpse that returns from the dead is discovered by the blue glow that is visible above its grave. The Romanian *strigele* (spirits of witches who are unable to find a resting place) are seen as little points of light floating in the air.

Bram Stoker used this motif to heighten the atmosphere of mystery near the beginning of *Dracula*. As Jonathan Harker traveled through the darkness in a stagecoach toward his rendevous with Dracula:

> Suddenly, away on our left, I saw a faint flickering blue flame. The driver saw it at the same moment; he at once checked the horses, and, jumping to the ground, disappeared into the darkness. I did not know what to do, the less as the howling of the wolves grew closer; but while I wondered the driver suddenly appeared again, and without a word took his seat, and we resumed our journey. I think I must have fallen asleep and kept dreaming of the incident, for it seemed to be repeated endlessly, and now looking back, it is like a sort of awful nightmare. Once the flame appeared so near the road, that even in the darkness around us I could watch the driver's motions. He went rapidly to where the blue flame

arose—it must have been very faint, for it did not seem to illumine the place around it at all—and gathering a few stones, formed them into some device. Once there appeared a strange optical effect; when he stood between me and the flame he did not obstruct it, for I could see its ghostly flicker all the same. This startled me, but as the effect was only momentary, I took it that my eyes deceived me straining through the darkness. Then for a time there were no blue flames, and we sped onwards through the gloom, with the howling of wolves around us, as though they were following in a moving circle.

In 1722, the appearance of a corpse light caused a stir in Narragansett, Rhode Island:

There has lately a surprising appearance been seen at Narraganset, which is the occasion of much discourse here, and is variously represented, but for the substance of it, it is matter of fact beyond dispute, it having been seen by abundance of people, and one night about 20 persons at the same time, who came together for that purpose. The truth, as near as we can gather from the relations of several persons, is as follows. This last winter there was a woman died at Narraganset of the small pox, and since she was buried, there has appeared, upon her grave chiefly, and in various other places, a bright light as the appearance of fire. This appearance commonly begins about 9 or 10 of the clock at night, and sometimes as soon as it was dark. It appears variously as to time, place, shape and magnitude, but commonly on or about the grave, and sometimes about and upon the barn and trees adjacent; sometimes in several parts, but commonly in one entire body. The first appearance is commonly small, but increases to a great bigness and brightness, so that in a dark night they can see the grass and bark of the trees very plainly; and when it is at the height, they can see sparks fly from the appearance like sparks of fire, and the likeness of a person in the midst wrapt in a sheet with its arms folded. This appearance moves with incredible swiftness, sometimes the distance of half a mile from one place to another in the twinkling of an eye. It commonly appears every night, and continues till break of day. A woman in that neighbourhood says she has seen it every night for these six weeks past.

I knew more than I cared to know as zero hour approached. Nothing that the lights might signify—from murdered corpses and restless souls to witches' graves and plague victims—seemed to bode well for those who encountered them. I had decided not to share these findings with my fellow . . . legend trippers. Was I really a legend tripper, too? Dr. Rational hated to think of himself in that context. After all, he was a scholar, not a thrill-seeker. But, my decision to remain silent was in keeping with my resolution to keep him on a short leash. I would begin this adventure with no preconceptions; I was a blank slate for experience to write upon.

If we had taken this legend trip *after* the release of the *Blair Witch Project*, I might have been spooked despite my vow to forget everything I knew about lurking evil. Walking through the woods toward the lot, we were telling jokes and laughing. Then Joe reported seeing some lights. I suggested there might be houses through the trees. Jennie responded that there were no houses over there. Then she asked me if, when I'm in her house, I "pick up any feelings."

There was a pause before I answered, "No." Then another pause. "I'm insulated, though."

"What do you mean you're insulated?"

"I'm just naturally insulated from those things."

"Being a folklorist," Mary-Lou sniffed, with mock serious-ness, "he's an objective observer."

I stammered a bit on my explanation. I really didn't want to get into the split personality of a professional folklorist, how the child inside, who wanted to suspend his disbelief, was in a con-stant battle with the grown-up. "I, I think I'm, I'm just emo-tionally insulated."

Jennie said, "I should walk you down in there and see how *emotionally insulated* you are."

We discussed whether we should, indeed, go down into the boggy ghost lot. Paul said we had to turn off the flashlight, otherwise it would "wreck the whole thing."

Jennie tried to relieve our anxiety with, "It's just down in the hollow."

Paul said not to worry, he knew the way because he had to go down there every morning before school to move the family's cow from one field to the next.

The sounds of cars passing on Danielson Pike grew fainter as we descended into the hollow. After a while, Jennie said to me, "Hey, Mike. I don't like this area. I get very bad vibes here. Very, very bad."

We came to the edge of the trees and I asked how we could get down to the fields before us, dimly lit by the eyelash of a moon. Jennie responded, "Nobody goes in the fields at night."

"Why not?" I wanted to know.

"Because strange things happen! Nobody goes to the fields at night!"

"Well, we can't get in anyway. It's all fenced off," I said.

Jennie said, "Nobody goes to the fields at night. Do you understand?"

Despite her insistence, we found a path and continued on. Jennie kept asking if we really wanted to go down there. We walked in silence, which amplified the katydids' singing. For the first time, we could hear the faint chirping of crickets. At the edge of the fields, we looked further down, into a sunken hollow, overgrown with trees.

Jennie said, "Oh, that place down there. . . . "

Mary-Lou interjected, "That's creepy, down there."

Jennie didn't wait for Mary-Lou to finish before she shot back, "That's creepy. That is really, really . . . I don't like it down there. You see lights . . . you see everything."

"You don't want to go down there?" I asked.

"No," Jennie said. "David goes down there, but I'm really afraid."

We had another debate about whether to go down there or not. Jennie kept trying to convince us that it was a bad idea. Mary-Lou agreed. We decided to press on, with Jennie objecting along the way. As we walked in silence, the insect sounds again rose to prominence. Jennie told us that if we continued on the path, we would come to Dolly Cole Pond. She used to go there during the day to draw, but stopped because she "just didn't like the feelings around it."

"It's beautiful land!" she exclaimed. "You couldn't ask for better land. But it's got bad vibes."

We had traversed the field and just entered the woods in the hollow. The sounds of cars grew closer as we approached what I took to be Tucker Hollow Road. Then, what some of us dreaded, but others hoped for, happened. At the same time, we all saw small points of light, bouncing around near the ground, just as Jennie and David had described. For a very long moment, we stood still, transfixed, with our eyes darting around to follow the lights. I couldn't believe I was actually seeing the legendary lights!

Joe separated from the group and bent down for a closer look. "I think they're bugs," he said, "with the light hitting them from the cars going by . . . their white bodies."

Jennie shot back, sarcastically, "Oh, yeah, sure. Oh, yeah. Little tiny bugs . . . through the air . . . and the car lights. Um, huh. Good explanation."

"Because I thought I saw it fly by," Joe responded rather sheepishly.

Paul chimed in, "*Don't be a rational adult, here.*"

Mary-Lou chuckled. "It just doesn't cut it, you know what I mean?"

Paul asked, "Do you always take the easy way out, Joe? Huh?"

"What do you mean?" Joe responded.

I clarified Paul's intent for Joe, "With your explanation."

Joe just laughed, and Mary-Lou made the mock-scary "ooo-wee-ooo" sound. The walk back to the house was quick-paced and hushed. Jennie hardly spoke. It had been Joe's turn to be Dr. Killjoy Rational, and after he burst Jennie's supernatural bubble, I wanted to rewind the tape and play the scene again. Take two: this time, nobody sees the glowing bugs.

I remember vividly the day my older sister told me that Santa Claus was actually our parents. I was six years old and a door closed forever.

A kind word or a touch on the shoulder might have softened the blow.

CHAPTER 8
Never Strangers True Vampires Be

T his one burial was really weird," the voice at the other end of the phone was saying. "It looks like this guy was buried long enough to decompose, dug up, some of his parts were rearranged . . . and then he was buried again." The voice belonged to Nick Bellantoni, Connecticut State Archaeologist. Nick said that he was aware of my research on the New England vampire tradition and thought that I might be able to shed some light on these peculiar findings in the town of Griswold, Connecticut. He told me that earlier in the year, 1990, three boys were having fun sliding down the slopes of a recently excavated section of a gravel pit about two miles from the village of Jewett City. As one of the boys descended, two human skulls seemed to fly out of the ground, accompanying the horrified youngster to the bottom of the pit. The boys reported their find to the local police, who, at first glance, wondered if there might be a serial killer in town. Closer scrutiny revealed that the remains were quite old, suggesting that the state archaeologist was a more suitable investigator than the medical examiner.

Nick Bellantoni's on-site investigation indicated that the skulls came from a small, unmarked cemetery, which was being worn away by a privately operated sand-and-gravel mine. The partial remains of eight individuals had eroded out from the cliff. Nick told me that he and his crew had excavated the burials that were perched dangerously close the edge of the cliff and had begun research to determine who was interred in the cemetery.

Since soil erosion was occurring at an alarming rate, and it was impossible to stabilize the bank, the landowner asked Nick to excavate the entire cemetery and reinter the remains in another location. Nick told me that they were seeking funding to proceed with the excavations. Forensic anthropologist Paul Sledzik, Curator of Anatomical Collections at the National Museum of Health and Medicine in Washington, D.C. (and a Rhode Island native), also had been invited to assist in the investigation. My interest rose with each revelation. When Nick said that he would contact me when work resumed so that I could visit the site, I practically had one foot out of the door.

A check of the map revealed that Griswold's primary village was Jewett City, the home of Horace Ray. After nearly a decade of frustration, I was again on the trail of the Ray family vampire. Montague Summers had written that Horace Ray died of consumption in 1846 or 1847, and that two of his three sons followed him to the grave, the last in 1852. According to Summers, when the third son showed the signs of consumption, the bodies of his two brothers were exhumed and "burned on the spot." But Summers led me astray with his remark that the event, as reported in the *Norwich Courier*, took place on June 8, 1854. Believing that it would be a simple matter to find the newspaper article, in the summer of 1983, I drove to the Connecticut State Library and Archives in Hartford. I encountered a minor complication as I checked the newspaper index. There were *two* versions of the *Norwich Courier*, a weekly edition that appeared each Wednesday and a "daily" edition that was published on Tuesdays, Thursdays, and Saturdays. (I can't explain it either; even if you combine the weekly and daily editions, you still end up with just four publications a week—not my idea of daily.) This should be easy, I thought, plunking down in front of the microfilm reader. Several hours and a major headache later, I was back where I started. Having checked every daily and weekly issue from June, 1854, through the end of 1855, I found nothing. No vampire. No exhumation. No burning corpses. No "horrible superstition."

Hoping that a change of venue would lift my spirits, if not

cure my microfilm headache, I strolled to the State Archives of History and Genealogy. During the Depression, in one of their WPA projects, the state of Connecticut had paid researchers to visit every cemetery in the state and record the headstone inscriptions. Flipping through the 3x5 cards was a welcome relief from the whirling vertigo of the microfilm reader. I did not find a Horace Ray who fit the time and place provided by Summers, but there was a card for an Elisha H. Ray, who died at the age of 26 in 1851 and was buried in old Jewett City cemetery. Could Elisha have been one of the two sons whose bodies were exhumed and burned?

I seemed to have hit a dead end. Then, after our phone conversation, Nick Bellantoni sent me a photocopy of the "missing" *Norwich Courier* article. Working back through recent sources, he had found that the article appeared in the May 24, 1854 edition of the *Norwich Weekly Courier* under the headline, "Strange Superstition." The article states that the bodies were exhumed on *May* 8, not June 8—a small error that had created a lengthy stalemate.

A strange and almost incredible tale of superstition has been related to us of a scene recently enacted at Jewett City. It seems that about eight years ago, a citizen of Griswold, named HORACE RAY, died of consumption. Since that time, two of his children—both of them sons, we believe, and grown to man's estate—have sickened and died of the same disease, the last one dying some two years since. Not long ago, the same fatal disease seized upon another son, whereupon it was determined to exhume the bodies of the two brothers already dead, and *burn them.* And for what reason do our readers imagine? *Because the dead were supposed to feed upon the living,* and that so long as the dead body in the grave remained in a state of decomposition, either wholly or in part, the surviving members of the family must continue to furnish the sustenance on which the dead body fed. Acting under the influence of this strange, and to us hitherto unheard of, superstition, the family and friends of the deceased, accompanied by various others, proceeded to the burial ground at Jewett City, on the 8th inst., dug up the bodies of the deceased brothers, and burned them on the spot. The scene, as described to us, must have been revolting in the extreme; and the idea that it could have grown out of a belief such as we have referred to, tasks human credulity. We seem to have been transported back to the darkest age of unreasoning ignorance and blind superstition, instead of living in the 19th century, and in a State calling itself enlightened and christian [sic].

One of the recent articles that Nick had found appeared in the *Norwich Bulletin* on Halloween of 1976. The author's research indicated that the father probably was Henry B. Ray, not Horace Ray. The first member of the family to die was Lemuel Billings Ray, the second eldest son. According to his tombstone, he died in March, 1845 at the age of twenty-four. Four years later, the father expired. In 1851, the twenty-six-year-old son, Elisha H., died. Two sons remained: James Leonard, who lived until 1894, and Henry Nelson who, according to town hall records, was born in 1819. The author was unable to locate either a death record or tombstone for Henry Nelson, concluding that "the plight of the young man in whose behalf the family must have undergone such horrors" was unknown.

The other recent source provided by Nick also asserted that there was no documentation of Henry Nelson's death. "Unfortunately," David E. Philips wrote in *Legendary Connecticut*,

> there is neither a gravestone nor any document to confirm the date of Henry Nelson Ray's death. But since there is a date of death (either on a marker in the Jewett City Cemetery or in the Griswold town

records) recorded for all other members of the family, it is entirely probable that Henry Nelson survived his "fatal" illness of 1854. The young man who caused his family's vampire panic may well have lived to a ripe old age. If so, the surviving Rays were undoubtedly convinced that their anti-vampire "medicine" had saved his life.

As I write these words, I am looking at the two photographs of Henry N. Ray's headstone that I took ten years apart. Philips probably did not find Henry N.'s gravestone for the same reason that I couldn't find the rest of the Rays. We both expected the family stones to be close together, in the typical New England pattern. He found the father, the mother and, except for Henry Nelson, the children. I found Henry Nelson, and was baffled by the absence of the others. It was actually very easy for me to locate Henry Nelson's gravestone, since it was in a newer section of the cemetery, just inside the main gate. The small, plain granite gravestone, with a low profile, appears too modern to have been made in the mid–nineteenth century. The inscription reads simply, "Henry N. Ray / 1820–1854". It took several visits to the cemetery and a phone call to Mary Deveau of the Griswold Historical Society before I finally found the headstones of the rest of the family. They are grouped together in the oldest part of the cemetery, which is tucked away out of sight. Mary said that many of the Ray family graves, including Henry Nelson's, were moved in the early 1900s, which explains the newer-looking stone. Town records indicate that Henry N. was born in 1819, while the gravestone lists 1820. Such discrepancies, especially when stones are replaced long after death, are not uncommon. If Henry N., who died in 1854, was indeed the consumptive son, the ritual apparently did *not* work for him. When Mary showed me documentation that Henry N.'s young wife and children also died of consumption, that conclusion seemed sadly accurate.

A few weeks after our initial conversation, Nick Bellantoni gave me an update on the cemetery investigation at Griswold. In 1690, a couple from Boston, Nathaniel and Margaret Walton, established a farm in the northwest corner of Griswold (which was part of the town of Preston until 1815). The eldest of their five sons, John, became a Congregational minister, known in the region as "John the Scholar." Their second son, Nathaniel, and his wife, Jemima, remained on the family farm. In 1757, Nathaniel purchased a plot of land from a neighbor for use as a family burial ground. The cemetery was active until the early 1800s, when the members of the Walton family began a westward trek in search of better farm land. The cemetery continued to be used by another, unidentified family until about 1830, after which it was abandoned. The uninscribed fieldstone markers eventually were reclaimed by the land, and the Walton Family Cemetery faded from memory until its dramatic rediscovery in November, 1990.

Nick also sent me a reference to yet another vampire incident in Connecticut. This one was reported in 1888 by J. R. Cole, in his *History of Tolland County, Connecticut*:

In the old West Stafford grave yard the tragedy of exhuming a dead body and burning the heart and lungs was once enacted—a weird night scene. Of a family consisting of six sisters, five had died in rapid succession of galloping consumption. The old superstition in such cases is that the vital organs of the dead still retain a certain flicker of vitality and by some strange process absorb the vital forces of the living, and they quote in evidence apocryphal instances wherein exhumation has revealed a heart and lungs still fresh and living, encased in rottening and slimy integuments, and in which, after burning these portions of the defunct, a living relative, else doomed and hastening to the grave, has suddenly and miraculously recovered. The ceremony of cremation of the vitals of the dead must be conducted at night by a single individual and at the open grave in order that the results may be decisive. In 1872, the Boston Health Board Reports describe a case in which such a midnight cremation was actually performed during that year.

The report doesn't actually describe what took place in the cemetery that night. Were all five sisters disinterred and their corpses examined to find the one with "fresh and living" heart and lungs? Or did they burn the organs of all five? The stipulation that the ceremony had to be carried out by a single individual, at night, was striking, unlike any other case I had encountered. The term "vampire" is never mentioned.

I checked every gravestone in the old cemetery in West Stafford several years later and found no evidence of five sisters dying in rapid succession. There are four possible explanations: their stones are among those that are illegible or missing; they were buried in unmarked graves; one (or more) of the sisters was married and interred under a different surname; or, they were buried in another cemetery, such as the Universalist cemetery just down the road, dating from about 1799.

I had made several half-hearted attempts to find the Boston Health Board Reports that, in 1872, according to Cole, described "a midnight cremation"—in Boston, I assumed. Then, in the Summer of 2000, with the assistance of the Internet to narrow down potential sources, I launched an all-out effort. My personal odyssey of July 24, 2000, exemplifies both the frustrations as well as the small, unforeseen triumphs of following the vampire trail. I left on the 8:13 A.M. train from Providence, almost trembling at the prospect of finding a vampire exhumation in Boston. None had yet been documented in a city. My destination was the Massachusetts State Library, to examine an 1872 publication entitled, *Third Annual Report of the Board of Health, Massachusetts*. Scanning the table of contents, I found nothing that would seem to point to consumption and curative measures, nor any red-flag terms such as "superstition." I plowed through the 300-odd pages, knowing it was probably a futile exercise.

With mounting desperation, I turned to "consumption" in the card catalogue. There was a small sign on both large banks of the card catalogue informing patrons that works prior to 1975 were in the catalogue. All later issues were to be found in the electronic database. I was thinking that the card catalogue would soon join vampire exhumations and consumption as antiquated curiosities when I was shaken from my state of suspended animation. There was a cross reference on the consumption card. Since the researcher was directed to "see Tuberculosis," I concluded that this entry dated from the late nineteenth century. (I wondered, were there ever cards under a subject head of "Consumption"?) I found two intriguing entries, both authored by a Dr. Henry I. Bowditch. One title suggested that Dr. Bowditch adhered to a theory that consumption was the result of geography and topography.

It was lunch time, and since I had no faith that Bowditch would mention, much less discuss, folk cures for consumption, I took the T to South Station, intending to head back to Providence. I was annoyed to see that I had missed a train by fifteen minutes and would have to wait more than three hours for the next one. I debated whether to browse Borders Bookstore and Tower Records or try my luck with Bowditch. Bowditch won by circumstance. Walking in the direction I supposed Tower Records to be, I emerged onto the Commons and found myself just across the street from the State House. I took this as an omen and went, with confidence, back into the State Library.

The librarian told me that the two Bowditch works were in Special Collections. ("*Special* Collections"—I'm apprehensive, if not downright queasy, at the thought. Will I measure up? Are my hands and fingernails clean? Are my needs sufficiently pressing?) I recovered from this moment of self-doubt in time to hear the librarian giving me directions from the third floor to the basement home of Special Collections. Apparently, I missed an important instruction and took the wrong elevator, for I emerged into a basement cul-de-sac housing some state agency not remotely connected to libraries or books. I was informed by two passersby that, yes, they had heard of Special Collections, but that, no, I couldn't get there from here (not without going back up to the first floor, then crossing over from the east wing to the west and, from there, going back down to the basement). I managed to accomplish this task with only one more stop for directions.

When I finally arrived at Special Collections, the door was locked. A small computer-generated sign read, "Will be right back. Please wait." OK, why not? I sat in a chair placed conveniently next to the door, under a bulletin board with all sorts of "inspiring" notices. The chair looked worn and the seat cushion was stained. I sagely concluded that Special Collections was understaffed and not generously funded. The librarian really did come right back though, and she proved helpful and sympathetic (I didn't much mind having to put "anything you don't need"— that is, everything but a pencil and notebook—into an ancient wardrobe).

I first checked Bowditch's "pamphlet" on the geographic correlations of consumption. The frontispiece was headed, "Boston Board of Health, 1872," which sent my pulse racing. It was back down to 60 bpm by the time I finished skimming Bowditch's transcribed speech to the Boston Board of Health. His bottom-line argument was that living in damp, perhaps especially cold *and* damp, places was the major cause of consumption. I perused pages of testimony and statistical correlations mustered to demonstrate Bowditch's "law." There were many case histories, mostly sad, of entire families being decimated, with a few bright spots (such as the family member who was spared because he spent most of his time at sea, away from the boggy farm). Among all of the anecdotal evidence, I found not one reference to exhumations, vital organ burning or any of the other morsels I sought. Certainly, no "midnight cremation." I was doubting my premonition that missing the train and bumping into the library was a sign that I would find the missing puzzle piece.

But I still had to review the pamphlet, *Consumption in New England*. A few sentences into the manuscript, I had the eerie feeling that I had been there before. Comparing the two manuscripts side-by-side revealed that Bowditch's address to the health board had been transcribed and published under two different titles (I stifled the thought that Dr. Bowditch had padded his resume). Just to be sure, I flipped through the pages again. My eye somehow caught the word, "disinterred," and I paused to read a passage I had missed the first time. A Dr. J. L. Allen, of Saco, Maine, had been one of Bowditch's correspondents who had provided data regarding their cases of consumption and how they correlated to geography. Bowditch wrote that Dr. Allen, "a practitioner of long standing," had noticed two ridges of land that were identical in every respect save for the amount of moisture in the soil.

> Almost every family has been decimated on the wet part, while almost all upon the dry portion have escaped. . . . One ridge is quite dry, the other is literally filled with springs. Nowhere can a spade be driven a few feet into the ground, without meeting water. In fact, in former times, the superstitious frequently had their friends, who had died of consumption, disinterred, and Dr. Allen invariably found the coffins filled with water, however shallow may have been the graves.

While this brief passage does not refer to any specific instance that might be investigated, and does not provide specifics regarding what procedures were followed after disinterment, it does suggest that vampires were being sought in Maine in the early nineteenth century. And, perhaps equally intriguing, it seems to imply that a medical doctor, Dr. Allen himself, was routinely present at the exhumations. I didn't find the Board of Health Report I was looking for, but the trip to Boston was amply rewarded. Dr. Rational has no explanation for omens (or hunches, if you prefer), yet he cannot disregard them.

I continued to search for the 1872 Boston Board of Health

Report and was successful at the Archives of the City of Boston, which contained the Annual Reports of the Boston Board of Health, spanning the years from 1872 to 1880, as well as the document that established the Board of Health in 1872. Alas, I found nothing remotely related to the vampire practice. But the latter document did promulgate regulations on the interment of the dead. The following passages suggest why the Board of Health might have been aware of, and perhaps reported on, a vampire incident: "No person shall remove any dead body, or the remains of any such body, from any of the graves or tombs in this city, or shall disturb any dead body in any tomb or grave without the license of the Board of Health or the City Council. . . . No grave or tomb shall be opened from the first day of June to the first day of October, except for the purpose of interring the dead, without the special permission of the Board of Health." The reference to obtaining the permission of the City Council led me to go through their minutes, too. Again, nothing. The trail towards Boston's "midnight cremation" still beckoned.

As I drove to Griswold, Connecticut (about ten miles west of the Rhode Island state line, bordering West Greenwich and Exeter), I mulled over the evidence provided by Nick Bellantoni. When I arrived at the site, Nick and two assistants were in the final stages of the excavation. Several skeletons lay exposed in their opened graves. A young woman with a clipboard was sitting cross-legged on the ground next to Burial 20, sketching the locations of the bones of a nearly complete skeleton of a man in his early thirties. Almost all of the twenty-seven whole or partial skeletons had already been placed in acid-free tissue and bubble wrap and transported to the Archaeological Laboratory at the University of Connecticut for storage, awaiting their reinterment in the nearby historic Hopewell Cemetery.

One exception was Burial 4, the "weird" one that Nick had mentioned on the phone, which had been sent to the Museum of Health and Science for analysis by Paul Sledzik. The complete skeleton of this man, the best preserved of the cemetery, had been buried in a crypt with stone slabs lining the sides and top of the coffin. On the lid of the hexagonal, wooden coffin, an arrangement of brass tacks spelled out "JB-55," presumably the initials and age at death of this individual. When the grave was opened, JB's skull and thighbones were found in a "skull and crossbones" pattern on top of his ribs and vertebrae, which were also rearranged.

Two adjacent burials appeared to be related to JB One, a 45- to 55-year-old woman, had "IB-45" spelled out in tacks on her coffin lid and the other, a child, aged 13 to 14, had "NB-13" on his/her coffin. The layout of the cemetery indicated that people had been buried in clusters as opposed to the typical well-ordered rows. The seven closely spaced graves in the northern cluster were of small children, suggesting a disease epidemic within the family or community. In fact, about half of those buried in the cemetery never reached their teens. Death records from the nearby town of Norwich show that there was a measles epidemic in 1759 and a smallpox epidemic in 1790, either of which could be represented in this cemetery. An 1801 account in a history of Griswold states that, twenty-five years earlier, "consumptions . . . proved to be mortal to a number" of people.

In light of the biomedical evidence uncovered, JB must have been an imposing figure. Rugged and tall, at six feet, he probably walked with a limp, due to severe osteoarthristis of the left knee, and hunched over, from a healed fracture of his right collarbone that was never set. Surely he was in pain, not only from the arthritis, but also because of chronic dental disease. Examination of JB's remains also revealed lesions of the second, third, and fourth ribs, indicating chronic respiratory disease, most likely pulmonary tuberculosis, but possibly some other disease, such as typhoid, syphilis, or pleuritis. In any event, J.B.'s condition probably would have been interpreted as consumption, as Nick and Paul subsequently observed:

Regardless of the specific infectious etiology of pulmonary disease in this individual, symptoms of a

chronic pulmonary infection severe enough to produce rib lesions would have probably included
coughing, expectoration of mucous [sic], and aches
and pains of the chest. Such symptoms, if not actually caused by pulmonary tuberculosis, would likely
have been interpreted as consumption by 19th century rural New Englanders.

No other cases of tuberculosis could be discerned in the excavated skeletons. Paul and Nick concluded that "the physical
arrangement of the skeletal remains in the grave indicate that no
soft tissues were present at the time of rearrangement, which
may have been 5 to 10 years after death. No other burial had
been so desecrated at the cemetery."

JB's decapitation and the rearrangement of his leg bones led
me back to the story of the "Welsh wizard" that appeared in
Witchcraft in Old and New England (quoted in Chapter 3). After
his death, the wizard kept coming back to terrorize his neighbors until, finally, "a brave English knight" had his body dug up
and beheaded. Was this a common approach to keeping a corpse
from returning to bother the living? Did it have a precedent in
the ancestral regions of New England, in northern Europe, especially Great Britain? It became clear as I researched these questions that what had been done to JB's corpse was far from a
unique occurence.

Archaeological evidence indicates that this practice goes back
at least to the Iron Age, more than three thousand years ago. A
number of Celtic sites show similar ways to deal with apparently
dangerous corpses, including "tying the body, prone burial, displacing parts of the skeleton, partial cremation." At one burial
site, nearly half of the eighty skeletons were missing the skull,
and there were "others in which the skull was present but separated from the trunk." Many of these graves had been reopened
after burial. British archaeologists who discovered late
Roman–British and pagan Anglo–Saxon cemeteries, dating
from the third to the seventh centuries, containing corpses that

had been decapitated, concluded that such burials were not uncommon. Their excavations disclosed that the detached head was normally positioned towards the lower end of the corpse, most often between or next to the lower legs or feet. But skulls have been found on or beside the pelvis, on the chest, by the arms, and near the neck. In one of the burials, the head had been removed and placed between the thighs, and the lower legs had been cut off and buried beside the upper arms. In most of these cases, there is no evidence showing whether decapitation was the cause of death or occurred after death. The same archaeologists also found the earliest recorded case of tuberculosis in Britain—an adult woman with a possible case of spinal tuberculosis (or Pott's disease). Several of her vertebrae were affected and the condition was diagnosed as "long-standing and . . . almost certainly due to healed tuberculosis." No decapitations were found at this cemetery.

The archaeological record does not provide explicit answers regarding why such measures were undertaken. For that, we must turn to written history. A medieval historian wrote about a raging pestilence that was attributed to the ghost of a man killed shortly before the onslaught of the misfortune. "To remedy the evil they dug up his body, cut off the head and ran a sharp stake through the breast of the corpse. The remedy proved effectual, for the plague ceased." Employing more than one method, in this case decapitation and staking, is not unusual. Murderers whose spirits were feared and those thought to be vampires might receive the same treatment. In 1591, a German shoemaker of Breslau, a suicide, was suspected of being a vampire. His body was exhumed, "then its head was cut off, it hands and feet dismembered, after which the back was cut open and the heart taken out." A German source of 1835 noted the following:

> In East Prussia when a person is believed to be suffering from the attacks of a vampire and suspicion falls on the ghost of somebody who died lately, the only remedy is thought to be for the family of the

deceased to go to his grave, dig up his body, behead it and place the head between the legs of the corpse. If blood flows from the severed head the man was certainly a vampire, and the family must drink of the flowing blood, thus recovering the blood which had been sucked from their living bodies by the vampire. Thus the vampire is paid out in kind.

The telltale presence of flowing blood fits snugly with the New England tradition of seeking "fresh" blood in the suspected vampire's heart. And here we have an explicit explanation for drinking the vampire's blood. Ingesting the ashes of the burned heart seems but one step removed.

The simplest rationale for the practice of decapitation is that

> "the soul was believed to reside in the head, so that the removal of the latter ensured the complete and final separation of the soul from the body. The placing of the head by the legs may have been intended as a reminder to the soul that it was now time to set off on its journey, for which it could no longer use its bodily legs—as was often emphasized by placing boots elsewhere in the grave."

The same scholar speculated that decapitation might "liberate the spirit and remove any fear of haunting."

In much closer proximity to JB and Connecticut is "a strange Russian story," collected in upstate New York in the early 1940s, that related the "digging up the corpse of a very active ghost, cutting the head off the corpse and putting it between his legs and then reburying him" to keep him from returning from the grave. Given the firmly established precedents in northern Europe—and at least one bit of evidence suggesting it was known, if only through narrative, in New England—it does not seem extraordinary that the practice would make an appearance in Connecticut.

After my visit to the site, Nick Bellantoni, Paul Sledzik, and I conferred. Combining our experiences in archaeology, physical anthropology, history, and folklore, the best conclusion we could reach was that JB had been exhumed to counteract the spread of tuberculosis. Here, in short, was the first truly tangible, physical evidence for the vampire tradition in America. If we could see into the grave of one of these vampires, what would we expect to find? Probably a skeleton that would have

1) been disrupted after death;
2) shown evidence of tuberculosis; and
3) been found in a cemetery from the same time and place as other New England vampire accounts.

JB fit these three criteria, and no other interpretation of his unusual remains even approached the coherence of the following scenario: An adult male, JB, died of pulmonary tuberculosis or a similar infection interpreted as tuberculosis by his family. Several years after the burial, one or more of his family members contracted the disease, including, possibly, his 45-year-old wife, IB, and his 13-year-old son or daughter, NB. As a last resort—to spare the lives of the family and stop consumption from spreading into the community—JB's body was exhumed so that his heart could be burned. When his body was unearthed, however, JB was found to be in an advanced stage of decomposition. Perhaps his ribs and vertebrae were in disarray as a result of the desperate search for the remains of his heart. Finding no heart, JB's skull and thighbones were arranged in a "skull and crossbones" pattern.

It was not difficult to explain the presence of the vampire tradition in Eastern Connecticut. Not only does it border on Rhode Island's South County—a hotbed of vampire activity, as we have seen—it also shares a common ethnic heritage, dialect, and other customs. Indeed, the town of Griswold was "partly settled" by emigrants from South County in the early 1800s. A town historian described these Rhode Islanders as "profane and uneducated," writing that "their clownish manners and their lack of schools were all objects of ridicule and contempt. They were accounted ignorant and vicious."

The discovery of the Walton family cemetery, and the moderate amount of media attention given its excavation, has led to the creation of at least three works of fiction: a novel, a short story, and a poem. If you knew about JB, the opening paragraph of the young adult novel, *The Apprenticeship of Lucas Whitaker*, might send shivers down your spine:

The Connecticut countryside, 1849

> The grave was dug. Carefully, Lucas Whitaker hammered small metal tacks into the top of the coffin lid to form his mother's initials: HW, for Hannah Whitaker. Then he stood up to straighten his tired back. All that was left was to lower the pine box into the cold, hard ground and cover it with dirt.

It is more than coincidence that this passage recalls the Walton family cemetery in Griswold. The author, Cynthia DeFelice, had read several newspaper articles that summarized the discovery of JB and the interpretations offered by Nick, Paul, and me. In her foreword, she acknowledges the factual basis for her fictional narrative, which, for the most part, treats the vampire superstition with sympathetic understanding.

Fleeing the farm that embraces the remains of his entire family, dead of consumption, the young Lucas wanders aimlessly through the Connecticut countryside until he answers a "help wanted" sign in the fictional town of Southwick. As an apprentice to Doc Beecher, Lucas is introduced into both the wonders and limitations of medicine in the middle of the nineteenth century. When Doc admits that he is helpless in the face of consumption, Lucas asks why he doesn't use the "cure" that he, Lucas, had learned of too late to save his own family.

> "I didn't really understand the cure, how it worked. But now I do, thanks to you."
> Doc appeared startled. "How's that Lucas?"

Lucas was surprised by Doc's question. "Well, you said—you said—lots of things. You said doctors don't always know what to do."

Doc smiled bleakly. "True enough."

"And you said that old witch woman—"

"Moll Garfield?"

"Yes. You said she knows a lot even though people call her a witch, and if she used hair from a dog that bit you it might cure the bite. And you told me how you can protect yourself from getting smallpox real bad by making sure you get just a little bit of it. So, when I thought about the cure, the one Mr. Stukeley did . . . "

"Yes?"

"Well, it seemed the same."

Lucas explains how breathing the smoke of the burning heart and making medicine from the ashes seemed just like an inoculation. And that removing the heart was sort of like bleeding people to get the bad blood out or cutting off a person's festered leg because it was making the rest of him sick. And then, as if to explain his own involvement with the "cure," Lucas continued. "Remember you said that sometimes you think the good of what you do isn't in what you do so much as in the—the kindness you show in doing it?"

As Lucas works through his own understanding of the relative merits of medical science versus folk practices, the reader is given a reasonably accurate depiction of life, disease, and death in rural nineteenth-century New England. There are some familiar names, including a Sarah Stukeley, and even an Everett Peck! And, not surprisingly, Lucas's neighbors had learned the "cure" from their Rhode Island relatives. One of DeFelice's sources probably was an article that appeared in the *Washington Post* around Halloween of 1993, in which my explanation for the "cure" is quoted:

"It is sort of homeopathic magic, like taking the hair

of the dog that bit you," said Bell. "It's what an inoc- ulation is, and in that sense is not that far removed from current scientific thinking."

Paul Sledzik coauthored, with mystery writer Jan Burke, a short story that centers around a vamp ire scare in a fictional Rhode Island village. In "The Haunting of Carrick Hollow," the narrator, Dr. John Arden, returns home after medical school to set up his new practice. He has occasion to recall tragic events that had occurred five years previously, in 1892, when he left school to attend to his family's consumption crisis. His younger brother, Nathan, was ill, and his father, Amos, an apple farmer, seemed haggard.

"Half my orchard has been felled," he remarked, and I knew he was not talking of the trees, but of the toll consumption had taken on his family. "First Rebecca, then Robert and Daniel. Last month, your mother— dearest Sarah! . . . "

"Noah and I are healthy," I replied, trying to keep his spirits up. "And Julia is with her husband in Peacedale. She's well."

Two days before he died, Daniel told John that he had dreamt that Rebecca and Robert came into his room and sat on his bed. Now, Nathan was worried that his own dead mother would come for him, because he had heard the tales of Mr. Winston, who had been telling everyone in the village that consumption was caused by vampires.

When John seemed incredulous that anyone would believe such things, his father answered, "In the absence of any cure, do you blame them for grasping at any explanation offered to them? Grief and fear will lead men to strange ways, Johnny, and Winston can persuade like the devil himself!"

The Winston character, who plays the role of belief specialist, is not at all likable. Wealthy and conniving, he attempts to force others to go along with his demand to exhume the dead. In his speech before a town meeting, Winston says,

"I have great sympathy for my neighbor, Amos Arden. The death of his wife and three children is a terrible loss for him. But in consumption, the living are food for the dead, and we must think of the living! The graves must be opened, and the bodies examined! If none of their hearts is found to hold blood, we may all be at peace, knowing that none are vampires. But if there is a vampire coming to us from the Arden graves, the ritual must be performed! This is our only recourse." The room fell silent. No one rose to speak, but many heads nodded in agreement.

Arden bows to the pressure, but asserts that no one but him will touch his wife. He explains to his son, "I don't do this because I believe it will cure consumption. But it is a cure for mistrust. A bitter remedy, but a necessary one." Adding to the anguish, the elderly town doctor pronounces Nathan's condition "hopeless."

The description of the exhumed corpses is gruesomely accurate, as would be expected with Paul, a forensic anthropologist, as coauthor. The sons and daughter were mummified, with "dry skin stretched tight over their bony frames." But the mother, who had been buried only three cold months, appeared "remarkably like the day we buried her. . . . Her nails and hair appeared longer, and in places, her skin had turned reddish." Of course, "fresh" blood was found in her heart, and it was dropped into the nearby fire. Returning home, John and his father find the dead Nathan cradled in the arms of his brother, Noah.

At medical school, John Arden learns that the condition of his mother's corpse was not unusual. And he learns about tuberculosis, too. Returning to his hometown, he visits the older town doctor, who gives him some advice: "Remember, John, that folks here are quite independent, even when it comes to medicine. They take care of their own problems, using the same remedies their grandparents used. It's hard to fight their traditions." Arden takes a special interest in treating tuberculosis and finally is able to convince his fellow citizens that medical science, not superstition, ultimately holds the best course of treatment. Angry that they had been persuaded by Winston to desecrate the bodies of their loved ones, the villagers give Winston a fitting reward.

Paul Sledzik's knowledge of New England's vampire tradition is apparent throughout the story, as we encounter a blending of now-familiar motifs from the cases of Mercy Brown and Sarah Tillinghast. Amos complained that half of his orchard, that is, half of his children, had died, just as in Snuffy Stukeley's dream. Night visits by the deceased augured impending death. Buried only from January to March, 1892, the body of Sarah was exhumed and found to be in an apparently remarkable state. And the venerable doctor's grasp of the townspeople echoes Everett Peck's characterization of his own forebears: they were independent people who took care of their own problems. A significant difference between the tradition and the story probably is explainable in terms of the narrative's need for an antagonist: Winston is consummately evil, whereas his counterpart in actual communities was more than likely genuinely attempting to help his neighbors. And, of course, the actual folks did not use (perhaps did not even know) the term "vampire."

Inspired by an article in the *New York Times* that summarized both the discovery of JB's remains and the Ray family incident, Michael J. Bielawa, a poet and librarian in Connecticut, composed "The Griswold Vampire."

> A good February fog
> is a wonderful thing to be with
> in the Connecticut woods.
>
> Until you hear the stories told, down at the one pump
> station.
> Always a warning as much as an invitation,
> The old men will grin and spit . . .
> "At night, Don't be found on the cemetery road."
>
> The route inevitably changes.

And the wind will whisper something very old,
'Why can't they pass, and leave it alone
that crumbling gate
where trees lean away from the sleepless stones.'

But no. The living will always arrive, never on time,
looking for the Griswold vampire.

Beyond the wall,
Amidst the frozen wind-piled leaves
A member of the historical society
rubbed his muddied knee
rising from realigning a stone . . .

"Never strangers true vampires be," he said,
"the loved ones they knew
upon whom they'd have to feed.
Demon lust for their family still living,
old Yankees did believe."

The car moves on.
These visitors will forget, and the New England stories soon wither forgotten;
But as the strangers wave good-by
to the ancient guide who stands at the gate
waiting . . .

The driver laughs with his friends
and unnoticed,
the rear view mirror cradles no reflection.

The finding of JB's grave still seemed incredible to me. Nick
Bellantoni said that, as far as he could determine, the Walton
cemetery was the first Colonial farm family cemetery ever excavated. What are the odds that it would hold a vampire?

CHAPTER 9
Ghoulish, Wolfish Shapes

C olonial houses on Providence's Benefit Street are like casseroles at a church supper: too much of a good thing. Yet, the yellow colonial house across the street from my office attracts attention. The door, at street level, opens directly into a stone-lined cellar. Since the house is set gable end to the street and built into a steeply rising hill, the main entrance is approached by climbing a flight of granite steps, then entering the yard through a gate. On the gatepost, four signs, in neatly lettered French, seem to warn of the wirehaired terriers, whose yapping muzzles bob above the low picket fence as if attached to yo-yo strings.

Attention	Chien Fort	Chien	Oubliez le
Chien	Méchant	Lunatique	Chien
Bizarre	et Pou		Attention
	Nourri		au Maitre

Fans of H. P. Lovecraft (1890–1937), and they are legion in Rhode Island, know the house at 135 Benefit Street as the "shunned house," the title of one of his short stories. I don't believe the signs are there to warn unwary strangers about the hyperactive dogs; rather, I think the owners of the house are sharing an inside joke with Lovecraft devotees who enjoy tracking down the places that he insinuates into his tales. The hidden meaning of their signs—directing visitors to beware of a

Exeter Grange and Chestnut Hill Baptist Church, Exeter, Rhode Island. Mercy Brown is buried in the cemetery behind the church. *Courtesy of Alex Carerta.*

EXHUMED THE BODIES.

—

Testing a Horrible Superstition in the Town of Exeter.

—

BODIES OF DEAD RELATIVES TAKEN FROM THEIR GRAVES.

—

They Had All Died of Consumption, and the Belief Was That Live Flesh and Blood Would be Found That Fed Upon the Bodies of the Living.

Above left: *Providence Journal*, March 19, 1892, The newspaper article describing Mercy Brown's exhumation as a suspected vampire. *Courtesy of Michael E. Bell.*

Above right: Gravestone of Mercy Brown, Chestnut Hill Cemetery, Exeter, Rhode Island. Her body was exhumed on March 17, 1892 in a desperate attempt by relatives to save the life of her dying brother. *Courtesy of Michael E. Bell.*

Everett Peck, a descendant of Mercy Brown, whose family story about her started the author on the trail of New England's vampires. *Courtesy of Michael E. Bell.*

The author in front of the crypt where Mercy Brown's corpse was kept prior to performing the vampire ritual. *Courtesy of Alex Caserta.*

Records of Births, Tillinghast Family 1763–1786, Town Records, Exeter, Rhode Island.
Several members of the Tillinghast family died in rapid succession. About 1799, Sarah
Tillinghast's body was exhumed and her heart was removed and burned to prevent fur-
ther deaths in the family. *Courtesy of Michael E. Bell.*

Plain Meeting House, West Greenwich, Rhode Island. Nellie Vaughn, a legendary
vampire, is interred in the cemetery behind this church. *Courtesy of Michael E. Bell.*

West Greenwich, Rhode Island. The entrance to the cemetery where Nellie Vaughn is buried. *Courtesy of Michael E. Bell.*

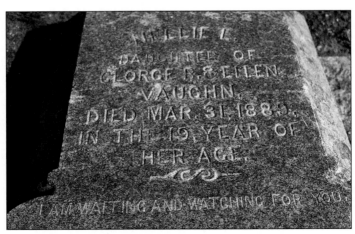

Gravestone of Nellie Vaughn. The inscription "I am waiting and watching for you." probably led to her legendary status as a vampire. *Courtesy of Michael E. Bell.*

Gravestone of Nellie Vaughn. Part of Nellie Vaughn's legend is that no grass will grow on her grave. *Courtesy of Michael E. Bell.*

Young Family Cemetery, Foster, Rhode Island. In the early 1800s, several members of the Young family died of consumption. *Courtesy of Michael E. Bell.*

Top left: Gravestone of Nancy Young. Her corpse was exhumed in the summer of 1827 and burned so ill family members could breathe the smoke and be cured. *Courtesy of Michael E. Bell.*

Top right: Excavated grave of JB, Walton Family Cemetery, Griswold, Connecticut. Long after decomposition, JB's body was exhumed and some of his bones were rearranged perhaps as an attempt to keep him from leaving his grave. *Courtesy of Connecticut State Museum of Natural History.*

Gravestone of Henry N. Ray, Jewett City Cemetery, Griswold, Connecticut. The bodies of two of Henry's brothers were exhumed on May 8, 1854 and burned in the hope of saving Henry's life. *Courtesy of Michael E. Bell.*

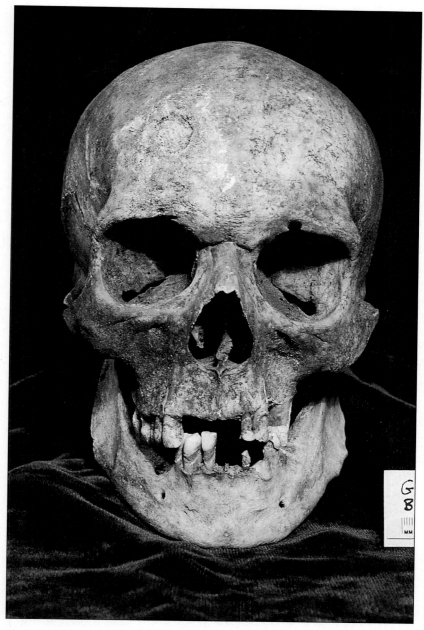

Skull of JB. He is probably the only suspected American vampire whose remains have been studied by scientists. *Courtesy of National Museum of Health and Medicine, Washington, D.C.*

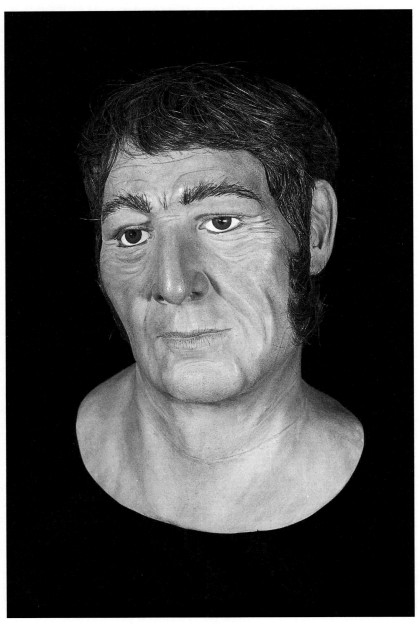

A reconstruction of JB's head made from his skull by forensic artist Sharon Long. *Courtesy of National Museum of Health and Medicine, Washington, D.C.*

bizarre, undernourished, mad dog, then instructing them to forget the dog and heed the master—is plain to those who have read "The Shunned House" (1937).

Lovecraft fans come in several varieties. I'm the casual sort who appreciates his embedding of history, local landmarks, and genealogy into outrageous fantasies. Lovecraft's subtle transmutations of factual material glide by unchallenged, unless one seeks esoteric conversations with like-minded fans. Ordinarily, I'm not up for the task. Having read "The Shunned House," though, I knew that Lovecraft alluded to the Mercy Brown event, stopping short of naming names. I didn't think much about it until I began to follow a trail of entries in Ernest Baughman's *Type and Motif-Index of the Folktales of England and America*. Under the heading "Vampire sucks blood of victims (usually close relatives) by unknown means," I found references to vampire stories collected in Rhode Island, Vermont, and New York. I put the last two on hold to follow the Rhode Island trail, which revealed some links that the word "fascinating" only begins to portray. Vampires and werewolves and . . . Tillinghasts? Oh, my!

I picked up the trail at Baughman's reference to Charles M. Skinner's *Myths and Legends of Our Own Land* (1896). Skinner tells readers that his entries were "gathered from sources the most diverse: records, histories, newspapers, magazines, oral narrative—in every case reconstructed." Alas, Skinner "reconstructed" the tales (which I take to mean that he took the liberty of rewriting them in his own words), and he did not provide his sources. Still, Skinner's two-volume collection is, in itself, a valuable source for legends. In his tale "The Green Picture" (the one Baughman cited as a vampire story), the Mercy Brown incident from Exeter seems to function as a sort of explanatory device, saying, in effect, "there are people in this region who actually believe in vampires."

> In a cellar in Green Street, Schenectady, there appeared, some years ago, the silhouette of a human form, painted on the floor in mould. It was swept and

scrubbed away, but presently it was there again, and month by month, after each removal, it returned: a mass of fluffy mould, always in the shape of a recumbent man. When it was found that the house stood on the site of the old Dutch burial ground, the gossips fitted this and that together and concluded that the mould was planted by a spirit whose mortal part was put to rest a century and more ago, on the spot covered by the house, and that the spirit took this way of apprising people that they were trespassing on its grave. Others held that foul play had been done, and that a corpse, hastily and shallowly buried, was yielding itself back to the damp cellar in vegetable form, before its resolution into simpler elements. But a darker meaning was that it was the outline of a vampire that vainly strove to leave its grave, and could not because a virtuous spell had been worked about the place.

A vampire is a dead man who walks about seeking for those whose blood he can suck, for only by supplying new life to its cold limbs can he keep the privilege of moving about the earth. He fights his way from his coffin, and those who meet his gray and stiffened shape, with fishy eyes and blackened mouth, lurking by open windows, biding his time to steal in and drink up a human life, fly from him in terror and disgust. In northern Rhode Island those who die of consumption are believed to be victims of vampires who work by charm, draining the blood by slow draughts as they lie in their graves. To lay this monster he must be taken up and burned; at least, his heart must be; and he must be disinterred in the daytime when he is asleep and unaware. If he died with blood in his heart he has this power of nightly resurrection. As late as 1892 the ceremony of heartburning was performed at Exeter, Rhode Island, to

save the family of a dead woman that was threatened
with the same disease that removed her, namely, consumption. But the Schenectady vampire has yielded
up all his substance, and the green picture is no more.

The sinister mould on the basement floor, interpreted as a vampire, coupled with the mention of the Exeter case of 1892, sent me
back for a closer reading of "The Shunned House," which also
includes those elements. Writing in the first person, Lovecraft
weaves fact and fiction into a seamless, gripping narrative whose
focal point is an abandoned house built into a hillside on Benefit
Street in Providence, odd in that its gable end faces the street and its
small door opens directly into the cellar. Community legend had it
that no one would live in the house because "people died there in
alarmingly great numbers." As a youngster, Lovecraft avoided the
house, fearing its bad odors and especially the weirdly shaped,
phosphorescent fungi that grew on the dirt floor of the cellar that
the front door opened into. Aided by the tales of his uncle, Dr.
Elihu Whipple, a medical doctor and a lover of local history and
legend (who often conversed "with such controversial guardians of
tradition as Sidney S. Rider and Thomas W. Bicknell"), Lovecraft
pieced together the morbid history of the shunned house, built,
according to his story, in 1763 by William Harris for his wife,
Rhoby Dexter, and their four children.

Things were bad from the beginning. The first child born in
the house to Harris and his wife was stillborn. ("Nor was any
child to be born alive in that house for a century and a half,"
according to Lovecraft's text.) Soon, the older children began to
die, too. Although the doctors made a diagnosis of "infantile
fever," people said it was a "wasting-away" condition. Then the
servants, and then Harris himself, succumbed, and the widowed
Rhoby "fell victim to a mild form of insanity, and was thereafter
confined to the upper part of the house." Her older sister, Mercy
Dexter, moved in to manage the household. By this time, those
servants who had not died, fled. Seven deaths and a case of
insanity, all in the space of five years, made securing new servants

next to impossible. Mercy at last found Ann White, "a morose woman" from Exeter, who, as Lovecraft wrote,

> first gave definite shape to the sinister idle talk. Mercy should have known better than to hire anyone from the Nooseneck Hill country, for that remote bit of backwoods was then, as now, a seat of the most uncomfortable superstitions. As lately as 1892 an Exeter community exhumed a dead body and cere-moniously burnt its heart in order to prevent certain alleged visitations injurious to the public health and peace, and one may imagine the point of view of the same section in 1768.

Ann White was soon discharged, but life in the house continued its downward slide.

The violent fits of Rhoby Harris increased in fury. "Certainly it sounds absurd to hear that a woman educated only in the rudiments of French often shouted for hours in a coarse and idiomatic form of that language, or that the same person, alone and guarded, complained wildly of a staring thing which bit and chewed at her." She died the next year. As the tragic years rolled by, it became clear to people in the community that the evil was not in the family, but in the house and, specifically, the cellar. "There had been servants—Ann White especially—who would not use the cellar kitchen, and at least three well-defined legends bore upon the queer quasi-human or diabolic outlines assumed by tree-roots and patches of mould in that region."

Lovecraft elaborated:

> Ann White, with her Exeter superstition, had prom-ulgated the most extravagant and at the same time most consistent tale; alleging that there must lie buried beneath the house one of those vampires— the dead who retain their bodily form and live on the blood or breath of the living—whose hideous legions

send their preying shapes or spirits abroad at night. To destroy a vampire, one must, the grandmothers say, exhume it and burn its heart, or at least drive a stake through that organ; and Ann's dogged insistence on a search under the cellar had been prominent in bringing about her discharge.

Even so, Ann's tale made sense to many because of the way it "dove-tailed with certain other things": the ravings of Rhoby Harris, who muttered of "the sharp teeth of a glassy-eyed, half-visible presence;" the servant who had preceded Ann White complaining that something "sucked his breath" at night; the death certificates of fever victims of 1804 showing that "the four deceased persons" were "all unaccountably lacking in blood;" and the land that the house was built upon once being used as a cemetery (although the graves all had been transferred to the North Burial Ground prior to the building of the Harris house).

After he interviewed surviving family members concerning the house, Lovecraft turned to the historical record. He found the French connection in one Etienne Roulet, who had leased the land in 1697. The Roulets had used a plot behind their small cottage as a family graveyard—and Lovecraft found no record of a transfer of graves. The Roulets, from the small village of Caude in France, were part of the unfortunate group of Huguenots who settled in East Greenwich in the late seventeenth century, but eventually abandoned their property in the face of unrelenting intimidation by neighbors who laid claim to land the Huguenots believed they had purchased. After fleeing to Providence, Etienne Roulet ("less apt at agriculture than at reading queer books and drawing queer diagrams") had been given a clerical post "in the warehouse at Pardon Tillinghast's wharf, far south in Town Street" in Providence. Speculation and gossip concerning such activities as witchcraft followed the Roulets. Lovecraft, in his "wider reading," came upon an "ominous item in the annals of morbid horror" that recounted the trial of a Jacques Roulet, condemned to be burned at the stake in Caude, France, in 1598. "He had been found covered with blood and shreds of flesh in a wood, shortly after the killing and rending of a boy by a pair of wolves. One wolf was seen to lope away unhurt." For some unexplained reason, the wolfman was spared the death penalty by the parliament in Paris and locked away in a madhouse.

In light of this new evidence, the "anthropomorphic patch of mould" in the cellar acquired an increased terror, and Lovecraft noticed that above it rose "a subtle, sickish, almost luminous vapour which as it hung trembling in the dampness seemed to develop vague and shocking suggestions of form, gradually trailing off into nebulous decay and passing up into the blackness of the great chimney with a foetor in its wake." Lovecraft and his uncle, Dr. Whipple (filling a role similar to that of Dr. Van Helsing in *Dracula*) decided to spend the night in the cellar, augmented with scientific apparatus to analyze and, if necessary, destroy the evil entity, which they surmised was "traceable to one or another of the ill-savoured French settlers of two centuries before, and still operative through rare and unknown laws of atomic and electronic motion." One of their weapons, a flamethrower, was to be used "in case it proved partly material and susceptible of mechanical destruction—for like the superstitious Exeter rustics, we were prepared to burn the thing's heart out if heart existed to burn." Since the outcome of Lovecraft's tale has no direct bearing on the issues at hand, I won't spoil a good story by revealing its conclusion without purpose.

I could speculate that Lovecraft knew of Skinner's "Green Picture" or, perhaps, the unascribed source used by Skinner. The parallels suggest more than simple coincidence. The core of both tales is an odious mould on a cellar floor (Skinner's "silhouette of a human form, painted on the floor in mould" and Lovecraft's "anthropomorphic patch of mould"), whose description matches up, feature for feature. Both tales refer to three explanatory legends that account for the mould, including that the ground beneath was the site of an old cemetery (Dutch vs. French) and that it is the grave of a vampire. Of the human-shaped stain on the basement floor, Lovecraft wrote, "Later I heard that a similar notion entered into some of the wild ancient tales of the common folk—a notion likewise alluding to ghoulish, wolfish shapes taken by smoke from the great chimney, and queer contours assumed by certain of the sinuous tree-roots that thrust their way into the cellar through the loose foundation-stones."Then, of course, there are the allusions to the Exeter case of 1892, attached to the end of "The Green Door" but, consistent with Lovecraft's narrative style, woven into "The Shunned House" in several strands, with varying degrees of subtlety. Lovecraft may have had a playful smile on his face when he introduced Mercy Dexter (though not from Exeter) and Ann White (not Brown, the Exeter maid/vampire expert).

The house that Lovecraft calls the Stephen Harris House was built about 1764 for John Mawney, a physician. One of the first houses built on Benefit Street, it was in the Mawney family for many years, but by the time Lovecraft penned his short story, it had been abandoned and was in sad disrepair—favorable elements for a haunted house.

We are familiar with the Sidney S. Rider that Lovecraft's Uncle Elihu Whipple enjoys conversing with. He's the historian who first printed the story of Snuffy Stuke in 1888, omitting the family name of Tillinghast. And what a coincidence that Lovecraft's Frenchman-cum-werewolf, Etienne Roulet, happened to find employment with Elder Pardon Tillinghast, Snuffy's great-great-grandfather! Thomas W. Bicknell, the other "controversial guardian of tradition" in Whipple's circle, actually published a five-volume history of the state in 1920 that included a chapter on the French Huguenots in Rhode Island. Etienne Roulet is nowhere to be found in this chapter, nor is he listed in the state's cemetery database. But Jacques Roulet does indeed appear in the historical record, perhaps most accessibly to Lovecraft and other English readers, in Montague Summer's *The Werewolf*. By the time this book appeared in 1934, Summers had already published two books on witchcraft and two on vampires, the second of which contained a citation of the William Rose case in Rhode Island (discussed in Chapter 4).

In his chapter on the werewolf in France, Summers included several accounts of cases that had come before Judge Pierre de Lancre (1553–1631). De Lancre had written extensively about his tenure as a trial judge for cases involving those accused of witchcraft. He had interviewed (perhaps taking depositions under duress?) both the witnesses and the accused. Believing that his predecessors had been too soft on witches and their ilk, De Lancre undertook to set things right. He boasted of having burned 600 of the heretics. Following is Summers' synopsis of one of De Lancre's published accounts of a werewolf trial over which he presided in 1598:

> In the remote and wild spot near Caude, Symphorien Damon, an archer of the Provost's company, and some rustics came across the nude body of a boy aged about fifteen, shockingly mutilated and torn. The limbs, drenched in blood, were yet warm and palpitating, and as the companions approached two wolves were seen to bound away into the boscage. Being armed and a goodly number to boot, the men gave chase, and to their amaze [sic] came upon a fearful figure, a tall gaunt creature of human aspect with long matted hair and beard, half-clothed in filthy rags, his hands dyed in fresh blood, his long nails clotted with garbage of red human flesh. So loathly was he and verminous they scarce could seize and bind him, but when haled before the magistrate he proved to be an abram-cove [a cant word among thieves, signifying a naked or poor man; also a strong, "lusty rogue, with hardly any cloaths on his back: a tatterdemallion"] named Jacques Roulet, who with his brother Jean and a cousin Julien vagabonded from village to village in a state of abject poverty. On 8th August, 1598, he confessed to Maître Pierre Hérault, the lieutenant général et criminel, that his parents, who were of the hamlet of Gressiére, had

devoted him to the Devil, and that by the use of an unguent they had given him he could assume the form of a wolf with bestial appetite. The two wolves who were seen to flee into the forest, leaving the body of the slain boy whose name was Cornier, he declared were his fellow padders, Jean and Julien. He confessed to having attacked and devoured with his teeth and nails many children in various parts of the country whither he had roamed. As to his guilt there could be no question, since he gave precise details, the exact time and place, where a few days before, near Bournaut, had been found the mutilated body of a child, whom he swore he had throttled and then eaten in part as a wolf. He also confessed to attendance at the sabbat. This varlet was justly condemned to death, but for some inexplicable reason the Parliament of Paris decided that he should be rather confined in the hospital of Saint Germain-des-Prés, where at any rate he would be instructed in the faith and fear of God. It would seem that the wretched creature was a mere dommerer who could hardly speak plain, but uttered for the most part animal sounds. The full details of the case are not clear.

I recalled that the anonymous author of "The Vampire Tradition" (the article pasted into a scrapbook in the Arnold Collection of the Providence Public Library) speculated that the tradition was brought to Rhode Island by "the French Huguenot settlers who lived at Frenchtown, below East Greenwich, in the early part of the eighteenth century." What are the grounds for this connection? In his chapter on the Huguenots in Rhode Island, Bicknell is nothing but aglow with praise for these "people of singular purity and austere virtues." He writes that it was a "suicidal act" for Louis XIV to revoke, in 1685, the Edict of Nantes, thus ensuring the exile of "the most valuable citizens of France,—artisans, scientists, men of learning and of good wealth, industrious, virtuous, freedom loving, law abiding men and women." A possible motive for Rhode Islanders' animosity toward the Huguenots, and, thus, a willingness to blame them for introducing ghastly superstitions, hinges on two events. It appears that the Huguenots were deceived by an unscrupulous group of land speculators (based in Massachusetts) and, as a result, almost all of them were driven out through continual harassment, including destruction of their homes and their church, by neighbors who had claims to land the Huguenots believed they had purchased. That, combined with the beginning of war between England and France, and perhaps religious prejudice as well, made the French Huguenots an unwelcome group, and convenient scapegoats.

I thought it might be worth looking through Lovecraft's other works and was surprised—delighted, really—to see the village where I live, and its landmarks, mentioned in his short novel *The Case of Charles Dexter Ward* (1927–28). Following the trail of his ancestor, Joseph Curwin—a wizard and alchemist who abandoned Salem for Providence soon after the witch trials began— leads Ward to the ghastly discovery of Curwin's pact with evil in the pursuit of immortality. Ward's doom is sealed, as he is possessed by Curwin. Lovecraft writes into his novel a vampire scare in Pawtuxet Village that centers around Rhodes-on-the-Pawtuxet, a community landmark from the Victorian era that still stands less than two blocks from my house. During the time of these nocturnal assaults, Charles Ward's parents were becoming increasingly alarmed at his "haggard and haunted" visage, and his nighttime excursions. In fact,

> most of the more academic alienists unite at present in charging him with the revolting cases of vampirism which the press so sensationally reported about this time, but which have not yet been definitely traced to any known perpetrator. These cases, too recent and celebrated to need detailed mention, involved victims of every age and type and seemed to cluster around two distinct localities; the residential hill and

the North End, near the Ward home, and the suburban districts across the Cranston line near Pawtuxet. Both late wayfarers and sleepers with open
windows were attacked, and those who lived to tell
the tale spoke unanimously of a lean, lithe, leaping
monster with burning eyes which fastened its teeth
in the throat or upper arm and feasted ravenously.

Benefit Street is no stranger to either hauntings or horror
writers. Nearly a hundred years before Lovecraft, the street was
frequented by Edgar Allan Poe (1809–1849), whose work
Lovecraft admired and imitated. From the Providence
Athenaeum at 251 Benefit (a favorite haunt of both Poe and
Lovecraft), Poe often strolled the several blocks to the John
Reynolds House (c. 1785) at 88 Benefit Street to visit Sarah
Helen Whitman (1803–1878), to whom Poe was romantically
attached. Just north of the Reynolds House, between Benefit
Street and North Main Street, is St. John's (formerly, King's)
Churchyard, a cemetery dating back to the early 1700s. Lovecraft
wrote to a friend about feeling some vampiric presence and
seeing a corpse light in the cemetery, experiences that recall the
"almost luminous vapor" emanating from the cellar floor of the
shunned house:

> About the hidden churchyard of St. John's—there
> must be some unsuspected vampiric horror bur-
> rowing down there & emitting vague miasmatic influ-
> ences, since you are the third person to receive a
> definite creep of fear from it . . . . the others being
> Samuel Loveman & H. Warner Munn. I took Loveman
> there at midnight, & when we got separated among
> the tombs he couldn't be quite sure whether a faint
> luminosity bobbing above a distant nameless grave
> was my electric torch or a corpse-light of less describ-
> able origin!

Lovecraft later wrote in a letter (1937) that "Poe knew of this place, & is said to have wandered among its whispering willows during his visits here 90 years ago."

Poe, himself, wrote several vampire stories. His vampires are subtle, implicit, undesignated. In "The Oval Portrait" (1842), for example, the life essence of an artist's model is drained as her portrait emerges on the canvas. The magical transference is completed at the final sitting, as the model dies and the painting assumes the vitality of life. But it is Poe's short story, "Ligeia" (1838), that has New England parallels. "Ligeia" begins with a quote from Joseph Glanvill (1636–80), an English clergyman and philosopher who was chaplain to King Charles II, but, more to the point, also a believer in the spirit world and witchcraft. He refuted atheism by attempting to prove scientifically that witches and ghosts exist.

> **And the will therein lieth, which dieth not. Who knoweth the mysteries of the will, with its vigor? For God is but a great will pervading all things by nature of its intentness. Man doth not yield himself to the angels, nor unto death utterly, save only through the weakness of his feeble will.**

The story's narrator, after years of reflection, finds "some remote connection between this passage in the English moralist and a portion of the character of Ligeia"—his wife.

Early in the narrative, we get hints of Ligeia's supernatural qualities: This woman of "strange beauty . . . came and departed as a shadow." Then Ligeia grew ill, becoming pale with "the transparent waxen hue of the grave." "Words are impotent to convey any just idea of the fierceness of resistance with which she wrestled with the Shadow . . . in the intensity of her wild desire for life . . . solace and reason were the uttermost folly." On the day of her death, Ligeia asks her husband to repeat some verses she had recently composed. The last two were:

But see, amid the mimic rout,
A crawling shape intrude!
A blood-red thing that writhes from out
The scenic solitude!
It writhes!—it writhes!—with mortal pangs
The mimes become its food,
And the seraphs sob at vermin fangs
In human gore imbued.

Out—out are the lights—out all!
And over each quivering form,
The curtain, a funeral pall,
Comes down with the rush of a storm,
And the angels, all pallid and wan,
Uprising, unveiling, affirm
That the play is the tragedy, "Man",
And its hero the Conqueror Worm.

Fleeing "the dim and decaying city by the Rhine," the narrator repairs to the "wildest and least frequented portions of fair England," where he meets "the successor of the unforgotten Ligeia— the fair-haired and blue-eyed Lady Rowena." But he comes to loath her "with a hatred belonging more to demon than to man." Like her predecessor, Rowena begins to languish. Emaciated and pallid, she suffers bouts of night sweats and fever that alternate with apparent recovery. Ligeia seems to haunt more than the narrator's memory: "I had felt that some palpable although invisible object had passed lightly by my person . . . and I saw . . . a faint, indefinite shadow of angelic aspect—such as might be fancied for the shadow of a shade." Then he becomes "distinctly aware of a gentle footfall upon the carpet, and near the couch" where Rowena was raising a glass of wine to her lips. In that instant, he "saw, or may have dreamed" he saw, "three or four large drops of a brilliant and ruby colored fluid . . . fall within the goblet, as if from some invisible spring in the atmosphere of the room." Four nights after drinking the wine, the Lady Rowena is dead.

Watching the corpse of his newly dead wife, the narrator's "passionate waking visions of Ligeia" are interrupted by a low and gentle sobbing. He turns to Rowena's corpse to see that a slight "tinge of color had flushed up within the cheeks." Rowena still lived! But before he can take action, there is a relapse: "the color disappeared from both eyelid and cheek" and "the lips became doubly shrivelled and pinched up in the ghastly expression of death." This scene is repeated throughout the night, as Rowena appears to revive, then relapse, and the narrator is haunted by visions of Ligeia. Near dawn, the corpse stirred "now more vigorously than ever" and, "arising from the bed, tottering, with feeble steps, with closed eyes, and with the manner of one bewildered in a dream, the thing that was enshrouded advanced boldly and palpably into the middle of the apartment." Transfixed, unable to move, the narrator begins to doubt the identity of the shrouded figure. He wonders, "had she then grown taller since her malady?" He approaches her. "Shrinking from my touch, she let fall from her head, unloosened, the ghastly cerements which had confined it. . . . And now slowly opened the eyes of the figure which stood before me. 'Here then, at least,' I shrieked aloud, ' . . . can I never be mistaken—these are the full, and the black, and the wild eyes—of my lost love—of the lady—of the LADY LIGEIA."

Poe's Ligeia appears to share some features with the New England vampire in a poem by Amy Lowell. In her lengthy narrative poem, "A Dracula of the Hills," Lowell (1874–1925) shuns the European-derived literary vampire and turns, instead, to the New England vampire superstition. Lowell's vampire, Florella, follows the traditional New England pattern, killing silently from the grave, beginning with her most beloved, her husband. Lowell's dark, atmospheric story is set in western Massachusetts during the late 1800s. Like the other free-verse poems in her posthumous collection *East Wind* (1926), Lowell's vampire narrative unfolds in the style of the traditional ballad, developed more through dialogue, rendered in dialect, than description, leaping from scene to scene, and lingering on the crucial episodes that move the plot towards its dramatic climax.

Becky Wales, the narrator, recalls an incident that occurred when she was a young girl living "t'other side o' Bear Mountain to Penowasset." While her good memories seem "all jumbled up together," Becky relates that there are "some fearful strange things I can't never lose a mite of, no matter how I try." Whether you call it a custom or superstition (" 'Twarn't th' first time th' like had happened, I know"), Becky says,

> Seein's believin' all th' world over,
> An' 'twas my own father seed
> An' others besides him.

Because she was a young girl, she wasn't allowed to view the ghastly act.

> But I watched th' beginning's;
> An' what my eyes didn't see, my ears heerd,
> An' that afore other folks' seein' was cold, as you might say.

Florella Perry, "Fragile as a chiney plate," contracts consumption and finally is confined to bed. As she withers, she vows:

> "But I won't die. You'll see.
> I'll find some way o' livin'.
> Even ef they bury me, I'll live.
> You can't kill me, I ain't th' kind to kill.
> I'll live! I'll live, I tell you,
> Ef there's a Devil to help me do it!"

After "Dr. Smilie said ther' warn't nothin' to do for her," Florella "took a notion to see Anabel Flesche . . . a queer sort of woman . . . she lived in a little shed of a place over Chester way." Despite Anabel's knowledge of "herbs and semples . . . an' things like that

... Florella didn't change none" but kept "sinkin' an' sinkin' "
until "ther' warn't nothin' lef' of her but eyes an' bones." Becky's
mother and Miss Pierce "used to take it in turns to watch her."
The night before Florella died, Becky heard the whippoorwills
and knew "Florella's time was come." Before she died, she "was
jest plumb crazy ... worryin' 'bout th' life was leavin' her, an' all
eat up with consumption." Becky describes the sight of Florella's
corpse at the funeral:

> I can't a-bear to look on a corpse
> An' Florella's was dretful.
> Not that she warn't pretty;
> She was. Even her sickness hadn't sp'iled her beauty.
> She was like herself in a glass, somehow,
> An old glass where you don't see real clear.
> 'Twas like music to look at her,
> Only for her mouth.
> Ther' was a queer, awful smile 'bout her mouth.
> It made her look jeery, not a bit th' way Florella used
> to look.

Not long after the funeral, Florella's husband, Joe, began to show
the dreaded symptoms. When Joe reveals that he was consulting
with Anabel Flesche, Dr. Smilie vows, "I'll see that hussy stops
her trapesin' ... Rilin' up a sick man with her witch stories ...
I'll witch her, I'll run her out o' town if she comes agin." One
day, while Becky is on "death watch" for her friend, Joe, "all of a
sudden crash down come Florella's picture / on th' floor with th'
cord broke." Joe sees it as a death omen, that, "It can't go on
much longer." Becky begins picking up the pieces when she
notices that Florella's picture has been cut, "All about th' mouth
too. / It make it look th' way Florella's corpse did an' give me a
turn." Her fears that Joe would wake up and see the picture
proved unfounded, for Joe never again woke up. Taken ill in
Winter and dead by Autumn, Joe had gone down more quickly,
and more peacefully, than his wife.

Soon after Joe's funeral, Becky's father encounters the witch, Anabel Flesche. She suggests, "in a queer, sly way," that Florella loved life, and that "Joe's gone, but ther's others." Taking Anabel's hint, the father joins Jared Pierce in discussing the situation with the Selectmen. "Then some old people rec'llected things which / had happened years ago, / An' puttin' two an' two together, they decided to see / for themselves." At night, "so's not to scare folks," with lanterns, pickaxes, and spades they raise the coffin and open it.

Florella's body was all gone to dust,
Though 'twarnt' much more'n a year she'd be'n buried,
But her heart was as fresh as a livin' person's,
Father said it glittered like a garnet when they took th' lid off th' coffin.
It was so 'live, it seemed to beat almost.
Father said a light come from it so strong it made shadows
Much heavier than th' lantern shadows an' runnin' in a diff'rent direction.
Oh, they burnt it; they al'ays do in such cases,
Nobody's safe till it's burnt.
Now, sir, will you tell me how such things used to be?
They don't happen now, seemingly, but this happened.
You can see Joe's grave over to Penowasset buryin'-ground
Ef you go that way.
The church-members wouldn't let Florella's ashes be put back in hers,
So you won't find that.
Only an open space with a maple in th' middle of it;
They planted th' tree so's no one wouldn't ever be buried in that spot agin.

Lowell's poem begs scrutiny. I wonder if Lowell, herself, saw any similarities between her Florella and Poe's Ligeia? In some respects, Florella is like a Swamp Yankee version of Lady Ligeia. Both are strong-willed and unable to let go of life, determined to defeat death, even if it entails draining the life from the living. Ligeia's conquest though, is more dramatic, as she saps the essence of her husband's new wife, bodily supplanting her successor. Where might Lowell have learned of the vampire tradition? Born into a wealthy, aristocratic, and prominent family in Brookline, Massachusetts (very near Boston), and educated at home and in exclusive schools, Amy Lowell's knowledge of the vampire tradition surely must have been secondhand. She wrote that her upbringing was "very cosmopolitan" and that "the decaying New England" had been "no part of my immediate surroundings." Regarding the native Yankee, she admitted to being "a complete alien." Fortunately, it didn't take exhaustive research to find her source. In a letter to Glenn Frank, editor of *Century Magazine,* Lowell wrote in 1921: "The last case of digging up a woman to prevent her dead self from killing the other members of her family occurred in a small village in Vermont in the '80's. Doesn't it seem extraordinary?" She said her source was the *American Folk-Lore Journal.*

Bing! A bell sounded in my head. Baughman's folktale index, which had directed me to Charles M. Skinner's tale of the insidious patch on the cellar floor, also listed an account from Vermont that appeared in the *Journal of American Folklore* (*JAF*) in 1889. Could the report below have been Lowell's source?

Even in New England curious and interesting material may be found among old people descended from the English colonial settlers. About five years ago an old lady told me that fifty-five years before our conversation the heart of a man was burned on Woodstock Green, Vermont. The man had died of consumption six months before and his body buried in the ground. A brother of the deceased fell ill soon after and in a short time it appeared that he, too, had consumption; when this became known the family decided at once to disinter the body of the dead man and examine his heart. They did so, and found the heart undecayed, and containing liquid blood. Then they reinterred the body, took the heart to the middle of Woodstock Green, where they kindled a fire under an iron pot, in which they placed the heart and burned it to ashes.

The old lady who told me this was living in Woodstock at the time, and said she saw the disinterment and the burning with her own eyes.

. . . The old lady informed me that the belief was quite common when she was a girl, about seventy-five years ago, that if a person died of consumption and one of the family, that is, a brother or sister, or the father or mother, was attacked soon after, people thought the attack came from the deceased. They opened the grave at once and examined the heart; if bloodless and decaying, the disease was supposed to be from some other cause, and the heart was restored to its body; but if the heart was fresh and contained liquid blood, it was feeding on the life of the sick person. In all such cases, they burned the heart to ashes in a pot, as on Woodstock Green.

The details of this case don't quite jibe with the brief description tion Lowell wrote in her letter. The Woodstock vampire was a man, not a woman, and the event, though *reported* in the 1880s, apparently took place some fifty-five years before, in 1834.

I searched the early volumes of the *Journal of American Folklore* (published quarterly, beginning in 1888) to see if I could find a better match. I did not. But I did encounter some items that made me wonder if Lowell had preceded me along this trail some seven decades before, looking for material to include in her two volumes of narrative poetry set in rural New England (*Men, Women and Ghosts* and *East Wind*). The 1891 *JAF* included a note describing several death omens from New York's Champlain Valley, near the Vermont border, including the call of the whippoorwill and the deathwatch. Five pages in front of this article, the poet James Russell Lowell, Amy's first cousin, had contributed some nursery rhymes from Maine. Immediately following the Champlain Valley note was James Russell Lowell's obituary. Three years later, a *JAF* article on New England funerals included an anecdote illustrating the custom of viewing the corpse. Young girls who were coerced into looking at the ghastly remains of a woman who had been burned to death had nightmares for weeks afterward. The article also related the common belief that death is foretold by "the falling of a picture from the wall, especially if it were the portrait of the same individual." And, in "A Dracula of the Hills," we once again encounter the widespread corpse light tradition, in the form of a light "so strong it made shadows" radiating from Florella's tainted heart.

Amy Lowell's high regard for the romantic poetry of John Keats (himself a consumptive) led her to write a biography of him. Certainly, she was well acquainted with his two vampire poems. Both "The Lamia" and "La Belle Dame sans Merci" were composed in 1816 and center around an implicitly vampiric female. In ancient Greece, after Lamia bears Zeus' children, a jealous Hera kills them. In a rage, the spurned Lamia seeks revenge, feeding on the flesh and blood of the children of others. Lamia is a bogeyman in early folklore. Stories about her were told to control the behavior of young children. Tradition later transformed her into a shape-shifting succubus who could appear to young men as a beautiful woman. After seducing them, she sucked their blood and ate their flesh. It is upon this latter image that Keats based his poem in which Lycius succumbs to the shape-shifting lamia, who drains his vitality until he becomes like her and is finally saved, against his wish, by Apollonius.

"La Belle Dame sans Merci" takes the form of the traditional

English and Scottish ballad, consisting of twelve, four-line stanzas. In this short narrative poem, a knight relates how he was enchanted by a beautiful woman, pale with "wild wild eyes," and, after accompanying her to her elfin cave and kissing her, he fell asleep. He dreamed that he "saw pale kings and princes too, / Pale warriors, death-pale were they all; / They cried—'La Belle Dame sans Merci / Hath thee in thrall!' " He awakens alone on a cold hillside and finds that, he too, is pale and withering.

The romantic movement to which Keats was a strong contributor spawned an interest in indigenous cultures and ancient roots. Reacting against the ordered world of the Enlightenment and its belief in reason, romantics sought spiritual fulfillment, beauty and truth in the natural environment rather than the artificial world of the intellect. But, since nature also has a dark side, romantic fiction frequently went beyond the ordinary world to reveal a shadowy supernatural realm, tinged with horror, dread, death, and decay. A romantic writer, such as Keats, could explore the dual nature of humankind through an established figure of folklore, the vampire. He did not have to create, as Robert Louis Stevenson would later do, a Dr. Jekyll and Mr. Hyde.

Perhaps Lowell's choice of the specific "Dracula" instead of the generic "vampire" for her poem's title is telling. The term "vampire" did not appear in the *Journal of American Folklore* articles nor in her letter to Glenn Frank in which she comments on the "extraordinary" custom. Did she make the connection herself? Or had she used other sources of the New England superstition? Her choice of the literary Dracula suggests that Lowell assumed her readers would know the novel and be able to link Florella with the Count. By the early 1920s, when Lowell had completed this poem, Dracula was well on the road to total domination of the vampire genre; the terms "Dracula" and "vampire" had become synonymous. How did this occur?

The New England vampire tradition, as incorporated into the works of Lovecraft and Lowell, has had no discernible effect on the popular imagination. Indeed, even the impact of the *European* folk vampire has been less formidable than we might believe. Although the vampire was a genuine figure in the folk traditions of Europe, and remained so in isolated areas of Eastern Europe well into the twentieth century, in the urban centers of Western and Northern Europe the vampire was known principally through written communication. And writing, unlike the malleable oral tradition, freezes texts and images.

Augustine Calmet's recounting of the Arnod Paole incident of the early 1730s had an enormous influence on succeeding generations of writers. In 1746, he described, in *Dissertation on Those Persons Who Return to Earth Bodily*, how a series of unaccountable deaths in the Serbian village of Medvegia prompted a visit by a team of medical officers. Villagers claimed to have seen the reanimated corpse of Paole, an army veteran who broke his neck falling off a hay wagon. In their investigative report, *Visum et Repertum (Seen and Discovered)*, the officers described the apparent vampire attacks on villagers and the exhumations of Paole and several other suspected vampires. When unearthed, Paole's ruddy corpse appeared undecayed, there was fresh blood on his face and shirt, and he had grown new nails and skin. As the villagers drove a stake through his heart, Paole groaned and bled profusely. They burned his corpse and reburied the ashes. Legend has it that Paole, while on duty in Greece with the army, had been sucked by a vampire, an event that he eventually disclosed to his wife, Mina. (Is it coincidence that Mina is the name Bram Stoker chose for Jonathan Harker's fiancée, later wife, who assumes a prominent role in hunting down Dracula?)

The vampires of literature have taken on some of the more sensational features of folk vampires, but they have become character types in their own right, designed to fulfill their Gothic mission of embodying the dark side of human nature. Even though no other literary vampire has matched the immense popularity of Bram Stoker's *Dracula*, published in 1897, several predecessors brought vampires into the world of art and entertainment. Coleridge introduced readers to "Christabel" in 1816, the same year that Keats composed "The Lamia" and "La Belle Dame sans Merci." John Polidori's *The Vampyre, A Tale* (1819) was extremely successful and, like the later *Dracula*, spawned numerous derivative works: plays, comic operettas, vaudevilles, and even operas. In this novel, Lord Ruthven is a thinly disguised Gothic villain with a thirst for blood. Most of his characteristics belong to literature, not folklore: Ruthven bites his victims' necks to suck their blood, is immortal, pale, egotistical, influenced by the lunar cycles, and associated with Satan. He has supernatural strength, hypnotic power—which he uses to develop master-slave relationships— and he travels, sometimes great distances, in search of his prey. Like his mortal Gothic counterparts, the misanthropic Lord Ruthven is ruthless, immoral, vengeful, and world-weary. Another widely read vampire tale was *Varney the Vampire or The Feast of Blood*, a serialized thriller (with more than one hundred weekly installments begun in 1847) that might be regarded as a legitimate precursor to the "Dark Shadows" television soap opera. Sir Francis Varney bears a striking resemblance to Lord Ruthven: he is pale, with fang-like teeth and long fingernails, and he bites the necks of his female victims to suck their blood.

Stoker used these earlier literary models, as well as elements from vampire folklore, to create what became the prototype for all subsequent vampires of literature and popular culture. Even though the one-dimensional vampires of fiction pale in comparison to the diverse and colorful vampires of folklore and history, it is Dracula's shadow that falls over the entire vampire landscape. (Actually, demons, ghosts, and ogres cast no shadows. Stoker's Dracula to the contrary, folk tradition generally does not apply this characteristic to vampires.) Jennie and Paul Boldan's version of the Foster vampire story reflects the length of Dracula's shadow, which extends even to the remotest parts of New England. I have often wondered if it is possible to imagine a vampire without having Dracula's image intrude.

CHAPTER 10
The Unending River of Life

With the assistance of Jane Beck, Director of the Vermont Folklife Center, I found a more detailed description of the vampire case mentioned in the 1889 issue of the *Journal of American Folklore* (*JAF*)—the incident that I concluded Amy Lowell had used as the basis for her poem, "A Dracula of the Hills." Jane referred me to an article, published in *Vermont Life* in 1966, that described *two* vampire exhumations, some thirteen years apart, in the town of Woodstock. The article begins by quoting, verbatim, the description that was published in *JAF*. But the author, Rockwell Stephens, cites as the source a front page article that appeared in Woodstock's weekly newspaper, the *Vermont Standard*, in the fall of 1890, under the headline, "VAMPIRISM IN WOODSTOCK." The opening sentence of this article provides yet another source: "The following remarkable story is reprinted here as given in the *Boston Transcript*." I'm guessing that the Boston newspaper picked up the story from *JAF*, and that it's possible Amy Lowell learned of the Vermont vampires from the newspaper rather than from the less accessible academic journal.

The earlier of the two Woodstock cases was taken from an unpublished manuscript, housed in the stacks of the Norman Williams Public Library on Woodstock Green, entitled "Memoirs of Daniel Ransom." The Ransoms were an early and distinguished family in their town. Frederick Ransom, of South Woodstock, was a student at Dartmouth College when he died of consumption in 1817. His father had Frederick's body exhumed and his heart taken out and burned, hoping in vain to save the rest of his family. Frederick's mother (1821), sister (1828), and two brothers (1830 and 1832) died of the disease, but his younger brother, Daniel, was spared. Daniel was in his 80s when he wrote the following account of the incident in his memoirs:

> Frederick Ransom, the second son of my father and mother, was born in South Woodstock, Vermont, June 16, 1797 and died of consumption February 14th, 1817, at the age of about twenty. He had a good education and was a member of Dartmouth College at the time of his death. My remembrance of him is quite limited as I was only three years at the time of his death and I date my remembrance of anything at a visit of Dr. Frost to Frederick in his sickness. Keeping shy of the Doctor, fearing he would freeze me. It has been related to me that there was a tendency in our family to consumption, and that I, who now in 1894 am over eighty years old, would die with it before I was thirty. It seems that Father shared some what in the idea of hereditary diseases and withal had some superstition, for it was said that if the heart of one of the family who died of consumption was taken out and burned, others would be free from it. And Father, having some faith in the remedy, had the heart of Frederick taken out after he had been buried, and it was burned in Captain Pearson's blacksmith forge. However, it did not prove a remedy, for mother, sister, and two brothers died with that disease afterward.

The other case from Woodstock, which occurred in 1830, is the one that first appeared in the *Journal of American Folklore* in 1889. When the brother of a man who had been dead and buried for six months began to show the signs of consumption, the family had the deceased brother's body exhumed and examined.

Finding his heart "undecayed, and containing liquid blood," it was removed, and his body was reinterred. The heart was carried to The center of Woodstock Green, where it was burned to ashes in an iron pot. This brief description was recorded over fifty years after the event from "an old lady" who had seen "the disinterment and burning with her own eyes." When the story appeared in Woodstock's weekly newspaper, in 1890, the writer had added some particulars not included in the *JAF* article of the previous year:

> We may as well help the old lady's recollections in this matter and fill in with further details what she has left incomplete. To be particular in dates, the incident happened about the middle of June, 1830. The name of the family concerned was Corwin, and they were near relatives of the celebrated Thomas Corwin, sometime Senator in Congress from Ohio. . . . With regard to the cause of the illness that had seized the brother of the deceased, there was a general consensus of opinion among all the physicians at that time practicing in Woodstock. These embraced the honored names of Dr. Joseph A. Gallup, Dr. Burnwell, Dr. John D. Powers, Dr. David Palmer, Dr. Willard who recently died in New York, not to mention other members of the profession at that time residing in Woodstock and held in high repute at home and abroad. These all advised the disinterment as above described, all being clearly of the opinion that this was a case of assured vampirism. Only there was a slight controversy between Drs. Gallup and Powers, as to the exact time that the brother of the deceased was taken with consumption. Dr. Gallup asserted that the vampire began his work before the brother died. Dr. Powers was positively sure that it was directly after.
>
> The boiling of the pot on Woodstock Green, spoken of by the old lady, was attended by a large concourse of people. The ceremonies were conducted by the

selectmen, attended by some of the prominent citizens of the village then residing on the common. It will suffice to name Honorable Norman Williams, General Lyman Mower, General Justus Durdick, B. F. Mower, Walter Palmer, Esq., Woodward R. Fitch, of old men of renown, sound minded fathers among the community, discreet careful men. The old lady has forgotten to state what was done with the pot and its ghastly collection of dust after the ceremonies were over. A hole ten feet square and fifteen feet deep was dug right in the center of the park where the fire had been built, the pot with the ashes was placed in the bottom, and then on top of that was laid a block of solid granite weighing seven tons, cut out of Knox ledge. The hole was then filled up with dirt, the blood of a bullock was sprinkled on the fresh earth, and the fathers then felt that vampirism was extinguished forever in Woodstock. Eight or ten years after these events some curious minded persons made excavations in the Park, if by chance anything might be found of the pot. They dug down fifteen feet, but found nothing. Rock, pot, ashes and all had disappeared. They heard a roaring noise, however, as of some great conflagration, going on in the bowels of the earth, and a smell of sulphur began to fill the cavity, whereupon, in some alarm they hurried to the surface, filled up the hole again, and went their way. It is reported that considerable disturbance took place on the surface of the ground for several days, where the hole had been dug, some rumblings and shaking of the earth, and some smoke was emitted.

These additional details were so astonishing, I had difficulty deciding where to begin my investigation. But it was clear that several issues begged closer examination. Medical doctors were not just in attendance, but were approving, even *recommending,* the procedure; their only point of debate seemed to be *when*, not whether, the vampire attacked. The ceremony was conducted openly in a public space by the town's selectmen, with other notables also in attendance. The remains of the heart were reinterred under a huge block of granite, and the blood of a bullock was sprinkled on the earth. When the site was excavated some years later, all traces had disappeared. There was an odor of sulphur and a rumbling disturbance that lasted for several days. This additional information—the source of which is not disclosed by the author—seemed to distance the Corwin case from all of the others I had investigated.

Stephens added some research of his own in 1966, including a sketch of the medical men who were said to have "advised the disinterment." He suggested a provocative link to Rhode Island's vampire tradition through the person of Dr. Joseph A. Gallup, describing him as a "Rhode Island doctor." But my genealogical search revealed that Dr. Joseph Adam Gallup was born in Stonington, Connecticut (adjacent to Westerly, Rhode Island) on March 30, 1769. One of the few physicians of his day to have formal training, he was a member of the first medical school class of Dartmouth College, graduating in 1798 with a bachelor's degree. Dr. Gallup moved to Woodstock in 1800 after practicing medicine briefly in Hartland and Bethel, Vermont. He was president of the Castleton Medical Academy and a lecturer in the medical department of the University of Vermont before he established the Clinical School of Medicine (later, the Vermont Medical College) in Woodstock in 1827. He died in his adopted town at the age of eighty.

Although in the article Gallup is characterized as a strong proponent of the vampire theory, I could find no endorsement, or even mention, of the vampire practice in his published medical treatises, including the 1815 *Sketches of Epidemic Diseases in the State of Vermont . . . with Remarks on Pulmonary Consumption*. Clearly, Gallup believed that the use of calomel and bleeding of the patient was the most effective treatment for consumption, a theory that put him in opposition to the "asthenics" of the day who held that such diseases should be treated with opium and brandy.

Dr. John D. Powers, who allegedly argued with Dr. Gallup about whether the vampire began its attacks before or after it died, learned medicine from his father, who had learned from older doctors in Massachusetts during the mid-1700s. Dr. Powers' on-the-job training was the typical path for physicians at that time. He arrived in Woodstock with the early settlers in 1774. The Dr. Burnwell mentioned in the article was probably Dr. John Burnell, who boarded with Dr. Gallup on first moving to Woodstock in 1809. Apparently, the plan was for Dr. Burnell to take over Dr. Gallup's practice so that the latter could spend more time managing his drugstore; for some unexplained reason, it was never implemented. But Dr. Burnell seemed to prosper and, by the time of the vampire incident, had established a reputation for successfully treating patients through vaccination. Whether any of the town doctors actually performed the dissection of the vampire's heart is not known.

The public nature of the ceremonies—held on the town common, with a large portion of the community, including its leading citizens, in attendance—sets the Vermont case apart from those in Rhode Island. I don't believe that this difference is because Vermonters were more open and accepting of the practice than Rhode Islanders. The contrast, I think, is derived from a difference in settlement patterns which, ultimately, may be rooted in differing worldviews. What drew me to this conclusion was a rather startling statistic: Rhode Island averages 260 cemeteries for each 100 square miles while in Vermont, there are twenty covering the same amount of land. Why would Rhode Island have thirteen times more cemeteries per square mile than Vermont? Cemeteries in Vermont reflect the early New England settlement pattern, with towns, spaced five to seven miles apart, centered around the meetinghouse, the primary public structure that was the focus of religious as well as social activities. Near the meetinghouse lay the graveyard and the town "common" or "green," where outdoor religious ceremonies were held, the militia trained, livestock collected, and criminals hanged.

But Rhode Island was born of religious dissension, which tended to scatter people across the countryside. Beginning in 1636, free thinkers, led notably by Roger Williams, Anne Hutchinson, and Samuel Gorton, fled the religious conformity imposed by the Puritans in Massachusetts. What Williams termed "a lively experiment" began as a colony of haphazard settlements of Baptists, Quakers, and Congregationalists and evolved into a secular and diverse state. Rhode Island's cemeteries reflect this freedom from centralized authority, as family plots greatly outnumber community graveyards. The typical Rhode Island cemetery was small, isolated at the edge of the woods that bordered the family farm, and surrounded by a fieldstone wall with an iron gate.

Since in Vermont it would be all but impossible to hold a private exhumation in a graveyard located near the center of town, the ceremony was destined to be public by default. With that in mind, a family might decide that it was prudent, if not necessary, to obtain some sort of town sanction. If such approval was not officially conferred (by a vote of the selectmen, for example), it may have been given informally by the mere presence of town officials and notables. The graveyard and town green would be in close proximity, and the green was the customary site for communal activities. If a blacksmith's forge with its handy furnace was nearby, practical Yankees might use it for extraordinary purposes.

The article states that the Corwin brother whose body was disinterred had been buried in the Nathan Cushing cemetery. But when Rockwell Stephens investigated, he found some dead ends:

> The cemetery is there, above the north bank of the Ottauquechee stream, flanked on the south and west by town roads and the east and north by the pastures and mowings of a modern dairy farm. But among the headstones dating to the early days of the town, none bears the name Corwin. Nor does the careful script on the pages of the Town register of births and deaths record a Corwin. The name is not found in

census or land records of Woodstock or the adjacent
Pomfret—which also used Cushing plots.

When Stephens' article was reprinted in an anthology of
Vermont legends, the editors concluded that the event itself had
never actually occurred:

> Although apparently entirely fictitious, the original
> recounting of the Woodstock vampire illustrates
> considerable narrative skill in that its tracing is pur-
> posely obscured by framing it as a story within a
> story, by the credibility lent to it in staging the action
> at a true and familiar setting, . . . and the interjection
> of the names of attesting witnesses who were promi-
> nent citizens (but at the time safely long-deceased).

Is this the only, or best, conclusion? Certainly, it is possible that
the newspaper account providing the name and cemetery was in
error or deliberately falsified. If a pseudonym was used for the
family involved, the choice of Corwin might be telling, as it has
some renown in New England. You may recall that, in Lovecraft's
Case of Charles Dexter Ward, Joseph Curwin, the evil vampire
figure, is a refugee from the Salem witchcraft trials. Lovecraft wrote
that, "His birth was known to be good, since the Curwens or Car-
wens of Salem needed no introduction in New England." As a
Lovecraft scholar noted, " 'Curwen,' 'Carwin,' or 'Corwin,' is
indeed an old Salem name, a 'Jonathan Corwin' being listed as a
judge in the Salem witchcraft trials along with Nathaniel
Hawthorne's ancestor, John Hathorne." Not only was Jonathan
Corwin one of the magistrates at the witch trials, his nephew,
George Corwin, was the High Sheriff—and a cruel one, too.
When Giles Corey was pressed to death with heavy stones in 1692
for not entering a plea to a charge of witchcraft, it was Sheriff
Corwin who used his cane to push Corey's protruding tongue
back into his mouth. Corey was said to have cursed both Corwin
and Salem. A vampire in the family seems an appropriate scourge.

Whether or not the name and place of burial are accurate, the supporting evidence of so many similar events in the region during that era seems to argue against concluding that the account is purely fictional. Besides, the initial "story within a story" was actually published in the *Journal of American Folklore*. It would have been an elaborate hoax, indeed. And for what purpose? Had I dismissed each case for which I could find no headstones or official records documenting the existence of participants, I would have had to conclude that many of the cases considered to this point did not happen. If there was any episode in the Woodstock account of 1830 that was nothing more than a good yarn, my vote would be for the mysterious disappearance of the iron pot containing the vampire's cremated heart (not to mention the seven-ton block of granite covering it), and the "great conflagration . . . in the bowels of the earth" that was accompanied by the smell of sulphur. These phenomena are the customary calling cards of the Devil, who dwells in the earth's interior and announces his presence with the odor of brimstone. The Devil carries off wicked people (or, in this case, the remains of their possessed parts), often causing earthquakes and shaking the foundations of houses before disappearing amid a terrible rattle. Perhaps the presence of this incident at the end of the 1890 account functions as a sort of moral tag, transporting a pagan ritual into the more comfortable realm of Christian doctrine.

Blood played a prominent role in the Woodstock vampire event of 1830: the physicians were debating the efficacy of bleeding their patients; the exhumers looked for "undecayed and liquid" blood in the heart of the suspected vampire; and "the blood of a bullock was sprinkled on the fresh earth" that covered the reinterred heart ashes. Why did blood, especially from the heart, occupy such a prominent position, not only in Woodstock, but in all of New England's vampire cases?

The vampire concept rests on two fundamental principles: the belief in life after death and the magical power of blood. The power of blood is derived from its association with life itself. Even people who knew nothing of death-causing microbes understood that, if one lost enough blood, one died. If blood itself is not the life, it must contain the essence, soul, or spirit of the life. (This concept, termed "vitalism," was carried well into the nineteenth century by physicians who viewed blood as the "paramount humor.") Believing it possible to transfer an organism's properties through its blood, Roman gladiators drank the blood of fallen opponents to acquire their strength and courage, and Egyptians bathed in it to restore health. Perhaps the most notorious practitioner of the revitalizing power of blood was Countess Elizabeth Bathory, the "Blood Countess." Born in 1560 in Eastern Europe, she grew up on the family estate in Transylvania. She and her husband delighted in finding new ways to torture those unfortunate enough to be among her many servants. She was arrested in 1610 and convicted of murdering as many as 650 young women and girls. The countess had bathed in their blood, believing that it kept her young and beautiful. She was sentenced to be confined in a room of her own castle, with air vents and a small slot for food, but no windows or doors. She survived fewer than four years in this state of deprivation.

Early on, people came to believe that the power residing in blood could be used for diverse purposes, good and evil, and many superstitions and magical practices grew up around blood. The blood of saints, kings, and innocents (such as children and maidens) was especially valued for its power to heal, and even restore life. Though the blood of a strong and courageous ally might protect the earth on which it falls, that of a malevolent spirit was kept from penetrating the ground, for its evil influence would remain, making the place dangerous. Since blood was a well-known vehicle for the soul or life, people believed that ghosts and vampires were eager to obtain it, as exemplified by the ancient European custom of pouring blood into holes bored in graves to "feed the dead." This belief also explains why revenants slip out of their graves at night to suck the blood of the living, and why Odysseus sacrificed sheep to placate the shades on his visit to Hades. Blood, a symbol of mortality, is also "the unending river of life."

The bright red blood from a consumptive's lung hemorrhages was said to be from the heart. If the blood was life, then the heart was its home. In folk speech, heart signifies center, essence, soul, courage. The heart was, in fact, long supposed to be the seat of passion as well as the locus of life itself. A commonplace phrase that appears in European balladry is "heart's blood," a combining of the two traditional locations of soul and power to signify the very essence of a person's life. In a traditional British ballad, when young Sir Hugh is stabbed with a penknife:

> Then out and cam the thick, thick, blood,
>   Then out and cam the thin,
> Then out and cam the bonny heart's blood
>   Where a' the life lay in.

In the folklore of northern Europe, a person who has been enchanted may break the spell by drinking human blood. A Norse ballad tells how a young man, who had been turned into a wolf by his stepmother, regained his human form by tearing out her heart and drinking her blood:

> He griped her fast with wolfish claw,
>   And then with deadly bite
> Tore out her heart and drank her blood
>   And so stood up a knight.

When I came across the Egyptian "Tale of the Two Brothers," I thought of Edwin Brown, hoping to restore his health by drinking, in water, the ashes of his dead sister's heart. In the tale, a man is wrongly accused of having an adulterous relationship with the wife of his brother. Although he proves his innocence, he removes his own heart and places it atop a cedar tree to keep it safe. The untruthful wife has the tree cut down, and the innocent man dies as a result. But he is restored to life when his brother finds the heart and makes him swallow it with cold water.

While beliefs concerning the restorative powers of blood and the heart are ancient, an incident recorded in the London *Daily Mail* in 1880 shows that they were carried into recent times:

> A strange and horrible Wendish superstition, which has been handed down from the Pagan ancestors of the Prussians . . . , has of late led with shocking frequency to the commission of a hideous crime, punishable, even under the merciful German laws, by life-long imprisonment. It is commonly believed among the poorer peasantry of Wendish extraction that several paramount medicinal virtues and magical charms are seated in the heart or liver of a dead maiden or infant of tender years, and that these organs, brewed with certain herbs into a beverage, will cure diseases or inspire the passion of love in their consumers. The practical result of this barbarous belief is the constantly recurrent violation of the grave's sanctity, and the mutilation of the corpses secretly disinterred from the consecrated ground in which they have been laid to rest. Last week two graves in the new cemetery of Weissensee were broken open during the night, the coffins contained in them forced, and the bodies of an unmarried girl and a male infant discovered next morning by the guardians of the burial-ground, mangled in the most revolting manner, the cavity of the chest in both cases having been completely emptied of its contents. A rigid search for the perpetrators of this ghastly offence is being instituted by the gendarmerie of the Weissensee district, but with small hope of success, as the superstitious savages, who have upon several occasions within the last few years committed several similar outrages, have hitherto invariably escaped detection.

The existence of liquid blood in the heart of an exhumed

corpse was viewed as unnatural, since it was interpreted as "fresh" blood. People understood that blood coagulates following death, which indeed it does. But they apparently did not know that blood can liquefy again, depending on the circumstances of death. The blood of a person who died suddenly, for example, has a tendency to reliquefy. That blood in its liquid state proclaims the presence of life complies with a widespread folk principle that underlies many beliefs and practices. "Liquid is life" goes back at least to the Greek conception of life as the "gradual diminishing of liquid inside a man." A corpse that has decomposed is dry, indicating that death is complete and the corpse is inert. Cremation dramatically hastens the drying process, removing life's liquid. But a corpse that has not sufficiently dried—one with liquid blood still in the heart, for example—would be viewed as incompletely dead. The remedy is to consummate the drying process by burning the heart or the entire corpse. Vampires need the liquid blood of the living—the river of life—to remain undead.

Many of us know the version of the folktale "Jack and the Beanstalk" in which the giant recites a short poem declaring his malicious intentions to the frightened, concealed boy: "Fee, fi, foe, fum, I smell the blood of an Englishman. . . . I'll grind his bones to make my bread." This episode took on an entirely new significance after I began researching the folklore of vampire practices. James Frazer, the author of the *Golden Bough* wrote that one way of "entering into communion with the dead . . . is to grind their bones to powder or to burn them to ashes, and then swallow the powder or the ashes mixed with food or drink." In addition, Frazer discovered that "sometimes the valuable qualities of an animal or of a person may be imparted to another by the more delicate and ethereal process of fumigation" or "washing" the person in the smoke of burning parts of the body. Frazer found these methods of "absorbing the virtues or appropriating the souls of deceased kinsfolk" to be widely practiced. He also noted that "just as the savage thinks that he can swallow the moral and other virtues in the shape of food, so he fondly imag-

ines that he can inoculate himself with them. Here in Europe we
as yet inoculate only against disease." Yet, Frazer, himself, was
born into a culture where doctors drained blood to remove evil
humors and transfused it to calm the insane. The distance
between the so-called savage and the European is perhaps not so
great. The crucial procedures followed in New England—
ingesting the ashes of a dead kin's heart in medicine or water, or
breathing the smoke from its burning corpse—extend far back
into the human experience. I find some comfort knowing that
nineteenth-century Vermonters were, in some ways, very much
like people who lived in a time before recorded history.

Shortly after marriage, the beautiful young bride grew pale and
began to pine away, sinking into a terminal consumption. Following an appropriate interval of mourning, the widower married again. His second wife, though not as comely as the first, was
healthy and attractive. But soon, she, too, evidenced the obvious
signs of the dreaded wasting disease. The family wondered if the
first wife's spirit somehow was draining the life from the second.

Does this scenario bring to mind Poe's "Ligeia"? When I
encountered this story, as I was following the vampire trail in Vermont, I thought of Ligeia devouring Rowena. But in this nonfic-
tional case that was recounted in an early history of the town of
Manchester, Vermont, Hulda was being consumed by Rachel:

> Esquire Powel's second wife was the widow of
> Joseph Harris and sister to Isaac Whelpley. Captain
> Isaac Burton married her daughter, Rachel Harris.
> She was, to use the words of one who was well
> acquainted with her, "a fine, healthy, beautiful girl."
> Not long after they were married she went into a
> decline and after a year or so she died of consump-
> tion. Capt. Burton after a year or more married
> Hulda Powel, daughter of Esquire Powel by his first
> wife. Hulda was a very healthy, good-looking girl,
> not as handsome as his first wife. She became ill

soon after they were married and when she was in the last stages of consumption, a strange infatuation took possession of the minds of the connections and friends of the family. They were induced to believe that if the vitals of the first wife could be consumed by being burned in a charcoal fire it would effect a cure of the sick second wife. Such was the strange delusion that they disinterred the first wife who had been buried about three years. They took out the liver, heart, and lungs, what remained of them, and burned them to ashes on the blacksmith's forge of Jacob Mead. Timothy Mead officiated at the altar in the sacrifice to the Demon Vampire who it was believed was still sucking the blood of the then living wife of Captain Burton. It was the month of February and good sleighing. Such was the excitement that from five hundred to one thousand people were present. This account was furnished me by an eye witness of the transaction.

Another source gives the date of exhumation as February, 1793, and states that Hulda, the second wife, died September 6th of that year. If there were, indeed, up to a thousand people present, then most of the town was there, as the 1791 census lists the population of Manchester at 1276.

Internal evidence suggests that the eyewitness account was recorded sometime between 1857 and 1872 by Judge John S. Pettibone (1786–1872), a veteran of the War of 1812 and, for many years, Manchester's representative to the state legislature. Long before his "Early History of Manchester" was published in 1930, it had languished in manuscript form. The year before its publication, a Mary C. Munson had donated the manuscript to the Vermont Historical Society. In an accompanying letter, she mentioned the "traces of the New England witchcraft delusion still lingering" during Pettibone's era and revealed her Burton family lineage:

The Capt. Isaac Burton, whose wives were the subject of the witchcraft incident, was a brother of my great-grandmother and I never heard any tradition of the incident from any one of the family. The only trace of an independent source came through the son of old Judge Fowler who told Miss Canfield he had heard his father tell the story as one he heard from the older residents of the town in his day.

This rather indirect evidence suggests that the "witchcraft" story was told by townspeople but did not become a vigorous part of the town's oral tradition, perhaps eventually fading from the collective memory.

A Vermont historian wrote that "nearly all the leading men of the first decades were immigrants," many of whom followed the Connecticut River north from Rhode Island and Connecticut. Timothy Mead, who presided over the ritual, was one of the first settlers in Manchester, arriving in 1764 from southeastern New York with several other proprietors who had been given land grants. Mead was one of the town's leaders, along with his friend and political confidante, Martin Powel (Hulda's father and Rachel's stepfather) and his fellow proprietor, Isaac Whelpley (Rachel's uncle). Mead married into the Burton family and was, according to Pettibone, not particularly religious, but generally good natured though "overbearing" and "high tempered."

While these early founders were educated men, there seemed to be a decline following the Revolutionary War, when, in Pettibone's opinion, Manchester became "an immoral place" where "drinking, gambling, and whoring were common." He attributed this moral slide to the effects of the war, when men became conditioned to gather in taverns and carouse. Manchester, like many of the newer towns that sprang up in southern Vermont in the years immediately preceding the Revolution, had the feel of a loose frontier town, certainly more tolerant than the older, decorous communities along New England's seaboard. Even the town's two doctors during the period seemed caught up in Manchester's degeneration: "Dr. Gould, a graduate of Yale College, and Dr. Asel Washburn were the physicians of Manchester. Dr. Washburn was esteemed as an excellent physician but his usefulness was much lessened by intemperance, and Dr. Gould became a drunkard."

Manchester was haunted by more than vampires, as it struggled toward respectability. Almost twenty years after the exhumation, a Manchester man named Russell Colvin disappeared. While no body was ever found, many suspected that he had been murdered by his unsavory brothers-in-law, Stephen and Jesse Boorn, with whom he had had a violent argument. For seven years, escalating town gossip blamed the brothers, but there was no hard evidence. Then, Jesse and Stephen's uncle, Amos Boorn, was visited by Colvin's ghost. "Three times in all, Russell Colvin's ghost came and stood beside the slumbering Amos. The ghost said that it had been murdered and that it wanted to show Amos the place where its body lay buried. Amos followed the ghost to the grave site," an abandoned cellar in a field that used to belong to Barney Boorn, the older brother of Amos and the father of Stephen and Jesse. Soon, others in town began having "strange dreams and unaccountable visions." The furor finally culminated in the arrest and conviction of the brothers. Stephen, who had confessed, was to be hung, and Jesse was sentenced to life in prison. But at the last minute, the missing Russell Colvin appeared. Was it really Colvin, or a paid impostor? The brothers, whose family had many ties to the principal participants in the vampire incident, including the Meads, Powels, and Whelplys, were legally exonerated. But, to this day, the case is unresolved and the mystery remains. In his fascinating book, *The "Counterfeit" Man*, Gerald McFarland examines this case in detail and paints a vivid portrait of early Manchester, which, like other towns on the western slopes of the Green Mountains, was known as a refuge for "religious liberals: freethinkers, deists, and universalists."

At the same time that Captain Burton was confronting the death of his second wife, the family of Lieutenant Leonard Spaulding, living about thirty miles southeast of Manchester in the town of Dummerston, was on the brink of extinction. Although they seemed to be vigorous and healthy, within a span of sixteen years, nine members of the Spaulding family, including the father, died of consumption. The children ranged in age from sixteen to thirty-seven. David L. Mansfield reported the event in his "History of the Town of Dummerston," which appeared in the *Vermont Historical Magazine* in 1884. The deaths began in 1782 with Mary, aged twenty, continued on a regular basis through the father's death in 1788, and culminated with the death of the last remaining son, twenty-seven-year-old Josiah, in December of 1798. Apparently the remaining three daughters lived well into maturity. Mansfield's account provides no dates and few details:

> Although the children of Lt. Spaulding, especially the sons, became large, muscular persons, all but one or two, died under 40 years of age of consumption, and their sickness was brief.
>
> It is related by those who remember the circumstance; after six or seven of the family had died of consumption, another daughter was taken, it was supposed, with the same disease. It was thought she would die, and much was said in regard to so many of the family's dying of consumption when they all seemed to have the appearance of good health and long life. Among the superstitions of those days, we find it was said that a vine or root of some kind grew from coffin to coffin, of those of one family, who died of consumption, and were buried side by side; and when the growing vine had reached the coffin of the last one buried, another one of the family would die; the only way to destroy the influence or effect, was to break the vine; take up the body of the last one buried and burn the vitals, which would be an effectual remedy: Accordingly, the body of the last one, [sic]

buried was dug up and the vitals taken out and burned, and the daughter, it is affirmed, got well and lived many years. The act, doubtless, raised her mind from a state of despondency to hopefullness [sic].

Looking at the sequence of deaths in the family, it appears that the exhumed body belonged to either Leonard, Jr. (the sixth to die, in 1792) or John (the seventh, who followed his twin brother, Timothy, to the grave in 1793).

The vine or root that was growing from coffin to coffin was an entirely new addition to my records of the vampire belief. What does it mean? My knowledge of the lore of grave plants did not extend to such ghastly connotations; however, it doesn't take a folksong scholar to recognize the familiar motif of lovers who, being prevented from embracing in life, intertwine in death through plants. A version of the ballad "Barbara Allen," collected in the Appalachians, includes the following verses:

> Sweet William was buried in the old church tomb
> Barbara Allen was buried in the yard.
> Out of sweet William's grave grew a green, red rose
> Out of Barbara Allen's a briar.
>
> They grew and they grew to the tall church door;
> They could not grow any higher.
> They linked and tied in a true lover's knot
> And the rose grew round the briar.

This motif appears in the medieval romance of Tristan and Iseult, where the vine grows only from one coffin, and the initial response is to cut it down.

> When King Mark heard of the death of these lovers, he crossed the sea and came into Brittany; and he had two coffins hewn, for Tristan and Iseult, one of chalcedony for Iseult, and one of beryl for Tristan. And he

took their beloved bodies away with him upon his ship to Tintagel, and by a chantry to the left and right of the apse he had their tombs built round. But in one night there sprang from the tomb of Tristan a green and leafy briar, strong in its branches and in the scent of its flowers. It climbed the chantry and fell to root again by Iseult's tomb. Thrice did the peasants cut it down, but thrice it grew again as flowered and as strong. They told the marvel to King Mark, and he forbade them to cut the briar any more.

This favorite theme in folk narrative, where that which is separated in life is united in death through the lasting embrace of plants, is found not only throughout Europe, but also in traditions from Northern Africa through the Middle East and as far away as China.

The kind of plant growing from the grave may be an index to the character of the deceased. In the folklore of southern France, for example, thorns or nettles growing on the grave are a sign of the damnation of the dead; if other plants grow, he is at peace; if a mixture, he is in purgatory. In German folksong, a blackthorn grows from the bodies of slain heathens while a white flower grows near the heads of fallen Christians; white lilies grow out of the graves of innocents who are put to death. Implicit in this motif is the belief, distributed throughout the world, that, at death, the soul or spirit of the corpse may enter into a plant, especially one that grows from its grave after burial. Ancient Europeans regarded trees as the abodes, not only of demonic spirits, but also of souls. Indeed, the wood nymphs, or dryads, of classical mythology had their lives linked to a certain tree. If the tree withered and died, they themselves pined away. Any injury to bough or twig was felt as a wound, and cutting down the tree put an end to them at once. In many Teutonic legends, the souls of the departed passed into trees, or continued to live in the trees that grew upon their graves. These indwelling spirits were supposed to have the power to both cause and cure disease. A related belief was that "the soul of the family-ancestor had passed into the tree growing in or before the homestead, and this tree accordingly became associated with the tutelary spirit of the family."

In *The Golden Bough*, Frazer compiled an enormous amount of ethnographic data showing the ancient and widespread beliefs that link human beings to plants. The following example expresses the magical powers, inherent in grave plants, that may be directed by the living: "A tree that grows on a grave is regarded by the South Slavonian peasant as a sort of fetish. Whoever breaks a twig from it hurts the soul of the dead, but gains thereby a magic wand, since the soul embodied in the twig will be at his service."

The shared concepts that underlie such seemingly disparate expressions as the eternal embrace of deceased lovers and a desperate attempt to terminate a consumption epidemic penetrate deep into the human past. Perhaps they are even the bedrock of belief that informs the vampire theory. If the vine growing from coffin to coffin was, indeed, a life token, the fate of the external soul or spirit within the grave would be bound up with the well-being of the vine. If the spirit was conceived to be benign or beneficial, then one would want to nurture the plant. On the other hand, if the indwelling soul was seen as evil or harmful, it would be prudent to destroy it.

Should the Spaulding family have allowed the vine to enter another grave to infect yet another soul, the curse would have been prolonged, opening the door to an endless chain of death. While I cannot know what the surviving Spauldings were thinking when the vine was cut, nor where they might have learned of the ritual, I can view their act against a background that links them to other, perhaps ancestral, traditions. For me, as in the case of the treatment of JB's remains, this makes an apparently singular act seem less extraordinary.

Through Lt. Spaulding's wife, Margaret, there are direct ancestral connections to both Celtic and Rhode Island traditions. She was daughter of Gabriel and Elizabeth (née Sprague)

Love of Providence. Her father was born in Ireland and immigrated to Warwick, Rhode Island. Her mother was a member of the powerful Sprague family that produced a number of political and economic leaders in Rhode Island. It was Amasa Sprague's murder that set off a chain of events which led to the abolition of capital punishment in the state and that many point to as the cause for the haunting of Sprague Mansion in Cranston (see Chapter 4). According to Mansfield's history of Dummerston, "Mrs. Spaulding . . . went on horseback, alone, every two years to visit her aged mother in Providence, R.I. as long as she lived, who died at the advanced age of nearly a hundred years" in 1802.

The Vermont families in which the vampire practice has been documented—the Ransoms, Burtons, Spauldings, and, possibly, the Corwins as well—all were early and respected citizens of their towns. It would be inaccurate to view them as ignorant and backward. Lt. Spaulding, a veteran of the French and Indian War, settled in Dummerston in 1772. This farmer, carpenter, and trader (selling, among other items, sugar, nutmeg, rum, and an occasional "pot of syder") became the town's first representative to the state legislature. At this time, families were streaming into Vermont to settle on land that cost next to nothing. But property disputes, with claims and counterclaims, were still raging when the first shots of the American Revolution were fired at Lexington on April 19, 1775. But were those really the first shots? An early history of the town of Dummerston reported that "Lt. Spaulding was the first man here, to start with his gun for the fight at Westminster, Mar. 13, 1775. He was knocked down and wounded in that skirmish."

At Westminster, just north of Dummerston, a sheriff's posse fired on a mob of farmers who were trying to stop the court in that town from doing business. The farmers, many of whom were indebted, believed that the courts were allied with wealthy speculators who were trying to divest them of their land. Although Vermont's "Westminster Massacre" preceded Lexington by more than a month, it didn't involve British soldiers per se (though the posse has been characterized as "officers

of the crown"). The death of one of the rioters is memorialized
on a slab of slate in the old burial ground at Westminster:

> In Memory of WILLIAM FRENCH, son to Mr.
> Nathaniel French, who was Shot at Westminster,
> March ye 13th, 1775, by the hands of Cruel
> Ministerial tools of George ye 3d, in the Court-house
> at a 11 O'clock at Night, in the 22nd year of his Age.
> Here William French his Body lies, For Murder
> his Blood for Vengeance Cries. King George the third
> his Tory crew tha with a bawl his head Shot threw.
> For Liberty and his Country's Good he Lost his Life,
> his Dearest Blood.

So, Spaulding, already a war veteran, jumped into the American War for Independence as early as anyone. He fought at the battle of Bennington, close enough to his home that his wife could hear the sounds of battle: "The day it was fought, his wife, who was in the garden gathering vegetables for dinner, heard distinctly the sound of the roaring cannon, nearly forty miles away." In 1777, General John Burgoyne had dispatched about 700 troops, mostly Hessians and Indians, under command of Lieutenant Friedrich Baum, to capture much-needed horses that the Americans had collected in the village of Bennington, Vermont. The battle that ensued was a stinging defeat for the British, and most of Baum's force—except for the Native Americans, who managed to disappear into the woods—were either killed or captured. The previous year, Spaulding had been wounded in the thigh at the battle of White Plains. The musket ball "remained in his leg as long as he lived; and was troublesome at times."

For his service in the French and Indian War and the Revolutionary War, Lt. Spaulding received a grant of land "lying west of Lake Champlain in New York state," which obviously he was never able to occupy. I noted the irony that the man, though wounded several times, survived terrible battles fighting Native

American, French, British, and Hessian soldiers, but finally succumbed, in 1788, to a microscopic organism.

While checking various folklore journals for examples of consumption cures (in the hope of finding more connections to, or examples of, the vampire practice), I came upon an article entitled "Henry David Thoreau as Folklorist." The author had extracted entries from Thoreau's journal that pertained to folk traditions, such as weather lore and home remedies. On September 29, 1859, Thoreau recorded the following: "I have just read of a family in Vermont who, several of the members having died of consumption, just burned the lungs, heart and liver of the last deceased, in order to prevent any more from having it." With no other information available, it's impossible to know if he might have been referring to the Corwin or Ransom incidents (or perhaps another one, as yet, undiscovered). Thoreau does not mention the vampire connection, and his entry seems to focus on the preventative aspects of the practice. Thoreau's interest in this event must have been more than idle curiosity. When he wrote this entry, he was already aware that he had consumption; he died of the disease less than three years later.

In the *Journal of American Folklore*, I found another item that clearly emphasized the medical aspects of the procedures. This example, collected in Grafton County, New Hampshire, and published in 1891, also contained no reference to vampires: "If the lungs of a brother or sister who died of consumption be burned, the ashes will cure the living members of the family affected with that disease." What seems to push this example towards the *medical*, and away from the *supernatural*, realm is the use of the lungs rather than the heart. After all, it is in the lungs of consumptives that the disease is located. Could this be considered a rudimentary attempt at inoculation? Was this so-called vampire practice simply a home remedy, or were these dead relatives actually vampires?

CHAPTER 11
Relicks of Many Old Customs

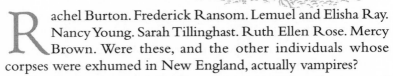

Rachel Burton. Frederick Ransom. Lemuel and Elisha Ray. Nancy Young. Sarah Tillinghast. Ruth Ellen Rose. Mercy Brown. Were these, and the other individuals whose corpses were exhumed in New England, actually vampires?

Close your eyes and imagine a vampire. What do you see? Bela Lugosi as Count Dracula in Universal Studios' 1931 movie, dressed in tuxedo and cape, with hair slicked-back from a widow's peak, face pale and pasty, prominent canine teeth protruding over cruel, red lips? When he says, "I am Dracula, and I bid you welcome," his Eastern European accent and distant politeness reinforce the coldness of his dark, penetrating stare.

Yes? I saw him, too, back in 1981, before my interviews with Oliver Stedman and Everett Peck spurred me to try and riddle out the mystery and meaning of Mercy Brown. The Dracula image also explains why my knee-jerk reaction to the question was, "of course they weren't vampires"—an answer that seemed to put me squarely in the camp of people outside of the community who were also trying to sort out what was going on at those ghastly graveyard scenes. For instance, a few days after Mercy's exhumation, in 1892, the *Providence Journal* published a discussion on vampires. The author set the scene for his definition of a vampire with a paragraph that left no doubt about *his* opinion:

> "Ugh!" says the person of refinement. "Horrible!" ejaculates even the reader of the horrible daily

papers. But those who believe in it express themselves thus: "It may be true," "You may find one there," "I always heard it was so," and "My father and grandfather always said so." From traditions of the vampire, it is, on the whole, pleasing to be free, but how singular that this old belief of the Hindoos and Danubian peoples should survive in Rhode Island! Had such a superstition been acted upon in White Russia or lower Hungary, Rhode Islanders would have read it as fiction, or a strange, wild falsehood, but this exhumation in the South County, in the town of Exeter, with the name of the persons authorizing it known in the county, and with a modern physician assisting, is a fact divested of mystery or fictional description.

To assist his readers in deciding for themselves if Mercy was really a vampire, the author offered the following discourse:

The vampire is described in the Century Dictionary as follows: "A kind of spectral being or ghost still possessing a human body, which, according to a superstition existing among the Slavic and other races of the lower Danube, leaves the grave during the night, and maintains a semblance of life by sucking the warm blood of men and women while they are asleep. Dead wizards, werewolves, heretics and other outcasts become vampires . . . and any one killed by a vampire. On the discovery of a vampire's grave, the body, which it is supposed, will be found fresh and ruddy, must be disinterred, thrust through with a whitethorn stake and buried, in order to render it harmless." In the Encyclopedia Britannica and other books, a similar description of the theory occurs. They all recount that the tradition comes from Europe, and did not originate among the

Indians. The earliest existence is said to have been in Southwestern Russia, Servia, Poland and Bohemia. . . . From 1730 to 1735 the tradition took on renewed life, and starting in Hungary, spread all over Europe, and to America. . . .

In all forms of the tradition, the vampire left its abode, and wrought its object, at night. When the full moon shone and the sky was cloudless, its opportunity was supposed to be the most favorable. It appeared as a frog, toad, spider, venomous fly, from that moment until it returned to the grave and its corpse home. Its active moments when wandering about were spent in sucking the blood of the living and this was invariably the blood of some relation or friend of the dead. From this feeding, the body of the dead became fresh and rosy. Another form of the tradition, but with far less acceptance, was that the soul of the living man or woman left the body in his sleep in the shape of a straw or a fluff of down. It was wafted to the victim on the night breezes and returned to the living without a warning of the visit, the victim being left pale and wan, and the vampire-man being freshened and invigorated. . . . For the eradication of the curse, the old method was always the digging up the body of the dead, the driving of a stake through the heart, the cutting off of the head, the tearing out and burning of the heart, or the pouring of boiling water and vinegar into the grave.

Leave aside, for the moment, the questions raised in this article concerning the tradition's origins and consider the image itself. With the exception of literary elaborations (I'm thinking of Sidney Rider's tale of Sarah Tillinghast) and contemporary caricatures derived from mass–media interpretations (Jennie Boldan's story of Nancy Young is a good example), descriptions of New England's vampires do not correspond to the Dracula image. Take the traits, one by one:

- no sightings of them outside of their graves at night (or any other time of the day);
- no empty coffins;
- no reports of them sucking people's blood;
- no marks on their dying relatives to suggest a vampire is feeding; and
- no mention of them having been wizards, werewolves or heretics during their lives.

Can we, with justification, label as "vampires" the New Englanders whose bodies were exhumed and deemed to be unnatural? Certainly not, if we use the standard vampire model, the "classic vampire" of our imaginations exemplified by the *Providence Journal's* summation above. But, what if we begin with a blank slate and ask, again, what is a vampire?

Blaming the dead for death seems but a short, logical step from the fundamental vampire concept that the dead have a life after death. The fear that the dead will prey upon the living, whether out of anger, jealousy, or a desire for revenge, unless certain steps are taken to appease or disable them, probably explains why the most primitive type of vampire is a reanimated corpse. This cause-and-effect relationship between the dead and death permeates our everyday folklore. Often, the connection lurks beneath the surface—implied, but not stated. "If a dead man doesn't get stiff at once, some other member of the family is going to die." This superstition, collected in early twentieth-century North Carolina, suggests a vampire-like connection between living and dead family members, bringing to mind the scene at the graves of the New England vampires, where their corpses appeared to be in an unnatural state. The belief that a corpse that does not do what people expect augurs impending death in the family has roots in England, as illustrated in the following personal experience collected in 1868 in West Sussex:

A woman who was speaking of the great mortality

which had occurred in a neighbouring family, where she had lived many years as a servant, told me of this curious superstition. She said, "The day after my master's death, one of his sisters-in-law came into the room and asked the nurse if she had ever heard that a limp corpse was a bad sign; and nurse made answer, 'La, miss! it's nothing but an old woman's saying.' But she winked at me; and when miss was gone she said, 'I didn't like to tell her the truth; but master's corpse not stiffening is a sure sign that death will be knocking pretty soon again at the door of this house for some other of the family;' and Miss Susan did not live many years after that herself".

The behavior of the New England vampires—infecting their close relatives with a lethal disease—links New England to a very large community. "Our pagan ancestors believed that sicknesses were caused by malignant demons—some of them the spirits of dead ancestors." This observation was made by two scholars who were tracing the roots of Pennsylvania German folk medicine, but its core belief has been found in Europe, India, Asia, and Africa. It seems strange to blame the ghosts of near relations for sickness and death, yet this familial connection is as persistent as it is widespread. Even now, in certain areas of the Phillipines, "to die," means joining "the ranks of the dead ancestors . . . who are often imagined as eager to bring the living into their abode." Especially feared are the *kalagkalag*, "the restless dead who some-times 'bother' the living relatives by sending them sickness of undiagnosed origin." The Wallachian *moroi*, a vampire from the region just south of the Transylvanian Alps, stays close to home, waiting for an opportunity to settle accounts with members of its own family. A *moroi* inhabits the body of a weaker relative by creeping into its heart, which it eventually devours. These notions certainly throw new light on the New England exhuma-tions, where the corpses's hearts were examined for "fresh" blood. Could it be that the disease-causing evil spirit, the vampire, moved from one corpse to another, devouring hearts as it traveled? And finding blood in the heart informed the exhumers that they had located the evil's abode? Viewed in this light, the vampire designation doesn't seem preposterous.

"Like the legend of the living dead, so the origin of the word *vampire* is clouded in mystery." This first sentence in a study of the history of the word *vampire* suggests that neither the term nor the creature itself will be easily pigeonholed. Theories advanced to explain the origin and development of the term reveal various attributes of vampires, as well as connections between vampires and other evil beings. One school of thought keys on the verb "to drink," arguing for an origin in ancient Greece or Lithuania. Others have traced the term through several Slavic synomyns back to the Turkish word for witch. Many scholars now agree that the term has a Slavic derivation, rooted in the Serbian word *bamiiup*. The vampire *concept*, of course, predates, and exists independently from, the word *vampire*, which did not enter the vocabulary of Northern and Western Europe until early in the eighteenth century. But a vampire by any other name would be as lethal.

Vampires and witches are frequently linked in folklore. The belief that vampires cannot drown because they always float on top of the water connects Romanian vampires to the witches of Europe and colonial New England, who were tested to see if they floated upon being thrown into water. Those who drowned were proclaimed innocent while those who rose to the surface were condemned as witches. This "ordeal by swimming" (*judicium aquae frigidae*) rests on the ancient doctrine that water, a pure element, will reject an evil doer. In Romania, one might easily confuse *strigele*, the spirits of witches, with *strigoi*, the most common name for vampires. The *strigele* are spirits of either living witches or dead witches who are unable to find a resting place. According to folk tradition, they are seen as little points of light floating in the air (once again, the corpse light, makes an appearance). But in Italy, the *strega*, or witch, can also play the part of a vampire insofar as "she sucks the blood of sleeping people through the little finger, thus inducing an inscrutable and therefore incurable marasmus." Marasmus is a gradual loss of flesh and strength, a condition similar to consumption.

The New England record is mute about *why* an individual might be transformed into a vampire, an odd silence that is in sharp contrast to the situation in Europe, where it seems easier to become a vampire than not. Suicides, excommunicates, perjurers, bastards, unavenged murder victims, those who died violently or drowned, the seventh child of the same sex, those born with a caul or with teeth, anyone who ate a sheep killed by a wolf, persons in league with the devil, or someone bitten by a vampire—all could become vampires. Among the Wallachians of southeastern Europe, a person's soul may become restless and "seek its former house and ... haunt close relatives" if the person was treated improperly while living, or if the "proper rituals and precautions at death and afterwards" were disregarded.

The consequences of not stopping a vampire are terrible, indeed:

> This reviving being, or *oupire*, comes out of his grave, or a demon in his likeness, goes by night to embrace or hug violently his near relations or his friends, and sucks their blood so much as to weaken and attenuate them, and at last cause their death. This persecution does not stop at one single person; it extends to the last person of the family, if the course be not interrupted.

A vampire not detected and neutralized leaves an ever-widening circle of devastation in its wake. After destroying its family, it will continue on to the people of the village and surrounding countryside. Was it this fear that motivated families and neighbors to pressure the head of an afflicted household, such as George Brown of Exeter, to allow the exhumation of his family?

If the vampire figure exists along a continuum, with no clearly defined borders, then how and where do we draw the line to define it? A conception that seems to fit all of the vampires that appear in the folklore record is suggested by Paul Barber in his insightful book, *Vampires, Burial, and Death*: "[A] vampire might be defined as a corpse that comes to the attention of the populace at a time of crisis and is taken for the cause of that crisis."

Barber approaches the vampire phenomenon assuming that eyewitness accounts of vampire exhumations came from people who were pretty much like you and me: ordinary folks who described what they saw in terms that were conventional for their time and place. He takes their descriptions at face value and reinterprets them from the perspective of forensic pathology. Scientists now know what happens to corpses during decomposition under various conditions. Many of the "supernatural" events reported by earnest onlookers may have been the result of natural processes. The supposed blood-sucking predilection, for example, may be just "a folkloric means of accounting for two unrelated phenomena: unexplained deaths and the appearance of blood at the mouth of a corpse." Barber speculates on the definition that a modern-day observer might formulate after viewing the exhumed remains of a suspected vampire: "A vampire is a body that in all respects appears to be dead except that it does not decay as we expect, its blood does not coagulate, and it may show changes in dimension and color." All of these conditions can result from the natural processes of decomposition, as Barber observed: "Our descriptions of revenants and vampires match up, detail for detail, with what we know about dead bodies that have been buried for a time." I have no doubt that the condition of the corpses exhumed in New England and declared to be "unnatural" could be explained within the framework provided by Barber.

Vampire lore, in New England, is a regional variant of a worldwide tradition, with particularly close ties to European practices. Once we remove Dracula's shadow, we can see, lurking in the folkloric countryside, a host of supernatural creatures, including fallen goddesses, demons, devils, witches, hags, ghosts, vampires, and werewolves. In the ever-changing landscape of this *danse macabre,* creatures and concepts merge and blend, divide and disperse. Ultimately, what unites these seemingly diverse folk traditions is the belief that a corpse, possibly animated by an evil spirit, is responsible for an otherwise inexplicable sequence of deaths. Reduced to its common denominator, the vampire is a classic scapegoat.

The corpses of Rachel Burton, Frederick Ransom, Lemuel and Elisha Ray, Nancy Young, Sarah Tillinghast, Ruth Ellen Rose, and Mercy Brown, to paraphrase Barber, attracted attention at a time when consumption was threatening to decimate their communities, and they were singled out as the cause of that crisis.

In that sense, *they were vampires.*

Now, how did vampires get linked to consumption? Once again, Barber pointed me towards an answer, this time with his statement that "the fear of the revenant was not entirely irrational. . . . Often people were afraid of contagion, without having defined its limits so closely as we have nowadays." Either theory—germ or vampire—could explain both the contagious and hereditary aspects of the disease as it was understood prior to the twentieth century. The germ/vampire can quickly proceed from being an individual problem to one involving a family and, if not checked, an entire community. Both vampires and germs are simultaneously tangible and intangible. The tangible parasite is so small as to be invisible to the naked eye, just as the parasitic vampire moves unseen among its living victims. Did the killer live within, laboring around the clock to destroy its host, consuming the lungs, eating away flesh, leaving behind a rotting mess and bright red blood, all froth and foam? Or did the killer live without, visiting his prey at night to feed on flesh and blood?

The disease's specific symptoms correlate well with vampire folklore. Consumption's victims suffer most at night, sweating profusely. They awaken, coughing and in pain (sometimes described as a heavy feeling, like someone has sat upon the chest). Strength, color, and appetite fade. As the disease progresses, ulcers and cavities develop in the lungs, creating a noticeably sunken chest (again, suggesting weight on the victim's chest). Night sweating and coughing grow worse and the sputum is thicker, now containing blood. Emaciation becomes extreme. One family member fades away, then another, and another. Nightly, it seems, something is draining the life of the family.

For centuries, both vampires and consumption have been portrayed as mysterious body snatchers, simultaneously lethal and life-giving, draining one's vitality while saturating one with sensuality and passion. The consumptive, like the vampire, has been depicted as diseased and disgusting yet erotically attractive. Dickens, in *Nicholas Nickleby*, saw tuberculosis as a disease where life and death "are so strangely blended, that death takes the glow and hue of life, and life the gaunt and grisly form of death." A consumptive's appearance thus ties him to death—and to the vampire. The consumptive was also one of the living dead, though doomed not by a curse, but by the failure of his fellow human beings to find a remedy.

We derive comfort from giving tangible form to phenomena beyond our understanding. The monsters of folklore, including vampires, "put a face on our fear of the unknown and help us explain and cope with the universe and the cycle of life and death." By personifying death and disease, we can more easily identify, objectify, and perhaps forestall one and eradicate the other. At the very least, seeing is relieving. "To me Death is a lecherous, sly, deranged old man," wrote Betty MacDonald in *The Plague and I*, a book about her experiences in a tuberculosis sanatorium. "I can see him hovering like a great bat over the emergency ward . . . . I can hear him shuffling up and down the corridor at night." Aretaeus, a Greek who practiced medicine in Asia Minor during the third century BCE, wrote a description of one suffering from phthisis (or the wasting of consumption) that could be the very picture of the vampire (I see Max Schrek as Count Orlock in the 1922 film *Nosferatu*):

> Voice hoarse, neck slightly bent, tender not flexible, somewhat extended; fingers slender but joints

thick; of the bones alone the figure remains, for the fleshy parts are wasted; the nails of the fingers crooked, their pulps are shriveled and flat, for owing to the loss of flesh, they neither retain their tension nor rotundity. . . . Nose sharp, slender; cheeks prominent and red; eyes hollow, brilliant and glittering; swollen, pale, or livid in the countenance; the slender parts of the jaws rest upon the teeth, as if smiling; otherwise of a cadaverous aspect. So also in all other respects; slender without flesh; . . . the whole shoulder blades apparent like wings of birds.

A clinical description of a consumptive, written in 1799, underscores the frightening aspects of this portrait:

The emaciated figure strikes one with terror; the forehead covered with drops of sweat; the cheeks painted with a livid crimson, the eyes sunk; the little fat that raised them in their orbits entirely wasted; the pulse quick and tremulous; the nails long, bending over the ends of the fingers; the palms of the hand dry and painfully hot to the touch; the breath offensive, quick and laborious, and the cough so incessant as to scarce allow the wretched sufferer time to tell his complaints.

The vampire is consumption in a human form, embodying an evil that slowly and secretly drains the life from its victims.

How did the vampire tradition become established in New England? I see three possible explanations. 1) The European colonists learned about it from Native Americans. 2) It developed apart from any other tradition (in the same way that agriculture and the bow-and-arrow were invented independently, and at different times, in both the Old and New Worlds). 3) The practice was imported, either directly by colonists or immigrants, or indirectly through written or print media.

The *Providence Journal* article that described Mercy Brown's exhumation in 1892 reported that local residents of Exeter claimed the vampire practice was "a tradition of the Indians." Blaming indigenous peoples for anything deemed unsavory or uncivilized has a long tradition in the region, beginning with the Puritans. But did the indigenous people of New England actually have vampires in their traditions? Once again, the question arises, What is a vampire? The answer to the first question depends on the answer to the second. In his vampire casebook, Alan Dundes argues that the vampire is not a universal figure:

> Widespread as the vampire is throughout eastern Europe, it is not true, as has been claimed, that "the belief in vampires is found all over the world". . . . This statement in the *Standard Dictionary of Folklore, Mythology and Legend* is demonstrably false. The vampire is *not* universal by any means. Native Americans do not have vampires. Nor do most of the indigenous peoples of Oceania have vampires. Fear of the dead is one thing; vampires in particular are quite another.

Stith Thompson obviously believed otherwise. In his *Tales of the North American Indians,* he lists a number of tales under the vampire heading ("corpse which comes from the grave at night and sucks blood"). A Cherokee legend, collected in North Carolina and published in the *Journal of American Folklore* in 1892, seems comparable to the European vampire tradition in several respects. First, "The Demon of Consumption," explains the existence of an inexplicable wasting away, which the tale's collector labels as "consumption," a disease introduced to Native Americans by Europeans.

In the olden days, before the white man's foot had

ever crossed the Blue Ridge, there resided in a cave
. . . a demon with an iron finger . . . . His food was
human lungs and livers, which he procured by his
power of personating any absent member of a family
. . . . The demon would . . . enter the house in the
form of the absent one, select his victim, begin
fondling his head, run his soft fingers through his
hair until the unsuspecting victim would go to sleep.
Then with his iron finger would he pierce the
victim's side and take his liver and lungs, but
without pain. The wound would immediately heal,
leaving no outward mark.

The one thus robbed would, on awakening, go
about his usual occupation, entirely unconscious of
the injury at the time, but would gradually pine away
and die. The monster, of course, did most of his mischief in the immediate neighborhood of his home.

In 1896, four years after the *Providence Journal* article linked
the vampire practice to Native Americans, George Stetson also
singled out a Cherokee tale as he explored the connection in
his *American Anthropologist* article on the New England vampire
tradition:

The Ojibwa have, it is said, a legend of the ghostly
man-eater. Mr. Mooney, in a personal note, says that
he has not met with any close parallel of the vampire
myth among the tribes with which he is familiar. The
Cherokees have, however, something analogous.
There are in that tribe quite a number of old witches
and wizards who thrive and fatten upon the lives of
murdered victims. When some one is dangerously
sick these witches gather invisibly about his bedside
and torment him, even lifting him up and dashing
him down again upon the ground until life is extinct.
After he is buried they dig up the body and take out

the liver to feast upon. They thus lengthen their own lives by as many days as they have taken from his. In this way they get to be very aged, which renders them objects of suspicion. It is not, therefore, well to grow old among the Cherokees.

Thompson includes a tale from a Northeastern tribe, the Abenaki, which the collector referred to as a "witch-story":

An old "witch" was dead, and his people buried him in a tree, up among the branches, in a grove that they used for a burial-place. Some time after this, in the winter, an Indian and his wife came along, looking for a good place to spend the night. They saw the grove, went in, and built their cooking fire. When the supper was over, the woman, looking up, saw long dark things hanging among the tree branches. "What are they?" she asked. "They are only the dead of long ago," said her husband, "I want to sleep." "I don't like it at all. I think we had better sit up all night," replied his wife. The man would not listen to her, but went to sleep. Soon the fire went out, and then she began to hear a gnawing sound, like an animal with a bone. She sat still, very much scared, all night long. About dawn she could stand it no longer, and reaching out, tried to wake her husband, but could not. She thought him sound asleep. The gnawing had stopped. When daylight came she went to her husband and found him dead, with his left side gnawed away, and his heart gone. She turned and ran. At last she came to a lodge where there were some people. Here she told her story, but they would not believe it, thinking that she had killed the man herself. They went with her to the place, however. There they found the man, with his heart gone, lying under the burial tree, with the dead "witch" right overhead. They took the body

239

down and unwrapped it. The mouth and face were
covered with fresh blood.

I can understand Thompson classifying these as vampire tales,
for they contain the following motifs: undead; shape-shifter; nocturnal attacks; stays close to home; unexplained wasting away;
mouth and face are covered with blood; monster is burned,
problem solved. But these examples raise the issue of translation,
literal and figurative, across linguistic and cultural boundaries. The
references to witches, demons, and consumption are framed in
European terms by folktale collectors of European extraction. I
cannot help but wonder if these tales seem analogous to European
tradition because of the circumstances of their collection. Whatever explanation one accepts to account for the parallels between
the Native American and New England traditions, it seems clear
that there is no genetic connection. Making one scapegoat,
Native Americans, responsible for the introduction of another
scapegoat, vampires, seems an unjustified expansion of blame.

Could it be that no one but New Englanders, themselves, are
responsible for their vampire practices? Faye Ringel Hazel, interpreting "some strange New England mortuary practices," wrote
that "it seems likely . . . that the vampire belief originated spontaneously in New England, in response to the increased incidence of and dread of consumption in the nineteenth century."
She concludes that the similarities between the New England
and Eastern European vampire traditions are the result of separate responses to "the same underlying need to explain the unex-
plainable mysteries of death, decay and survival." The two
personal-experience stories below were collected in Romania
and date from the first quarter of the twentieth century. Their
remarkable similarity to accounts from New England seems to
argue against Hazel's contention:

> Some fifteen years ago . . . an old woman . . . died.
> After some months the children of her eldest son
> began to die, one after the other, and, after that, the

children of her youngest son. The sons became anxious, dug her up one night, cut her in two, and buried her again. Still the deaths did not cease. They dug her up a second time, and what did they see? The body whole without a wound. It was a great marvel. They took her and carried her into the forest, and put her under a great tree in a remote part of the forest. There they disembowelled her, took out her heart, from which blood was flowing, cut it in four, put in on hot cinders, and burnt it. They took the ashes and gave them to children to drink with water. They threw the body on the fire, burnt it, and buried the ashes of the body. The deaths ceased.

Some twenty or thirty years ago, a cripple, an unmarried man . . . died. A little time after, his relations began to die, or to fall ill. They complained that a leg was drying up. [Perhaps polio or some other crippling disease?] This happened in several places. What could it be? "Perhaps it is the cripple; let us dig him up." They dug him up one Saturday night, and found him as red as red, and all drawn up into a corner of the grave. They cut him open, and took the customary measures. They took out the heart and liver, burnt them on red-hot cinders, and gave the ashes to his sister and other relations, who were ill. They drank them with water, and regained their health.

Surely, a more likely explanation for why the procedures employed in two widely separated regions are identical is that there is a cultural connection, even if it emanates solely from an ancient and common Indo-European heritage.

The remaining explanation for how the vampire tradition appeared in New England—that it was imported from the Old World—now would appear to be the most plausible. When George Stetson was preparing his article on New England's vampires in the 1890s, he corresponded with Rhode Island historian Sidney Rider, requesting information on the "vampire superstition in Rhode Island." In his first letter, dated December 11, 1895, Stetson asked: "I would like to know if you have any idea as to its origins in your state? Was it introduced by the Swedes or Welsh?" It seems odd that Stetson singles out the Swedes and Welsh. Perhaps he was seeking connections to Northern European and Celtic traditions. Unfortunately, I have not located Rider's replies to Stetson. A nineteenth-century newspaper article singles out as a possible source of the tradition, the French Huguenots who settled in East Greenwich, Rhode Island, in the early part of the eighteenth century. But the Huguenots, like the Indians, were perhaps just a convenient scapegoat, as there is no evidence linking them to the vampire practice.

If I were going on pure speculation, I would not have chosen Indians, Swedes, Welsh, or French Huguenots. I would look closer to Eastern Europe, the home of vampire traditions most like those in New England. Searching for clues that might establish such a conduit, I reviewed the earliest incidents with my mind open to inspiration. Vampire cases began appearing in the record just after the American Revolution. New England was the major source of soldiers for the Continental Army. The families of both Captain Burton and Lieutenant Spalding, Vermonters and veterans of the Continental Army, had resorted to the vampire practice in the early 1790s. Given that consumption was of epidemic proportions at that time, and flourished in overcrowded and unsanitary environments, I supposed that it had been rife in the British and Continental armies a decade or more earlier. Perhaps soldiers recruited from Eastern Europe to serve as mercenaries in both armies brought with them traditional methods for managing such plagues. I envisioned an army regiment or prisoner-of-war camp turning to measures of last resort, suggested by fellow soldiers (or perhaps prisoners) from Eastern Europe.

King George III was fortunate to have secured some 30,000 German mercenaries to fight in America, even though many

Germans were sympathetic to the colonists. The exportation of soldiers was actually a source of considerable income for German princes. Nearly half of the mercenaries never returned to Germany. While some of them were killed, of course, the majority chose to stay in America. I recalled the defeat suffered by Hessian mercenaries at the Battle of Bennington, in 1777, and that Lt. Spalding had fought there, within earshot of his home.

During the Revolution, as John Adams observed, "disease . . . destroyed ten men for us where the sword of the enemy . . . killed one." Not only did disease decimate the armies, but returning soldiers brought it home:

> Beginning in 1775, soldiers had taken disease home with them. Typhus, typhoid fever, and dysentery decimated towns and were especially deadly to small children. Everywhere the diseases were called the "camp fever" or the "camp distemper" or the "camp disorder." In the four hundred families of the First Church in Danbury, Connecticut, one hundred people had died of the camp distemper by November 1775, and according to the minister, many other towns had been similarly stricken. In the winter of 1776/1777, released prisoners of war and discharged soldiers, especially those from the invasion of Canada, spread disease that caused many deaths in Connecticut and Pennsylvania.

The American Revolution was revolutionary beyond securing separation from the British empire for the colonies. As two noted American historians described:

> war itself, then as always, stirred up and metamorphosed society and economy. It threw men of different colonies and different classes together. It brought in tens of thousands of British, thousands of French and German soldiers and sailors, who con-

> tributed something to the wealth, something to the
> habits, and something even to the stock of the
> Americans; it . . . loosened men from habitual loyal-
> ties and attached them to new ideas and institutions.

I wondered if one of those new ideas was how to deal with epidemic diseases such as consumption.

The voice I gave to this brainstorming speculation was published in a newspaper interview. It came back to haunt me, in
1995, when an article on the New England vampire tradition
appeared in the *Fortean Times*. Its author, Paul Sieveking, included
my conjecture: "Rhode Island folklorist Michael E. Bell has
researched 16 recorded instances of New England consumptives
being disinterred. . . . As the first recorded cases date from the
1790s, he suggests that the practice was introduced by European
mercenaries fighting on the American side in the Revolution—
though this sounds a trifle far-fetched." I don't remember lim-
iting my mention of mercenaries to just those who joined the
colonists, but, in any event, Sieveking was kind to characterize my
hunch as only "a trifle" outlandish. I have absolutely no proof,
and, thus, no justification, for adding a hypothetical Hessian to
the already crowded lineup of suspected vampire accomplices.

While a comparison of *practices* points to Eastern Europe, a
consideration of *ancestry* continues to whisper "England" in my
ear, even though the vampire belief seems never to have been
firmly established in English folk tradition. Still, the author of the
now-familiar account of the Vermont incident, published in
Journal of American Folklore in 1889, wrote that the practice was
among the "curious and interesting material" that he "found
among old people descended from the English colonial settlers."
In the same journal, there appeared, four years later, an article
that reiterated an English association but, like the earlier article,
failed to supply the detail that would give credence to the connection. C. A. Fraser, who collected "myths" and "weird tales"
from third generation Scottish Highlanders in Ontario, Canada,
wrote the following:

I was a little shocked to hear of a repulsive superstition which I have read of as being peculiar to certain parts of England,—I mean a horrible vampire story given in explanation of the ravages often made in a family by consumption. I did not meet this superstition myself, but was told that it was among them. Consumption was rife among them; it seemed to be hereditary. They looked so remarkably robust, and yet fell so easily prey to this disease, and it seldom lingered! It was nearly always a very rapid illness. These are sad memories. The matter always seemed so hopeless! In a sickroom superstition ceases to be either funny or graceful. I stood by sick-beds with a sore heart, knowing too well that the haste with which a doctor was procured would be fully equalled by the zeal with which his orders would be disregarded. They had faith in the physician, the man, but none whatever in his prescriptions.

My disappointment that Fraser did not elaborate on the procedures associated with this "repulsive superstition" were offset by encountering a new case that extended the practice beyond New England. Having by this time reviewed the medical establishment's dismal failure in treating consumption during the nineteenth century, I wasn't surprised to read that these Canadian Scots had little regard for the doctor's remedies (though it was nice that they had faith in the man).

When I checked on Scottish folk remedies for consumption, I found a cure that links "kirkyards" (that is, churchyards or cemeteries) and consumption. The following, collected in 1901 on the Shetland Islands, takes us within a step of the actual corpse:

A much-respected dissenting clergyman, still alive, called at this cottage . . . to inquire for a poor woman who was dying of consumption. On hearing she was no better, he inquired if they had used means to aid her recovery: "Yah," said her aged mother, "we gaed to the kirkyard, and brought *mould* frae the grave o' the last body buried, an' laid it on her breast. As this had nae effect, we gaed to the brig [bridge] ower which the last corpse was ta'en, an' took some water frae the burn below, an' made her drink it. This failed too, an' as a last resource, we dug a muckle hole i' the grund, an' put her in't".

Mold is associated with decaying matter, and grave mold (or dirt), when used in folk rituals, at least implies that the corpse's spirit inhabits the mold (which may actually contain matter from the decomposed corpse).

An example from the northern counties of England, recorded in the nineteenth century, shows a similar linking to products obtained from graveyards. A young man "was at last restored to health by eating butter made from the milk of cows fed in kirkyards, a sovereign remedy for consumption brought on through being witch-ridden." What tantalizes me most about this brief account is the linking of consumption with the witch-riding, or Old Hag, tradition. David Hufford, in his thorough study of this subject, found four identifying features of being hagged that apply equally well to many descriptions of vampire assaults: (1) awakening (or an experience immediately preceding sleep); (2) hearing and/or seeing something come into the room and approach the bed; (3) being pressed on the chest or strangled; (4) inability to move or cry out until brought out of the state by someone else or breaking through the feeling of paralysis on one's own. Hufford found another feature that connects the two traditions:

When comparing the accounts of vampire attacks to . . . Old Hag attacks, the characteristic detail in the former of the draining of either blood or spiritual essence stands out sharply. When we view this traditional belief from the subjective perspective of the victim, it is hard to avoid a comparison with the fatigue generally reported by those who suffer a series of Old Hag attacks in close proximity to one another. In fact, . . . even those who avoided actual attack became fatigued by their efforts at constant vigilance. Although more evidence is needed, it is possible to hypothesize that the traditional belief about the sustenance the vampire gains from his victims is at least in part based on the observation of this increasing fatigue.

The bulk of Hufford's research was based on accounts collected from people in Canada and the United States who, like New Englanders of the eighteenth and nineteenth centuries, did not use the term "vampire" when referring to experiences that they believed to be supernatural assaults. Mary Munson, a descendent of the Burton family of Manchester, Vermont, wrote of "the witchcraft incident" (rather than the vampire incident) when referring to the exhumation of Captain Burton's first wife. Witches and witchcraft were, of course, significant elements in New England's supernatural landscape. Could the evil that was supposed to reside in a dead relative's corpse have been understood as the result of some sort of witchcraft, unnamed or unknown?

In his book on European vampires, Montague Summers noted the practice, in England, of exhuming the corpse of a suspected revenant, cutting it into pieces, then burning the pieces in a furnace to halt its returning from the grave. The earliest record of such practices in England comes from twelfth-century English historian William of Newburgh, who recounted several cases of the dead coming back to assault the living. The solution for ending assaults by these *sanguisuga* (Newburgh used the latin term for "bloodsuckers") was to exhume the corpse and burn it.

Summers also includes the account of the vampire of Croglin Grange, provided to its author, Augustus Hare, by a Captain Fisher, descendent of the family that had occupied a place called Croglin Low Hall. First published in the late 1800s, the event initially was said to have occurred in the 1870s; later fieldwork in this region of Cumberland arrived at the much earlier date of the 1680s. In any case, evidence for the event itself is entirely legendary. In this narrative, a woman sleeping in the house is attacked by a vampire-like creature on two separate occasions. On the first, the creature, who has a "hideous brown face with flaming eyes," bites her violently on the neck. After an extended leave to Switzerland to recover, she returns to Croglin Low Hall only to be attacked again. But this time her two brothers are prepared, and they chase the creature away, wounding him in the leg with a pistol shot. They see him disappear into a vault in the nearby cemetery. The next day, accompanied by "all the tenants of Croglin Grange," they open the vault:

> A horrible scene revealed itself. The vault was full of coffins; they had been broken open, and their contents, horribly mangled and distorted, were scattered over the floor. One coffin alone remained intact. Of that the lid had been lifted, but still lay loose upon the coffin. They raised it, and there, brown, withered, shrivelled, mummified, but quite entire, was the same hideous figure which had looked in at the windows of Croglin Grange, with the marks of a recent pistol-shot in the leg: and they did the only thing that can lay a vampire—they burnt it.

Whatever popularity the vampire enjoyed in England during the eighteenth century (and perhaps even later) may be due to a "vampire scare" that began in a province of Hungary and spread to all of Europe, including England, between 1730 and 1735. Several authors have written that it was during this period that the word "vampire" entered the English vocabulary, usually attributed to the publication in two English periodicals of the case of Arnod Paole (or Arnold Paul), a suspected vampire (see Chapter 9). Another important vampire publication in English was *The Travels of Three English Gentlemen,* published in 1745 by the Earl of Oxford. He included in this account of his adventures in Germany a description of the vampire tradition excerpted from Johann Heinrich (John Henry) Zopfius's dissertation on vampires, published in 1733, a work I would not at first have judged to be crucial to my research. However, a phone call in September, 1999, from the Connecticut State Archaeologist, Nick Bellantoni alerted me to a call I might receive from a reporter for the *Hartford Courant* who was putting together a series on the early editions of the *Connecticut Courant,* the oldest continually published newspaper in the country. The reporter wanted to talk to me about a front-page article, headlined "The Surprising Account of those Spectres Called Vampyres," that appeared within a year of the newspaper's origin, on January 21, 1765. The first half of the article proved to be a verbatim rendering of the Zopfius essay that had been excerpted in English for *The Travels of Three English Gentlemen.*

The vampire described therein is the familiar classic bloodsucker:

> The Vampyres, which come out of the graves in the nighttime, rush upon people sleeping in their beds, suck out their blood, and destroy them. They attack men, women, and children, sparing neither age nor sex. The people attacked by them complain of suffocation, and a great interception of spirits; after which they soon expire. Some of them, being asked, at the point of death, what is the matter with them, say, they suffer in the manner just related from people lately dead, or rather, the spectres of those people; upon which, their bodies, from the description given of them by the sick person, being dug out of the graves, appear, in all parts, as the nostrils, cheeks, breast, mouth, etc. turgid and full of blood. Their countenances are fresh and ruddy, and their nails, as well as hair, very much grown. And, though they have been much longer dead than many other

bodies, which are perfectly putrefied, no[t] the least mark of corruption is visible upon them. Those who are destroyed by them, after their death, become Vampyres, so that to prevent so spreading an evil, it is found requisite to drive a stake through the dead body, from whence, on this occasion the blood flows as if the person was alive. Sometimes the body is dug out of the grave, and burnt to ashes; upon which, all disturbances cease.

The remainder of the article is the Earl of Oxford's description of reports of vampire activity, occurring between 1693 and 1738, in various districts of Eastern Europe. The article closes with an apparent endorsement of the vampire's existence: "however it may be ridiculed by many people, [the vampire practice may not be] altogether without foundation; since the Supreme Being may make wicked spirits his instruments of punishment here as well as plagues, wars, famines, & that he actually has done so, is sufficiently apparent from Scripture." The vampire as an instrument of God's punishment was not a novel idea, but its reiteration in this context did give me pause to consider the New England tradition's utter silence on what provokes a vampire attack. Perhaps there was a tacit understanding that consumption was just another sign of God's inscrutable sovereignty.

But what I found most intriguing about the 1765 newspaper article was the mention of destroying the vampire by burning its corpse to ashes, exactly the procedure employed in the cases from Jewett City, Connecticut, and Foster, Rhode Island—both within fifty miles of Hartford. Could this article have been instrumental in introducing a variant of the vampire practice to New England? Is it possible that methods for dealing with consumption/vampire attacks were imported at several different times, from several different sources? If the tradition was brought from the Old World to the New, there is no reason to assume that it arrived in just one place at one time. The variation that is apparent in the New England vampire tradition could have occurred through local adaptations from a single source, or it could have been introduced into the region from several different sources. Many of the beliefs and practices associated with the vampire tradition, and with consumption cures, are found in a variety of countries and cultures, in a multitude of configurations. Whether these "relicks of many old customs" arrived in New England, bundled together from one source at one time, or piecemeal, here and there from several sources over a period of time, I cannot yet say.

CHAPTER 12
A Ghoul in Every Deserted Fireplace

I enjoy getting phone calls from colleagues who say things like, "I've found something that I think might interest you." Robert Mathiesen, a Brown University professor, delivered just this message following a lecture I gave, in 1999, on the New England vampire tradition. During my presentation, I showed a map of New England with red dots marking each vampire incident. Robert said that a student in one of his courses had created a map showing the religious affiliations of New England colonies in the seventeenth century. All of the red dots on my map fell into areas designated as "tolerant," "separatist" or "unspecified" on his student's map. There were no red dots in the Puritan heartland. Robert recommended some works that discussed a magic worldview very different from the Puritan belief system that most of us associate with early New England.

So, when he called with something interesting, I was anticipating adding another red dot to my map. I wasn't quite correct; I needed *two* additional dots. Robert showed me some photocopied pages from a two-volume journal that had just been published. Incredibly, the very first entry described the author's participation in a vampire exhumation. On September 3, 1810, Enoch Hayes Place, a twenty-four-year-old Freewill Baptist Minister, set out for Vermont from southeastern New Hampshire to preach the word of the Lord. With his wife and young daughter (sick and "looking pale as death") in tears, and his grandmother pleading for him to stay, as Place wrote in the first entry of a journal that he would keep for fifty-five years, "I then turned my back upon them all, with tears in my eyes and went out of the house, took my horse and went on." Place had begun preaching three years earlier, a mere month after being converted, having been caught up in the sweeping religious revival known as the Second Great Awakening. A farmer, teacher, and strong advocate for education and the antislavery and temperance movements, Place remained, for most of his life, a minister in and around Strafford, New Hampshire.

Less than two days into his journey to spread the gospel, Place witnessed a "melincolly sight . . . as I never Saw before":

> Sep 4th — . . . I went this afternoon, to parson Geores meeting, which was at a Br Denitts; who was Sick with the Consumption. When I preached from these words Prov. 1–33, "But whoso harkeneth unto me Shal dwell safely, and Shall be quiet from the fear of evil." We had a good Season, Br George was well engaged, & the people there Bless God for the work he has done in that place—I then went on to Br Wilsons; where they were asembling for meeting. I preached from these words "The best of the Land is yet before." I had a deep Sense of the misteres of the Gospel, after meeting the people joined & Sung Some, beautiful hymns; which Comforted me much. I was then requested by Esqr Hodgdon, & others to attend the takeing up the remains of Janey D. Denitt, who had been dead, over two years, (she died with the Comsumption AE 21). She was the daughter of the beforementioned Sick brother— The people had a desire to see if any thing had grown upon her Stomach— Accordingly I attended. this morning wednesday Sep 5th a little after the breake of day with Br George, and a number of the neighbors. They opened the grave and it was a Solemn Sight indeed. A young Brother by the name of Adams

examined the mouldy Specticle, but found nothing
as they Supposed they Should—Suffis to Say it was a
melincolly sight to many I can Say of a truth I Saw
Such a Sight, this morning, as I never Saw before.
There was but a little left except bones and part of
the Vitals. Which Served to Show to all what we are
tending to. After the grave was filed up again, I went
with Sister Wilson to visit Br Denitt and prayed with
him where we had a good season to our souls Bless
God for it.

It may seem almost incomprehensible that Janey Denitt's exhumation was carried out by townspeople with the assistance of
Parson Georges and in the presence of Elder Place—not to mention that, after the event, Place went to visit and pray with Janey's
father. The lesson that Place drew from this "melincolly sight"
has to do with the frailty of the human condition on earth. In
place of the pious condemnation of the exhumation that we
might expect from conservative pillars of religion, we encounter
charity and compassion. He was at one with his flock.

The very same day, Place heard an account of a similar occurrence some years before in Loudon, a few miles to the west:

I then took breakfast with Br Willson's family; and
then went on to Br Shepherds in Gilmantown. Here I
Stoped for a while and rested my Self, then took
dinner, prayed took my leave of the family and went
on to Loudon. I Called at one Br Cates, and found them
will engaged being a distant relation to the Barrington
Cates. They requested a meeting. I concluded to Stop.
There was quite an asembly at meeting. I preached
from these words. Luke 2–29, 30, 31, 32. Now lettest
thou thy Servant depart In pease according to thy
word &c. (There being a number of old people
present) we had a good Season. The Lord being with
us of a truth. There was some weighty exortations,

delivered after Sermon. there being quite a reforma-
tion in that place. The people there told me of an
instant, in their neighbourhood simielar to this one. I
mentioned in barnstead of a Woman that had ben
dead eleven years. Who was taken up by the Shakers,
they found the Bones and eleven Sprouts that had
grown out of the bones, principally from the Stomach
bone, one from thence grew out through the top of the
Scull a number of others Stood up on the bone, all of
them resembling potatoe tops when grown in the
Seller, the persons that broke off those things Soon
died. it was all to no purpose to the Sick relation.

Reverend Place's actual participation in the exhumation ceremony puzzled me. I had been able to reconcile the participation
of the secular society—family, neighbors, community leaders, and
even medical doctors (though the extent and nature of their participation still has not been resolved). Even granting that the
supernatural worldview was a great deal more pervasive and influential than is often acknowledged or discussed, I was not prepared
to explain a religious accommodation of practices that suggested
a belief system quite apart from that of conventional Protestantism. When I learned of Rev. Place and his journals, I had
already begun to sketch in the general historical background of
New England's religious and secular belief systems, intending to
create a background against which to view the vampire practice
and the reactions to it by outsiders. Now, I needed to look again,
and more deeply than before.

The existence of the supernatural realm, including a varied
host of harmful spirits, was accepted by *all* segments of early
New England. Illness was viewed as a result of supernatural or
irrational causes, ranging from witchcraft to the predestinarian
notion that "God causes sickness." God and witchcraft were not
mutually exclusive. American colonists carried on an unbroken
tradition of witchcraft from sixteenth- and seventeenth-century
England, but they created their own variations. Puritan theology

encompassed relations, not only between God and His saints, but between devils, witches, and sinners, as well. In Puritan New England, if the official and folk supernatural realms did not coalesce, they at least ran in parallel streams. According to folklorist Richard Dorson, the Puritans

> did not swallow wholesale the old wives' tales and notions freely circulating among the folk, with which they were fully acquainted, but rather endeavored earnestly to screen out "superstitions" and "fabulous" elements from genuine evidences of sorcery and diabolism. The New England Puritan fathers took a median position on witchcraft lore, rejecting at one extreme the skeptics who denied the actuality of witches, and at the other the gullible who thought witches could transform themselves into beasts and birds.

The official Puritan stance also frowned on employing folk remedies that mustered supernatural forces. Dorson wrote that Puritan leader, Increase Mather,

> castigated those well-meaning persons who attempted folk remedies against witchcraft such as destroying wax images pricked with needles, or drawing blood from suspected witches, or bottling the urine of witches, or nailing horseshoes over the door, for having "fellowship with that hellish covenant" between the Devil and his witches. These widely practiced folk charms he dismissed as superstition, but at the same time he recognized the malevolent force of the dark covenants. . . . The art of "unbewitching persons" could only be learned from magicians and devils themselves, insisted Increase, and to practice this art in effect served the Devil's ends and worked for his salvation.

Although many of the miraculous providences—events through which God revealed himself, particularly his plans and judgments, by direct intervention in the affairs of humankind—concerned the appearance of ghosts and revenants, their role was strictly orchestrated within the confines of Puritan orthodoxy.

The Puritans in effect appropriated the currently circulating legends and folklore and pressed them into the service of their worldview. When the dead return in the remarkable providences, they do so to reveal a murder or other heinous sin. As Giles Corey, of Salem, Massachusetts, lay dying from the heavy stones placed upon his chest because he would not enter a plea to the charge of witchcraft, an apparition appeared to Ann Putnam. It was the ghost of the village idiot, who communicated to Ann that he, himself, had been pressed to death by Corey years before. The Devil had covenanted with Corey, promising that he should not be hanged for his crime. But "God's greater power ensured that Corey met a just retribution, by dying in the same manner as his victim."

Disease epidemics were part of the continuing struggle between God and Satan. The witchcraft outbreak in Salem Village, in 1692, followed a hard winter and an epidemic of smallpox, both of which served as proof that "a group of witches has allied themselves with Satan to destroy the Church of God and set up the kingdom of the Devil." There is, in this case, a linking of a contagious disease to supernatural agency, which is, of course, the foundation of the vampire practice in New England. But despite this common foundation, understanding how the vampire practice took hold in parts of New England (however it might have arrived there) requires looking to outlying areas where vampire accounts appear in the record and where very different worldviews held sway.

Rhode Island, in particular, was far removed from the Puritan influence, even though virtually surrounded by Puritans. In his *Jonny-Cake Papers*, Shepherd Tom Hazard described the state as "being filled with a host of sectarians and free thinkers, individualists one and all." Shepherd Tom, who "was bred in the strictest school of the Quakers' doctrine," wrote that he and his neighbors were fond of repeating "three articles of faith": "First, that ye love one another and your neighbor as yourselves. Second, that ye hate the Puritans of Massachusetts with a perfect hatred. Third, that ye hold the Presbyterians of Connecticut in like contempt." This other New England, radiating from the outlying towns in Rhode Island and eastern Connecticut, occupied the margins both philosophically and geographically. It extended up the Connecticut River Valley into Vermont and New Hampshire, and stretched into southern Maine. Its people were not especially religious in an orthodox sense, although many could be considered spiritual. During the colonial period, about 85 percent of New England's white population *did not* belong to any church, and, by the close of the eighteenth century, that figure had risen to 90 percent. Most of these "unchurched" New Englanders participated in various hybrid religions that have been classified as "folk," in the sense that they were unofficial combinations of Christian beliefs and various folk practices, many of them of a kind often referred to disparagingly as "superstitions."

These New Englanders experimented with a magical worldview that tapped into alchemy, astrology, divination, seeing stones, dowsing, and other practices that would have been viewed as part of the occult and, therefore, off limits to Puritans. The Puritans would have considered the vampire procedures to be diabolical practices that served the interests of Satan. But other Protestants could have reconciled such acts in the same way that they could, with equal ease and no apparent contradiction, consult almanacs and treasure dowsers as well as bibles and preachers. This was the heartland of the Quakers and Shakers and the source of later religious sects, such as the Mormons and the Oneida Community (whose founders both were from Vermont), that developed in central New York's "Burned-over District," so named because of its successive waves of unorthodox religious and spiritual movements based on idiosyncratic interpretations of Protestantism and imbued with an appealing supernaturalism. Joseph Smith, a treasure hunter by trade, found the golden tablets that became the basis for the Mormon religion by the use of seeing stones or, as they are commonly called, crystal balls.

"This mix of magic and religion influenced the untrained preachers who were commonplace after the Revolution." According to a scholar of American revivalism, "Dreams had meaning [for them], and the activities of beasts were oracles to the knowing. Birth, love, and death were assisted or held back by incantations. When a boy raised in this way became a preacher, it was not hard to reconcile his folk inheritance and his Christianity." Reverend Enoch Hayes Place's participation in the exhumation of Janey Denitt does not seem so mysterious in view of the eclectic belief system of his time and place.

This magical worldview cut across class, religious, ethnic, and linguistic boundaries. Along with the home remedies and supernatural lore that had been handed down in their own families and communities, people encountered the traditions of other groups. Shepherd Tom, a wealthy, landed Quaker from one of South County, Rhode Island's oldest families, made regular visits to a small hovel in the woods to have his fortune told by Sylvia Tory, a former slave. His brother, Joseph Peace Hazard, was a student of mysticism and spiritualism, a transcendentalist who went to seances and responded to dreams. He had "Druidsdream" and "Witches Altar" constructed as result of his supernatural experiences (see Chapter 3).

The prevailing, general interest in supernatural topics is recorded in old newspaper advertisements that promote itinerant lecturers, many originally from Germany and Eastern Europe, making the circuit from New Jersey and Pennsylvania into New England. For example, from 1760 to 1773, a German fortune-teller advertised his services in Rhode Island's English-language newspapers. Although this worldview has not received much attention, it appears to have touched many, if not most, Americans prior to the early 1800s. It is difficult to assess just how widespread the magical worldview was, as D. Michael Quinn observed in his examination of the New England roots of early Mormonism:

Without statistical sampling and opinion polls, it is impossible to know the actual extent of occult beliefs and magic practices among Americans during any time period. Anti-occult rhetoric and media attention could simply be the paranoia of the vast majority against a perceived threat by a numerically insignificant minority. On the other hand, anti-occult rhetoric by early American opinion-makers (clergy, legislators, jurists, newspaper editors, book authors) may have been the embattled effort of an *elite minority* to convert a vastly larger populace that was sympathetic to the occult. I accept the latter view of the situation. At any rate, literary sources and material culture show that occult beliefs and folk magic had widespread manifestations among educated and religious Americans from colonial times to the eve of the twentieth century.

As the eighteenth century unfolded, however, distinctions among magic, religion, and science became increasingly important to the elite, even though it still meant little to ordinary people, for whom the borders separating medicine and magic, and religion and the occult, were not sharply defined. By the time Mercy Brown's heart was cut from her body and burned, in 1892, a significant rift between the official and folk worlds had developed, at least from the viewpoint of the "civilization establishment" that included scientists, scholars, businessmen, clergy, politicians, and practitioners of the by-then dominant biomedical paradigm. Where official and academic culture began to divide the world into a variety of specialties, with their attendant specialists, the all-inclusive nature of folk culture persisted.

The lesson of the Mercy Brown event, according to the *Providence Journal* (and other newspapers of the day), was that "there are considerable elements of rural population in this part of the country upon which the forces of education and civilization have made scarcely any impression." The *Journal*'s editors, referring to "Deserted Exeter," found "the amount of ignorance and superstition to be found in some corners of New England ... more than surprising." Viewed from the pedestal of civilized man, the exhumation of Mercy Brown was yet another skirmish in the war between modern, scientific thinking and the primitive, unreflective superstitions inherited from a savage past. While the *Journal* waved the popular banners of "progress" and "civilization" before its readers, the *American Anthropologist*, through George Stetson's article of 1896 ("The Animistic Vampire in New England"), launched a scholarly attack on the lowly culture of Rhode Island's South County. Stetson commented that "it is a common belief in primitive races of low culture that disease is caused by the revengeful spirits of man or other animals" and suggested that rural Rhode Islanders harbored survivals from a lower level of cultural evolution as evidenced by this

> extraordinary instance of a barbaric outcropping ... coexisting with a high general culture. ... The region referred to [South County], where agriculture is in a depressed condition and abandoned farms are numerous, is the tramping-ground of the book agent, the chromo peddler, the patent-medicine man and the home of the erotic and neurotic modern novel. ... Farm-houses deserted and ruinous are frequent, and once productive lands, neglected and overgrown with scrubby oak, speak forcefully and mournfully of the migration of the youthful farmers from country to town. In short, the region furnishes an object-lesson in the decline of wealth consequent upon the prevalence of a too common heresy in the district that land will take care of itself, or that it can be robbed from generation to generation without injury, and suggests the almost criminal neglect of the conservators of public education to give instruction to our farming youth in a more scientific and more practical agriculture. It has been well said by a banker of well known

name in an agricultural district in the midlands of
England that "the depression of agriculture is a
depression of brains." Naturally, in such isolated conditions the superstitions of a much lower culture have
maintained their place and are likely to keep it and
perpetuate it, despite the church, the public school,
and the weekly newspaper.

In a footnote, Stetson provided statistics to corroborate his claim
that South County, particularly Exeter, was in decline: "The
town of Exeter, before mentioned, incorporated in 1742–'43,
had but 17 persons to the square mile in 1890, and in 1893 had
63 abandoned farms, or one fifth of the whole number within
its limits."

(I think that if there had been a Food and Drug
Administration at the time, it might have required that a warning
be posted prior to the performance of each vampire ritual:
"Surgeon General's Warning: Vampire rituals may not prove
effective against consumption, especially in advanced cases. Side
effects may include public ridicule.")

Stetson, of course, was not alone in his assessment, nor was he
totally misrepresenting the condition of rural New England. In
her monograph entitled "The New England Vampire Belief:
Image of the Decline," Faye Ringel Hazel writes:

The persistence of this vampire belief coincides with
the gradual decay of rural New England, as farms
were abandoned for more easily cultivated land to
the west. Beginning as early as the 1830s, and continuing to this day, the New England countryside has
reverted to woodlands. In the nineteenth century, this
process seemed to drain rural New England of its
most enterprising young citizens, leaving the old and
unfit behind. The results were appalling to contemporary observers. In 1869, the *Nation* asserted that
"Puritan stock is diminishing. . . . even that such of it

as remains is no longer what it should be" (411). Indeed, the editors note, "we are forever felicitating ourselves that the West is being peopled in great measure by the hardy citizens of Maine, but we are continually forgetting what sort of an effect this is likely to have upon Maine" (411).

Indeed, Hazel's citations from *The Atlantic Monthly* suggest that Stetson's blunt depiction of South County was almost mild in comparison with the picture of rural New England offered by other commentators:

In the notorious articles concerning "A New England Hill Town" which appeared in *The Atlantic Monthly* in 1899, the inbred inhabitants of the decayed hill towns of western Massachusetts are described in terms that recall similar Social Darwinist studies of the Appalachians and the Ozarks. The articles picture New England towns inhabited by dwarfs, giants, and idiots, all mutated from the ancient stock by what Rollin Hartt calls "natural selection the other end to—the survival of the unfittest" (572). . . . In such a climate of opinion, the audiences of scholarly journals or of scandal-sheet newspapers such as *The World* were ready to believe anything about the folk of backwoods New England. Any superstition or survival of ancient beliefs might linger in those benighted areas left behind by the westward march of American civilization.

Certainly, the editors of the *Providence Journal*, as well as George Stetson, would have agreed with the opening sentence of Hazel's monograph: "Of all the images of New England's decay and decline, none provides a more striking objective correlative than that of the vampire."

Amy Lowell used precisely this image in her vampire poem,

"A Dracula of the Hills," which unfolds in a rural New England that she viewed as a decaying, superstitious backwater, drained of its original hardy stock by the Civil War and movement away to the cities and out west (see Chapter 9). In 1917, she wrote in a letter:

> My bringing-up was very cosmopolitan, and my fore-bears for several generations have been much trav-elled people, and the decaying New England which [Robert] Frost presents and which, if you remember I also present in 'The Overgrown Pasture,' has been no part of my immediate surroundings. Therefore it is no grief to me to have it disappear.

She expressed the same sentiment a few years later, contrasting her attitude towards rural New Englanders with that of Robert Frost:

> . . . he [Frost] is much more sympathetic to them than I am, and makes excuses for their idiosyn-crasies. I pity them, and, in some ways, admire them, but, as far as time goes, I am a complete alien; not until I grew up did I know anything of the native Yankee. . . . But you remember that my cousin, Mr. James Russell Lowell, was one of the authorities on Yankee character of his day, and all I can think is that subconsciously I inherited a sort of general family acquaintance with the country people.

Robert Frost may have felt more kinship with the viewpoint that came from within the town of Exeter. Not surprisingly, it was exactly opposite of that proffered by outsiders. Local sources saw strength where others saw weakness. Following the death of Mercy's brother, Edwin, in May of 1892, the *Wickford Standard* (which covered the towns of North Kingstown and Exeter) pub-lished a lengthy commentary entitled "A Rhode Island Country Town." While there are no explicit references to the Brown family and the exhumations (a kind of discretion familiar in many of the documents pertaining to New England's vampire tradition), the article makes the best sense when viewed in the context of the notoriety this event generated when news of it was rapidly disseminated to the general public. The article begins with a description of Exeter that caused me to wonder if this is the same community that George Stetson and the *Providence Journal* were writing about:

> There is a quiet rural town in South County where the sun rises earlier and where its golden beams linger later than in most other places in Southern Rhode Island [Exeter's east-west stretch is the longest of any South County town]. It is widely known for its picturesque and romantic scenery, for its lofty terraced hills rising in rugged splendor one above another some of them reaching upward nearly six hundred feet above the level of the sea.

Unlike the outsiders, who saw a threat to civilization in the isolated rural areas, the Wickford commentary found the country to be a safe haven from the evil influences of urban life:

> If people are deprived of some of the conveniences of modern life, they are amply compensated by exemption from many of the temptations which undermine manhood and womanhood in more populous communities. No travelling theatrical troupe or circus company ever stops over night within its borders to poison the minds of the young or generate a feverish discontent with the conditions of honest labor and the routine of farm life. The citizens as a rule are honest, industrious, amicably-inclined and though living remote from their neighbors they are generous and social in their relations with each other.

The editorial emphasized the role of the community in times of illness, alluding to the advice given to George Brown by his neighbors:

> Perhaps in no phase of the life of these kind-hearted country people is their genuine goodness of heart more apparent than in cases of sickness and death, when their neighborly hands will linger long and lovingly in their efforts to perform in the most perfect manner the highest service which human power can render.

Finally, the commentary criticized journalists who denigrated the customs and exaggerated the beliefs of Exeter country folk:

> In conclusion it may not be amiss to say that this same town has been the subject of frequent newspaper articles during the past two or three years from the pens of young, ambitious city journalists. . . .
>
> So it would seem that these writers started out to find something sensational and unreal, and being somewhat unaccustomed to the conditions of country life have allowed their imaginations to picture a ghoul in every deserted fireplace, to parade the afflictions and misfortunes of those in distress before the public as something strange and wonderful. They have come to regard every man, the cut of whose clothes showed independence in dress, as a deluded believer in some superstitious impossibility. The people of this town may be fairly said to possess all the virtues and fewer of the vices than many communities, and it is equally true that the average education, general intelligence and freedom from superstition will compare favorably with any other town in the State, although it bears the name of "Deserted Exeter".

Other South County newspapers voiced similar opinions. Like the *Wickford Standard,* these local articles generally interpreted the Mercy Brown event as a demonstration of the positive values, such as compassion, concern, and mutual assistance, that characterize closeknit rural communities. A month after the event, the *Pawtuxet Valley Gleaner,* in its "Exeter Hill and Vicinity" column, ran the following commentary:

> We think that some one in "Deserted Exeter," who can afford it, should contribute an old shoe from which a medal can be made and suitably inscribed (never mind the expense we say) and then with appropriate ceremony have the said medal presented to the very (?) gentlemanly reporter whose graphic and herculean efforts recently appeared in the Providence Journal. " 'Nuff said".

These local newspapers were reinforcing a sense of group solidarity in the face of an outside threat. Outsiders used the same event to show that civilization had not yet triumphed everywhere and was being menaced by remnants of primitive thought and ignorance. Newspapers such as the *Providence Journal* were both censuring and asserting superiority over their rural neighbors. Whether or not the *Journal's* editorial stance was fair, the newspaper was undoubtedly correct in asserting: "It is probable that the theory was never practiced in this State under a better light of publicity, discussion and criticism."

The vituperative tone evident on both sides of this issue suggested that something deeper than a folk ritual was dividing these communities. The division between industrial Providence and agricultural South County was long-standing, rooted in economic and political concerns. But in the verbal battle over the exhumations, newer dichotomies also came into play as the beliefs and attitudes of evolutionists and modernists confronted those of romantics and antimodernists. This vampire war was part of a much wider struggle that pitted civilization against superstition.

The large debt amassed during the Revolutionary War became a source of strained relations between farmers and urbanized commercial interests in Rhode Island. The brunt of the war's financial burden was borne by farmers, since revenue from real-estate taxes had to offset revenues lost due to the disruption of trade and the British occupation of commercial port towns. In the ensuing struggle, farmers argued successfully for the issuance of paper money, thus allowing them to pay their debts to reluctant creditors with highly inflated currency. As Rhode Island was becoming the first urban, industrialized state in the Union, the state legislature was still dominated by rural interests, which steadfastly maintained a tax structure and voting requirements that ensured the continued disenfranchisement of the burgeoning cities in the north. This disparity led to an armed confrontation in 1842, the "Dorr War," which created greater representation for the northern industrial towns. The momentum continued to swing in the direction of cities during the nineteenth century, and farming communities lost their dominance. Well before 1892, the groundwork had been laid for the vampire war.

Another reason this event received widespread scrutiny is because it occurred at the end of the nineteenth century, a time that had experienced great changes in science and technology that were generally assigned positive labels such as "progress" and "advances in civilization." A vampire exhumation seemed very much out of place in 1892; it was an anomaly or, in the vocabulary of the era's anthropologists, a survival from a lower stage of cultural evolution. The exhumations carried out in the previous century received little, if any, attention from contemporaries. Perhaps there was an element of polite discretion involved but, in addition, practices that had not seemed extraordinary at the end of the eighteenth century were viewed by some as bizarre and threatening a century later.

With that issue in mind, I reviewed the vampire record, looking for commentary that would reveal attitudes about the practice. While the case of Captain Burton, in Manchester, Vermont, is the earliest on record, having occurred in 1793, it wasn't actually set down until many years later. It is likely that Judge John Pettibone collected the story from an eyewitness sometime between 1857 and 1872. When Pettibone used the following phrases to characterize the event, the nineteenth-century push toward civilization was well underway, so Pettibone, even though he was living in the same town, was, by then, judging a significantly different culture: "strange infatuation . . . strange delusion . . . altar in the sacrifice to the Demon Vampire who it was believed was still sucking the blood." While the Horace Ray case in Jewett City, Connecticut, was reported in the newspaper just two weeks after it happened in May, 1854, by that time, the author's disapproving tone was not out of place: "A strange and almost incredible tale of superstition. . . . The scene, as described to us, must have been revolting in the extreme; and the idea that it could have grown out of a belief such as we have referred to, tasks human credulity. We seem to have been transported back to the darkest age of unreasoning ignorance and blind superstition, instead of living in the 19th century, and in a State calling itself enlightened and [C]hristian." The same can be said for the "horrible vampire story" from Ontario, the "repulsive superstition" that "shocked" its collector in 1893.

The vampire report that has the earliest commentary attached to it was provided to me by one of those "I-think-I-have-something-of-interest" phone calls, this one from William Simmons in the fall of 1986. He had just completed a book on Native American history and folklore (*Spirit of the New England Tribes*), for which I provided some tales that I had collected in South County. We had discussed my interest in the vampire tradition, so, as he searched through old newspapers looking for Native American tales, he was on the lookout for any article that seemed relevant to my research. He presented me with two articles from the *Old Colony Memorial and Plymouth County* [Massachusetts] *Advertiser*. The first article appeared in the inaugural issue of the newspaper, May 4, 1822, under the headline "Superstitions of New England." The heading notes that it was taken from the *Philadelphia Union*:

In that almost insulated part of the State of Massachusetts, called *Old Colony* or *Plymouth County*, and particularly in a small village adjoining the shire town, there may be found the relicks of many old customs and superstitions which would be amusing, at least to the antiquary. Among others of less serious cast, there was, fifteen years ago, one which, on account of its peculiarity and its consequence, I beg leave to mention.

It is well known to those who are acquainted with that section of our country, that nearly one half of its inhabitants die of a consumption, occasioned by the chilly humidity of their atmosphere, and the long prevalence of easterly winds. The inhabitants of the village (or town as it is there called) to which I allude were peculiarly exposed to this scourge; and I have seen, at one time, one of every fifty of its inhabitants gliding down to the grave with all the certainty which characterises this insiduous [sic] foe of the human family.

There was, fifteen years ago, and is perhaps at this time, an opinion prevalent among the inhabitants of this town, that the body of a person who died of a consumption, was by some supernatural means, nourished in the grave of some one living member of the family; and that during the life of this person, the body remained [retained?], in the grave, all the fullness and freshness of life and health.

This belief was strengthened by the circumstance, that whole families frequently fell a prey to this terrible disease.

Of one large family in this town consisting of fourteen children, and their venerable parents, the mother & the youngest son only remained—the rest within a year of each other had died of the consumption.

Within two months from the death of the thirteenth child, an amiable girl of about 16 years of age, the bloom, which characterised the whole of this family, was seen to fade from the cheek of the last support of the heartsmitten mother, and his broad flat chest was occasionally convulsed by that powerful deep cough which attends the consumption in our Atlantick States.

At this time as if to snatch one of this family from an early grave, it was resolved by a few of the inhabitants of the village to test the truth of this tradition which I have mentioned, and, which the circumstances of this afflicted family seemed to confirm. I should have added that it was believed that if the body thus supernaturally nourished in the grave, should be raised and turned over in the coffin, its depredation upon the survivor would necessarily cease. The consent of the mother being obtained, it was agreed that four persons, attended by the surviving and complaining brother should, at sunrise the next day dig up the remains of the last buried sister. At the appointed hour they attended in the burying yard, and having with much exertion removed the earth, they raised the coffin upon the ground; then, displacing the flat lid, they lifted the covering from her face, and discovered what they had indeed anticipated, but dreaded to declare.— Yes, I saw the visage of one who had been long the tenant of a silent grave, lit up with the brilliancy of youthful health. The cheek was full to dimpling, and a rich profusion of hair shaded her cold forehead, and while some of its richest curls floated upon her unconscious breast. The large blue eye had scarcely lost its brilliancy, and the livid fullness of her lips seemed almost to say, "loose me and let me go."

In two weeks the brother, shocked with the spectacle he had witnessed, sunk under his disease. The mother survived scarcely a year, and the long range of sixteen graves, is pointed out to the stranger as an evidence of the truth of the belief of the inhabitants.

The following lines were written on a recollection of the above shocking scene:

I saw her, the grave sheet was round her,
  Months had passed since they laid her in clay;
Yet the damps of the tomb could not wound her,
  The worms had not seized on their prey.
O, fair was her cheek, as I knew it.
  When the rose all its colours there brought;
And that eye,—did a tear then bedew it?
  gleame'd like the herald of thought.
She bloom'd, though the shroud was around her,
  locks o'er her cold bosom wave,
As if the stern monarch had crown'd her,
  The fair speechless queen of the grave.
But what lends the grave such a lusture?
  O'er her cheeks what such beauty had shed?
His life blood, who bent there, had nurs'd her,
  The living was food for the dead!

It seems that the event occurred about 1807 and that the author (who apparently wrote both the article and the poem) was an eyewitness. A lengthy reply to this account was published in the next issue of the weekly newspaper. The letter, under the signature of "A Physician," took issue with some of the assertions about consumption that appeared in the first article, and the writer left little doubt that he believed his community had been unfairly singled out for ridicule:

Sir— . . . The writer indulges his imagination in ranting about the superstitious customs which specially prevail in the Old Colony, or Plymouth County, and this he fantastically locates in an insulated part of the State of Massachusetts. His first assertion is too extravagant to require refutation. If true it would imply a phenomenon which has never occurred in any part of the habitable world, "that nearly one half of the people die of consumption." Nor will it be credited, that one of fifty of the inhabitants fall a prey to this inexorable disease. It is impossible to conceive the motive by which the writer could be actuated in advancing a position so glaringly preposterous. . . .

[T]he average proportion of consumptive cases is about one to every five and a half deaths. This estimate applies to New England and the intermediate States, extending to the Carolinas. Instances, it must be conceded, too frequently occur of whole families having a constitutional predisposition to consumption, by which parents are bereft of children in the early periods of life. But the writer in the Philadelphia Union, cites one instance of a family in this vicinity consisting of sixteen persons, all of whom were victims of consumption. The number specified, as well as his fanciful ideas relative to the superstitious belief in the salutary effects to be derived from touching the entombed corpse, bear evident marks of great exaggeration. During a residence of nearly forty years in the district referred to, and favoured with opportunities of correct observation respecting this subject, the writer of this reply, has not been made acquainted, with but one solitary instance of raising the body of the dead for the benefit of the living: and this was done purely in compliance with the caprice of a surviving sister, reduced to the last stage of hectic debility and despair. Although the family and connections entertained not the smallest hope of beneficial conse-

273

quences, they could not in duty and tenderness refuse to indulge a feeble minded and debilitated young woman in a mean, on which she had confided her last fallacious hope. Inferences must be extremely incorrect when drawn from solitary instances, and it may with truth be affirmed, that the inhabitants of Plymouth County are equally intelligent, and not more remarkably addicted to superstition, than the generality of our race.

The insider's view evident in this letter is consistent with that which appeared some seventy years later in Exeter, with assertions that people in the community are just as intelligent and no more superstitious than people elsewhere. The physician takes the author to task for "indulging his imagination" in regard to the practice, and suggests that the incident described is greatly exaggerated. Yet he does admit to knowing of an exhumation that was carried out in the town. And his description calls to mind, once again, the decision made by Exeter's George Brown. Although the family did not believe the ritual would be efficacious, they complied out of a sense of duty and compassion. This rift between civilization and superstition—the vampire war— seems to have begun many years before Mercy Brown's corpse came to the attention of the *Providence Journal*.

The Plymouth account raises some other issues that, of course, I cannot ignore, even if they have no direct bearing on the vampire war. I was at first perplexed by the location of a vampire incident in Plymouth, the early gateway to New England and home of the Pilgrims. I checked again the map that Robert Mathiesen had shown me and discovered that Plymouth lies squarely within the southeastern section of Massachusetts that had a strong Separatist religious affiliation throughout the seventeenth century. It was not part of the Puritan tradition that stretched north from Cohasset (about midway between Boston and Plymouth) to Ipswich along the Atlantic Coast and to the southwest as far as Greenwich, Connecticut. Also excluded from the Puritan sphere were tolerant Rhode Island and the unspecified southern portion of adjacent Connecticut, in addition to northern New England, which became the states of Vermont, New Hampshire, and Maine. This territory, ringing the Puritan lands, takes in precisely those areas where a supernatural worldview was permitted to coexist, and even mingle, with Protestant sects and, not coincidentally, where the vampire tradition has been documented.

The remedy in the Plymouth case—simply turning the corpse over from face up to face down—is the only example of this procedure I've found in New England, adding yet another variant practice to the mix. (The stipulation that the rite be carried out at sunrise is a new addition, too.) Prone burials have an established precedence in folklore; they have been documented in Europe (among ancient Celtic peoples and others), Aboriginal America, India, and Africa. Burying a corpse face down (or prone) has been interpreted as a way to insure that it rests in peace and also prevents it from transforming into a vampire. Perhaps prone burial inhibits the vampire from finding its way to the surface because, according to some folk sources, the vampire will bite its way further down into the earth (folk vampires, unlike their literary and pop-culture counterparts, are not noted for being cunning or intelligent). An alternate folk explanation is that prone burial protects those attending the burial from the vampire's fatal gaze. In Romania and Macedonia, one of the signs that a corpse is a vampire is that, upon exhumation, it is found with its face turned downwards. The explanation offered in the following folktale from Transylvania is that the vampire's soul cannot return to its body if it has been turned into the prone position:

> An old man with some soldiers was driving a cart in Transilvania, trying to find where he could get some hay. Night came on during their journey, so they stopped at a lonely house in a plain. The woman of the house received them, put maize porridge and milk

on the table for them, and then went away. The soldiers ate the maize porridge, and after their meal looked for the old woman to thank her, but were unable to find her. Climbing up to the attic to see if she was there, they found seven bodies lying down, one of which was the woman's. They were frightened and fled, and, as they looked back, they saw seven little lights descending on the house. These were the souls of the vampires. Had the soldiers turned the bodies with their faces downwards, the souls would never have been able to enter the bodies again.

Ralph Merrifield, in his interpretation of ritual and magic through archaeological evidence, discovered a large number of prone burials in Britain dating from the late Roman and early Anglo-Saxon eras. He concluded that they revealed a "rite of separation . . . intended to ensure that the dead did not return," for it presumably indicated "to the soul the direction which it should travel." Paul Barber connects face-down burials to the well-known and widespread custom of reversing direction to ward off evil, a practice that folklorists call "widdershins." Of course, we all are familiar with the phrase that someone has "turned over in his grave" when something that would have been disagreeable to him occurs. According to Barber, the original notion that the corpse is preparing to return from the dead (perhaps to remedy the transgression) has been lost. And let's not forget that, according to Everett Peck's family story, Mercy Brown was found, upon excavation, to have "turned over in the grave."

The vampire war echoed a grander struggle. The apparent progress achieved by the late nineteenth century spawned two opposing views. One maintained that American culture, having just completed its "manifest destiny" of taming a New World from coast-to-coast, was on the verge of attaining the highest stage of civilization. The other was an antimodernist reaction by

"American intellectuals" who saw a "vulgarizing and deinvigo-rating tendency" accompanying "progress." They turned to the past, to "an older sense of community and tradition" to "under-stand their growing sense of alienation and loss."

While the newer notion of cultural evolution had its share of followers, the romantic idea of the "noble savage" continued, in various transformations, to hold the public imagination: the idea that the closer one is to nature, the land, and the direct labor involved in fulfilling one's various needs, the richer one is in a spiritual sense. By the late nineteenth century, the "latent hos-tility between town and country became more overt" and republican pastoralism became a more militant populism. Farmers were losing their independence as "railroad entrepre-neurs and commodity traders" gained increasing control over their economic life. "The ideal of an independent American folk" (as epitomized by the farmer) that had "energized political discourse throughout the 19th century" was in jeopardy, if not indeed already dead. Writing about the influence of folklore on mass culture, Jackson Lears provides an idealized romantic vision of these vanishing folk:

> Once upon a time, there was a place called tradi-tional society. People lived on farms or in villages, at one with nature and each other. For these preindus-trial folk, there was no separation between the home and the world, between labor and the rest of life. They worked hard but their lives were unhurried, governed by the rhythms of the seasons rather than the ticking of the clock, endowed with larger pur-pose by a supernatural framework of meaning. They passed the time, rather than saving or spending it, in easy sociability with people like themselves. Together they constituted a static, homogeneous social group, rooted in the soil and in face-to-face relationships. But the urban-industrial transforma-tion brought an end to this organic community.

> Religious beliefs eroded, social bonds stretched,
> class antagonisms formed and sharpened. People
> escaped the drudgery of the farm only to find them-
> selves huddling in fetid, anonymous streets, scur-
> rying to routine jobs in factories and offices.
> Through the brown fog of a winter dawn, they
> glimpsed the rise of modern society.

This same kind of romanticism actually helped stimulate the collection of what were conceived to be the "disappearing traditions"
of various folk groups, including European peasants and native and
black Americans. The impetus was to document for posterity, if not
actually preserve, the relics from more primitive, backward ways of
life. Some social reformers, though, used the existence of these
"backwater" communities as evidence of the need to press for
eliminating superstitions and other "survivals" deemed detri-
mental to the advancement of civilization in an enlightened age.
Their task as they saw it was to educate those who still suffered
under the delusions brought about by the faulty reasoning of previous ages—the "bastard science" of magic, as Sir James Frazer
termed it.

Viewed from the pedestal of "civilization," the Brown family
exhumations were yet another skirmish in the war between
modern, scientific thinking and the primitive, unreflective superstitions inherited from a savage past. But, the romantic "noble
savage" would not go away. The two sides of this dichotomy
placed very different values on folk traditions, such as the ritual
performed in Exeter's Chestnut Hill cemetery.

CHAPTER 13
Is That True of All Vampires?

March 15, 1995. I turned on the TV in time to hear the host of a show ask, "Could these strange ritual burials reveal an American cult of vampires?" Several months before, the show's producers had contacted me and requested an interview. I asked about the nature of the program, who else would be interviewed, and, most importantly, if they were interested in presenting some approximation of an historically accurate account. When I was told that Paul Sledzik and Nick Bellantoni, with whom I had consulted regarding JB and the Walton family cemetery in Griswold, Connecticut (see Chapter 8) had agreed to participate, I assented pending confirmation by Paul and Nick. The three of us discussed the project and agreed that if we did participate, there was a chance that we could tell what we considered to be the authentic story, at least as far as we understood it from the evidence we had. If we declined to be interviewed, then we would have no chance to alter what we were certain would be the inevitable, irresistible pull of the Dracula caricature. When Paul mentioned that the interviewer had asked him about a "cult of vampires," we resolved to present a united front in denying the reality of anything remotely resembling a cult. Somewhat sheepishly, Nick admitted that, unfortunately, he had carelessly used the word in a newspaper interview when attempting to describe the extent of New England's vampire tradition. The show's producers must have read the article and, of course, the term "cult" drew them like a magnet. We decided that, if the term was mentioned, we would seize the opportunity to place the story in its proper context of tuberculosis and folk medicine and argue strongly against the notion that there was some sort of regional coven of the undead—which is precisely what we did over breakfast with the network's crew on the day of the shoot.

Finally, we were ready to begin filming. "Lights." "Roll it." "5, 4, 3, 2. . . . " First question: "What's this about a cult of vampires here in New England?" Spontaneous laughter from Nick, Paul, and Michael. Incredulous, but knowing, laughter. What followed was an on-camera, reasoned, well-articulated discussion of tuberculosis epidemics, the failure of the medical establishment, and the desperate hope that folk medicine might end a family crisis hurtling towards disaster.

So, when I turned on the TV, I couldn't believe I was hearing the phrase "cult of vampires" again. But this time I didn't laugh. My heart sank and I muttered some words I save for special occasions (such as finding out I've underestimated my income taxes by several thousand dollars). Once again, I felt betrayed. It was bad enough that this vampire segment was coupled with yet another Elvis sighting and yet another exposé of the government's cover up of an alien presence. On the program, as it aired, the word tuberculosis, or even consumption, was never mentioned. The show's host got no closer than "thousands died of mysterious causes." A sick feeling accompanied the realization that I was going to see myself on national television and, through the magical technology of editing—by expert juxtapositioning, deletion, and contextualization—and the use of narration and voice over, I was going to imply that, yes indeed, a *cult of vampires had roamed the New England countryside.*

During the years that I have been working on this project, word has gotten around to the mass media. I have been interviewed for both local and national newspaper and television presentations, with the resulting products ranging from outstanding to absolutely dreadful. Too many, unfortunately, tend towards the latter. Around Halloween, interest mounts, sometimes approaching a feeding frenzy. It seems that, in each case, just before I turn on the television to see one of these programs for the first time, I experience what I imagine it would be like if I were in the midst of a string of bad relationships, I meet someone new, and I say to myself, "This time will be different." But, naturally, it isn't. Then I ask myself, "Why do I say 'yes'? What's wrong with me?" Dr. Rational scolds Mike for being a naive optimist and slow learner. With downcast eyes, Mike responds, "Yeah, I know." I write this with no hubris, for I know that what they seek is not me, nor my interpretations. It is the vampires—the classic vampires—not the victims of tuberculosis or scapegoats. Why?

Perhaps I need to begin with a more basic question: Why is no one threatened by vampires today? Neither the communities whose ancestors dug them up, nor the newspapers that were shocked and outraged at the spectacle, take vampires seriously any more. Several factors coalesced by the close of the nineteenth century to spell the end of the vampire practice. The Civil War, Lincoln's assassination, the meticulous experiments of a German scientist, an altered intellectual climate, and the publication of a novel, all helped transform the vampire narrative from hard news to entertainment.

After Robert Koch announced his discovery of the tubercle bacillus in 1882, the germ theory became the commonly accepted explanation for the spread of tuberculosis. Along with a different theory came a different method of treatment that, until the discovery of streptomycin in 1943, entailed the isolation of the patient. This, and other preventative measures based on the assumption that the germ could be transmitted both directly and indirectly from person to person, led to a steady decline in the incidence of tuberculosis in the United States. The correlation between contagion and germs is obvious; the link between contagion and vampires is perhaps more indirect. The significant difference is how the contagion is explained. A Greek-American informant provided an unusual, but logical, connection between germs and vampires: "When people die of a contagious disease, and no one will go near them and they bury them without a priest, without anything, they become vrykolakes" [vampires in Greek]. A person who died of a contagious disease might become a vampire simply because everyone, including the priest who is supposed to perform the rituals to prevent the corpse from becoming a vampire, is afraid to approach the corpse. In any event, by the close of the nineteenth century, a microorganism called *Mycobacterium tuberculosis* had replaced the vampire as contagion's scapegoat.

Chemical embalming as mortuary practice was rising in popularity at the same time that the germ theory was winning acceptance. Between 1856 and 1870, eleven embalming patents were filed with the U.S. Patent Office. The Civil War created a need for preserving a great number of corpses, often far from desired or convenient sites of interment. The embalming of public figures to lie in state created a greater popular awareness of the custom. Lincoln's assassination, and the subsequent public viewing of his body as it went by rail from Washington to Illinois, reinforced public acceptance of the two related customs of embalming and viewing the corpse. The funeral industry grew rapidly during the 1880s, but, as is the case with many customs, there was a split between city and country. The rural population was slower to accept the expanding role of the professional undertaker, whose work usually included embalming. Earlier in the nineteenth century, embalming was used as a sanitary measure, particularly during outbreaks of contagious diseases such as smallpox, diphtheria, scarlet fever, and yellow fever. In the latter half of the century, embalming became the socially prestigious choice. In addition to the cosmetic effects of embalming, removal of the blood also renders the corpse inert, preempting, as it were, the creation of a vampire by eliminating its prime constituent.

As the germ theory and embalming were becoming generally accepted, the debate between evolutionists and romantics was subsiding. It was widely believed that civilization had won (or was on the verge of winning) the war over superstition. With the beginning of the twentieth century, the antagonistic relations between town and country were also lessening, and editorialists for urban newspapers no longer had reason to find fault with their rural neighbors. Without fanfare, the vampire war was over. Combine the above ingredients and add the publication of *Dracula*, in 1897, and you have a recipe for transforming the unfortunate victims who died too young of pulmonary tuberculosis into fanged fiends still roaming the countryside. Perhaps a little fine-tuning of Dracula, making him more accessible to the public and the media, was all that was needed. Hollywood obliged, turning Bram Stoker's Count Dracula (and his many clones) into an industry within an industry.

Yet, having the necessary ingredients available doesn't explain why media workers (including print journalists, television newspeople, and film producers) obviously feel free to ignore apparent facts in favor of fascinating fictions. Media workers distinguish between hard news and soft news. Hard news is timely and deals with important events. Soft news is concerned with "human foibles" and the "texture of our human life." Those who develop soft news features often feel free to stretch the facts for the sake of "color" and, in fact, research has shown that many have difficulty ascertaining just what the facts are in the first place.

This distinction is supported by newspaper and magazine articles that revisit the Mercy Brown event. This flood began just over three decades ago, and shows no sign of ebbing. In one of the first modern interpretations of Rhode Island's vampires, the author of a 1970 *Yankee* magazine article asserted that "the family and friends" of Edwin Brown "unanimously agreed that it must be a vampire that was sucking his blood and causing his loss of strength." The blood-sucking motif was reinforced in "Horrible History at the Boston Boo-Centennial," which appeared in the *Providence Journal-Bulletin* in 1975: "It was a sudden deteriorating illness of Edwin A. Brown many years ago that caused his family and friends to believe a vampire must have sucked his blood, causing a once husky and healthy man to lose all his strength."

By 1980, it was a "ghoulish curse" that had stricken the

Brown family, and Mercy had acquired the attributes of the classic vampire: "Surely the fiend rested there and stole forth from the crypt to drink the spirit of her brother." Just one year later, this popular pattern was consummated with bites on the neck from the demonic, imperishable corpse of Mercy Brown: "The mother, Mary Brown, had died on Sept. 8, 1883, apparently of tuberculosis, but the local story was that she had died of a bite in the neck. The following year, on June 6, her daughter, Mary Olive, aged 20, followed her in death—and again a mysterious bloodsucker was blamed." The article relates that "a doctor prescribed a dose of ashes of Mercy's heart dissolved in tonic" to "exorcise the demon" from Edwin. This description of the Mercy Brown case concludes: "That vampire still roams free in Chestnut Hill Cemetery, and is said to rage around that midnight fire that glows anew every Halloween in Exeter."

In these accounts, a reanimated Mercy continues to haunt Exeter, an open-ended sequel that contrasts sharply with the outcome related in oral versions still told in South County. As Everett Peck remarked, burning the heart "took care of it." Ninety-two-year-old Oliver Stedman, a local historian from the adjacent town of South Kingstown, echoed this traditional understanding of the event's finality: "They went an' cut the heart out, and burned it, there, and then they figured the whole thing was all over, it was all right . . . they'd fixed it, there'd be no more vampire."

Three days before Halloween, in 1979, a headline in the *Providence Sunday Journal Magazine*, asked, "What really happened to Mercy Brown?" The reader is led to believe that Mercy is still an active vampire:

> Let the scientists and the rest of the skeptics have their say. In their own dark little hearts they know there are strange things that even they can't explain. Maybe nobody could tape Mercy's voice, for instance, because she wasn't there when the recorder was. Vampires DO roam.

A related article in the same magazine continued the undead motif with, of course, the required soft touch:

> Mercy Brown died nearly 88 years ago. She was the fourth from her family in nine years. Life had been drained from all of them. Vampirism was the cause, everyone knew that. So why couldn't Mercy whisper from the grave again? The undead do . . . don't they?

No one can accuse these authors of assaulting the reader with facts. The whispers from Mercy's grave were recorded by a couple, Ed and Sally, who had positioned a running recorder at the grave to determine if Mercy was trying to communicate from her coffin.

The publication of their attempt to record Mercy's voice from the grave created a new kind of legend trip to Chestnut Hill Cemetery, as others began leaving tape recorders running at the gravesite during the night. Several claimed to hear whispering from the grave when the tapes were played back, adding to the belief that Mercy continued to haunt the cemetery. A local television news magazine's subsequent broadcast of a segment on Rhode Island's vampires included a follow-up interview with Ed and Sally:

> Ed: We have something from the grave, . . . definitely what it is, we don't know, but there's something that come off that tape recorder.

> Narrator: Ed and Sally . . . visited Mercy Brown's grave and claim they have evidence to confirm their belief that Mercy was a vampire. Inspired by a TV movie in which a tape recorder picked up voices of the dead, Ed and Sally decided to make their own recording.

> Ed: Whenever you get around this cemetery, my

feeling is that definitely there is something that roams around here at night. It's just that type of a place. It's a lonely, pretty desolate place, and anything is possible down here. And . . . there's something there, definitely.

Narrator: What that something is, Ed and Sally believe they have on their tape recorder.

Ed: I've heard the tape numerous times. I've sat down by myself and listened to it, on many occasions. And I can pick up where it sounds like she's sayin', "Please help me."

When a portion of the recording was played back, it sounded to me like white noise and hiss created by using inexpensive tape in a low-end tape recorder. The newspaper reporter who had earlier written about Ed and Sally's tape, surprisingly, had reached the same conclusion: "An investigation showed . . . that the built-in microphone in Sally's tape recorder wasn't picking up the sounds of a pleading vampire. It was hearing the scraping of the tape reel rubbing against the sides of a poorly made cassette." But those seeking supernatural explanations would not be deterred:

Sally: We really didn't expect anything, you know, at first . . . and then all of a sudden hearing that. It was really horrifying. Even Ed, he was scared. He says, "Yeah, let's get out of here. There's something in there."

Ed: Well, Mercy Brown was supposedly a vampire. And based on what I've read, and what I've talked about, and what I've heard about—she was a vampire. And 'til proven differently, I figure that she was a vampire.

The scene faded as eerie music played in the background. Ed's closing argument above closely resembled a number of answers given by the 27 percent who responded "yes" to the survey question, "Do you believe it is possible that vampires exist as real entities?" posed in Norine Dresser's book, *American Vampires*. Answers included, "No one has proved otherwise" and "I have no evidence to disprove their existence." The media have adopted the same position: Mercy is guilty of vampirism until proved innocent (and, of course, no such proof would ever be admitted into evidence).

While I was amused by what I saw as the media's inadvertent self-parody in this case (Ed was "inspired by a TV movie"), there was a more substantial implication to consider. If Ed and Sally were indeed inspired by media depictions of the supernatural, then it seemed reasonable to look more deeply into the role of "spirit-belief specialists," which role the mass media often seem to assume. In small, close-knit communities, it is typically an individual who functions as one of the "influential authorities, whose opinion, by virtue of their social prestige, becomes decisive" in interpreting an event as supernatural. In the Mercy Brown case, I had concluded that William Rose (perhaps through his second wife, a Tillinghast descendent) might well have been the one who counseled George Brown regarding the supernatural nature of his family's distress (see Chapter 4). The press, television, and movies now seem firmly entrenched in the legend process. As active bearers of tradition, *they* are the storytellers and spirit-belief specialists who interpret and shape, for a large number of people, the supernatural nature of events.

Community insiders, such as Everett Peck, however, still refer to established folk tradition. During our interview, Everett projected a rational, down-to-earth, hardheaded view of his family's story, the events that spawned it, and recent attempts to attach supernatural elements to Mercy's grave: "Well, they got some kind of soundin' devices to hear, uh, they say they hear things. Well, now, damn, you ain't gonna hear nothin'. . . . There may not even be *bones* left." And Everett is justly indignant at the vandalism that seems to accompany the legend tripping.

In the context of a newspaper or television interview, however, supernatural experiences are not just accepted, they are actively pursued for their commercial appeal. Television interviewers and newspaper feature writers seek out individuals, such as Ed and Sally (and Jennie Boldan, of Foster), who are willing to express a belief in vampires. Although they are usually outsiders who hold fringe views (in relation to expressed convictions of longtime community residents), their interpretations are portrayed by the media as typical or representative of the community's prevailing beliefs. Based on the examples I've gleaned from recent newspaper and television treatments, as well as my own direct experiences, I can only conclude that the media do not want to hear, indeed will not listen to, perhaps *cannot* hear, views that are not compatible with the popular conception of a vampire as exemplified by the Dracula of film.

The relationship between mass culture and local legend is not entirely antagonistic, at least insofar as vitality (if not veracity) is concerned; mass culture "nourishes legendry—providing it with fresh subject matter and speeding its dissemination." Norine Dresser even suggests that folklorists add the term "tubal transmission" to their glossary since "the television tube has become the tribal storyteller." The influence of mass media on the vampire tradition has been especially potent. Valid or not, mass-media accounts of the Mercy Brown incident have become part of the legend. In some orally transmitted versions told by outsiders and newcomers to South County, Mercy actually leaves the grave to suck her victim's blood and must be destroyed by driving a stake through her heart. Unlike Everett's family story, these tales do not hinge on a medical problem in desperate need of solution. They focus, instead, on Mercy as one of the living dead.

Differences in storytelling contexts are likewise revealing. Everett provided a compact description of the narrative's normal setting when he explained that the family was in the cemetery to honor the dead on Decoration Day or at the adjacent Grange for Children's Day. The story unfolded naturally, clarifying the admonition to avoid Mercy's gravestone and the rock where her heart was burned. In this context, the family story of Mercy Brown is an explanatory legend, providing the rationale for a specific tabu. From Everett's perspective, the tale was told for a practical reason rather than for entertainment per se (although, of course, the tale certainly may have entertained family members) or the sheer delight of fright, functions that seem preeminent in outsider versions. For instance, I interviewed a man who said that he tells the story to his children every Halloween, then drives them that night to visit Mercy's grave. He told me that the way he heard the story, a stake was driven through Mercy's heart.

Someone who is expected to recount a "supernatural occurrence"—to become a storyteller, as it were—feels various social pressures, the nature and effect of which depend upon a number of factors. Such recountings, generally referred to as *legends* by folklorists, are stories set in the real world of historical time, usually with named characters and places. Although they are often told as true, their truth is usually at least partially questionable or open to debate. While legends revolve around a memorable, stable core, their form tends to be unstable. Exactly how a legend takes shape is subject, in part, to the composition of the group of people who happen to be present: such elements as their personalities, beliefs, and attitudes, and their relationships to one another, help determine what kind of story gets told. For example, in the legend of Mercy Brown as told by the mass media for a mass audience, the focus of the conflict has shifted away from a family's effort to stop the onslaught of consumption—a folk medical practice—towards an encounter with the classic vampire of popular culture.

Even though the media might imply, or even label explicitly, that such a story is "history," they are not following the rules of historical interpretation; they are playing the entertainment game. As we move away from the actual, historical event (in time or place), the tragic aspects diminish as the supernatural elements are elaborated. The narrative has changed from a story "about sickness caused and cured by magic" into one of "encounters with agencies of the supernatural world." Over the past century, newspaper, magazine, and television stories have transformed this teenaged farm girl, an unfortunate victim of tuberculosis, into a Dracula clone, a role that neither history nor folklore can justify for her.

As a storyteller, Reuben Brown presents an intriguing case. Everett described him as "an old man livin' today who can remember one of the twelve"—referring to the twelve men who "got together" and decided to go ahead with the exhumations in 1892. Everett said that Reuben may or may not talk to people about the story, depending on how he's feeling. I must have caught him at a bad time, because he did not respond to my request for an interview when I approached him not long after my visit to Everett. But, shortly before his death in 1984, the eighty-seven year old descendent of the Mercy Brown family consented to an interview with a reporter from the *Providence Journal*. Part of his narrative is remarkable in its conformity to the popular pattern:

> The whole fearful matter started with unexplained deaths, says Reuben Brown. Young girls, six or seven on one side of the Brown family, pined away and died. All of them "had a mark on their throats."
>
> "People figured they'd been bit by a vampire . . . they all had that mark on them and nobody knows who made it," says Brown.
>
> Some folks were sure that Mercy—already gone to her grave—was the vampire.
>
> A dozen people got together—members of Mercy's family and others in the town—and decided to open the grave and pull Mercy's body into the sun-light to perform a terrible task.
>
> Reuben Brown had a friend who was there.
>
> "I used to know a man who saw them when they

unearthed her. He said he saw them cut her heart
out and burn it on the rock . . . it appeared that Mercy
had moved in the grave. She wasn't the way she was
put in there. . . .

"But he said there were no more deaths after that.
That's what he said."

Reuben Brown adds this footnote: "My father
believed she was a vampire. He said all those girls
had the mark on their throat when they died."

For me, Reuben's version of the legend raised more questions
than it answered. If his tale accurately portrayed the events, why
would such a striking detail as "a mark on their throats" not be
published in the newspaper accounts of 1892? Why did Everett's
story not include this motif? Did Reuben relate the story as it
was told to him? Was he playing with the reporter and, indirectly,
the public at large? Did he fill in details he could not recall? Did
he add details so that his tale corresponded with popular expectations? How much of his narrative was received tradition and
how much was shaped by the social tensions and the network of
identity and status relationships that he conceived to exist during
his interview with the newspaper reporter? Perhaps the overar-
ching, single question, I might ask is: Did Reuben Brown see his
storytelling role as one of history or entertainment?

The split between hard news and soft news did not develop
overnight in the world of journalism. Sidney Rider, who published, in an 1888 issue of his *Book Notes*, the account of Sarah
Tillinghast's vampiric assault on her family in late eighteenth-
century Exeter, chided the *Providence Journal* for what he saw as
their inconsistent policy on this issue when they refused to print
his article:

Once upon a time the writer [Sidney Rider] sent to
the *Providence Journal* upon invitation, an article
entitled the "Belief in Vampires in Rhode Island," in
which the origin of the myth was discussed, and an

instance narrated. The article was returned in due time with this note:

Dear Sir:—The enclosed blood curdling tale is rather too gruesome for the Sunday *Journal*, but I should think you could easily expand it into an article for some other paper which likes the sensational. Yours truly, R. S. Howland.

The article was not expanded, but it was sent to the New York *Evening Post*, in which it appeared, and from which it was reprinted in *Book Notes* vol. 5, p. 37. How was my chastened spirit shocked at these glaring headlines which I saw in the *Journal* of the 19th March, '92:

EXHUMED THE BODIES.

Testing a Horrible Superstition in
the Town of Exeter.

BODIES OF DEAD RELATIVES TAKEN
FROM THEIR GRAVES.

They Had All Died of Consumption, and the Belief Was That
Live Flesh and Blood Would Be Found That Fed Upon the
Bodies of the Living.

Nothing ghastly in those lines surely, Brother Howland, nor blood-curdling, nor gruesome. *Que m'importe.*

During a newspaper or television interview, it is supernatural experience, not historical interpretation, that is actively pursued for its commercial appeal. Vampires that do not fit the Hollywood model need not apply, no matter how authentic their historical or folkloric credentials. While researching the vampire tradition with the assistance of Joe Carroll, an intern from the Anthropology Department at Rhode Island College, I was contacted by a well-known local television newsman. He wanted to do a feature on haunted places in Rhode Island, including the cemetery where Nellie Vaughn is buried. Research and fieldwork may be the most interesting parts of my work as a consulting folklorist for a state agency, but public-sector folklorists are rightfully asked to make their findings intelligible and relevant to the general public, who, ultimately, have paid the bill. Ever the optimist, I see such requests as opportunities to balance the media's tendency to sensationalize at the expense of authenticity with some down-to-earth data. At this point, Dr. Rational tends to become cynical and usually asks Mike, "Did you ever hear of a 'Pollyanna'?" Then he looks for ways to bow out. So, I decided that this was a good opportunity to initiate Joe into some of the public-sector aspects of my position and asked if he'd like to stand in front of the camera and answer questions about Nellie Vaughn, a tale with which he was intimately acquainted.

Prior to a location shoot at Nellie Vaughn's gravesite, the newsman, Joe, and I discussed the legend. I emphasized the strong probability that the story of Nellie Vaughn as a vampire was the result of mistaking her for Mercy Brown. The newsman brought up the fact that no grass grows on her grave. Both Joe and I offered our opinion that there was no need to resort to supernatural explanations. Most likely, we suggested, nocturnal adolescent visitors ("legend trippers, as we folklorists call them," I told the interviewer) have destroyed the vegetation, just as they have damaged the gravestone itself.

The segment on Nellie Vaughn opened with music from the movie *The Shining*. The host began, "There are supposed to be twelve vampires in Rhode Island. You can believe that or not. But if you ever go by the West Greenwich Baptist Meeting House at Liberty Hill and Plain Roads, you probably will see a cemetery behind it. And if you go into the cemetery and look up Nellie Vaughn, you'll see that no grass grows around her grave. Nellie died at nineteen in the 1890s [actually, 1889], but it is said she walks around here quite often. Does she drink blood? Who knows? On her headstone is the inscription, 'I'll be watching and waiting for you' [actually, 'I am waiting and watching for you']."

The scene then cut to the cemetery, with Joe standing in front of Nellie's gravestone, which was broken and lying on the ground. He said, matter of factly, "It's not really that sinister when you think about it. It's common for a lot of tombstones that are out here. It just simply means 'I'm in heaven, waiting.' Part of the legend is that no grass grows on her grave. . . . "

The host interrupted with a question. "Is that true of all vampires?"

The camera panned to Joe, stunned and groping for words. The question presupposed that Nellie was a vampire, so any answer that he gave would at least tacitly accept that point. An on-the-air moment of silence seems like an eternity. Finally, Joe said, "Uh, I don't know. I'm not sure of all vampires." Collecting himself, Joe tried to reintroduce rationality, "But I think it's because people come out here to her grave and try to dig it up."

His was just a voice in the wind. The scary music started again. Cut to the host: "It's no secret that Nellie is here," he said solemnly. "But it still remains a mystery about what she's doing."

That was the entire Nellie Vaughn segment. Still a mystery to me is the "mystery about what she's doing." I should have realized that Joe and I were fighting a tradition of soft news that was a stronger adversary than any vampire, real or imagined.

Why would anyone prefer fictional vampires to authentic ones? I hadn't given the question much serious thought until an encounter I had when I was lecturing about New England's vampires to a class of students attending a prestigious art college. As I related the stories of rural families who dug up the bodies of their loved ones and burned their hearts to save the living, I tried to convey the reasonableness of actions taken centuries ago. These were ordinary farmers, I explained, who were confronted with an illness that medicine could neither explain nor cure. So they did something people everywhere had done for as long as there is memory or record. They blamed the dead. Fundamentally, I argued, the New England vampire practice was perhaps better understood as folk medicine rather than supernatural belief. After class, a student complained that her image of vampires would never again be the same. At first, I felt apologetic that I had destroyed her long-held icon. Later, I wondered why a person would want to cling to a tired, trite symbol. In her wonderful book on American vampires, folklorist Norine Dresser devoted an entire chapter to the lure of the vampire. She wrote that the "sanitized and romanticized" vampire "appears to be an appropriate symbol for contemporary American life—he is lonely, secular, glorifies (sometimes abuses) power, and enjoys sexual freedom." Vampires in novels, such as those by Anne Rice, may be updated as rock stars and contemporary thrill seekers, but deep inside, where it really matters, they are still Count Dracula. Could any other figure serve so well as a metaphor for the darker side of human nature? What better food for the imagination than a creature that incorporates sex, blood, violence, shape-shifting, superhuman power, and eternal life?

By the early twentieth century, vampires had disappeared from their natural countryside setting. But they found a welcome home in the world of entertainment. In a sense, and ironically, those who argued during the nineteenth century that civilization was on the verge of eradicating the last vestiges of primitive survivals were correct, at least regarding vampires. Science *had* banished them, but they were eagerly adopted by a smitten popular media. Once the vampire practice became an oddity of history, rather than a ritual actually performed by people living only several miles down the road, everyone could relax and enjoy the horror vicariously. Today's newspaper readers and television viewers, confident in their sophistication and numbed by Hollywood's onslaught of celluloid vampires, can now be entertained by New England's "quaint vampires."

CHAPTER 14
Food for the Dead

I n the vast stretch of human history before the twentieth century, disease was an accepted part of life, ever-present and endured. In a momentous turnaround, almost everyone alive today in Western industrial states was brought up believing in the inevitable conquest of disease. After all, hadn't vaccines, antibiotics, modern hygiene, and aggressive public health campaigns all but eradicated such feared scourges as tuberculosis, pneumonia, small pox, polio, and measles? But on the way to a disease-free world, some terrible things have shaken our complacency. New infectious enemies, such as AIDS, Ebola, West Nile virus, and potent strains of food-poisoning bacteria have appeared, and some old ones, particularly tuberculosis and pneumonia, have reemerged. Viruses with exotic names and distant origins— Hanta, Hendra, Nipah—have shown the adaptability of microbial adversaries *and* the vulnerability even of modern medicine. Infectious diseases are now the world's leading killer of children and young adults, accounting for thirteen million deaths per year. In the United States, mortality from infectious diseases increased 58 percent from 1980 to 1992. Ironically, we are now closer to 1892 than we were in the 1950s, when breakthroughs such as Dr. Jonas Salk's polio vaccine were introduced.

"What is happening now is not surprising, or shouldn't be surprising," said Dr. D. A. Henderson, the director of the Johns Hopkins University Center for Civilian Biodefense Studies in Baltimore. "I think we've gone through a period when we believed we had whipped infectious diseases. But mutations and change are part of nature. What is surprising is the frequency and severity of the outbreaks."

Not surprisingly, the unfamiliarity of these viruses already has led to misdiagnosis and incorrect treatment. The medical community is under stress trying to diagnose ailments where the symptoms do not point clearly to a specific disease. The pressure is compounded by often having only hours or days to begin treatment.

To make matters worse, we are witnessing the evolution of bacteria resistant to specific medicines. Extensive, indiscriminate use of antibiotics may have put some microbes on an evolutionary fast track that keeps them always a step ahead. Antibiotic-resistant hospital infections are of particular concern. Each year, nearly two million patients in the United States contract an infection as a result of a hospital stay. About 70 percent of the bacteria causing such infections are resistant to at least one of the drugs most commonly used to treat them. In some cases, these organisms are resistant to all approved antibiotics, so patients must be treated with experimental and potentially toxic drugs.

Alarmingly, new strains of drug-resistant tuberculosis have appeared. In 1993, the World Health Organization declared tuberculosis to be a global emergency. Statistics issued in their recent Global Reports are frightening. Tuberculosis is still the world's leading cause of death due to an infectious agent, killing almost three million people each year. Much of the world's population is infected with tuberculosis, and about eight million new cases occur annually. Challenged now is the smug belief that tuberculosis is strictly confined to marginalized populations, such as those living in the Third World, newly arrived immigrants, the homeless, people with chemical dependencies, and those made vulnerable because of AIDS.

Even the commonly accepted belief that tuberculosis declined dramatically in the twentieth century mainly because of chemotherapy is now being questioned. As Barbara Bates has pointed out in her social history of tuberculosis, many observers "now attribute the decline of tuberculosis chiefly to socioeco-

nomic changes," primarily a rise in the standard of living accompanied by less crowded conditions in the cities. A more cold-
blooded, Darwinian explanation is offered by others: through the
process of natural selection, those susceptible to the disease simply
died off.

Spread by people on the move in a shrinking world, tuberculosis and the other newly virulent diseases, along with the
emerging diseases (many of which also are dispersed by vectors
such as birds, insects, and fish—not to mention mad cows), have
reintroduced uncertainty and fear. Today, few doubt the microbial
basis for these afflictions. Moreover, if evolutionary biologist Paul
Ewald is correct, a number of ailments not previously considered
as having a microbial origin, including Alzhiemer's, schizophrenia,
and certain forms of cancer and heart disease, would join the
recently added peptic ulcers as chronic infections, "slow-motion
plagues that are difficult to recognize and difficult to control."
Uncertainty swirls around a great many of the diseases—old, new,
and evolving—that are having a major impact on the world's
health.

The mystery resides not only in the nature of the plagues
unleashed from Pandora's box, but also in how they got there in
the first place, who opened the box, and why. Those outside the
mainstream are no longer opening graves for answers. Interacting
on the Internet instead of face-to-face, as in traditional societies,
they are looking to conspiracies perpetrated by various governmental agencies, including the Central Intelligence Agency, U.S.
military, and the Food and Drug Administration, or by radical
groups engaged in bioterrorism. Their "explanations" range from
various economic, political, and ideological agendas to biological
warfare gone awry to deliberate attempts to annihilate excess or
targeted populations. Years ago, Susan Sontag wrote that "cancer
is now in the service of a simplistic view of the world that can
turn paranoid." A host of infectious diseases have now joined
cancer. Paranoid suppositions have replaced horrible superstitions—and these paranoid theories are as hard to disprove as to
prove. Humbled by our own era's failure to conquer disease, per-

haps we can appreciate the fear and uncertainty that tuberculosis engendered one and two centuries ago.

It is no coincidence that the tuberculosis/vampire epidemic accompanied the industrial revolution and increasing urbanization in New England. Industrialization began at Slater Mill, in Pawtucket, Rhode Island, in 1792; the first reported vampire case occurred in 1793. In other parts of the United States, tuberculosis did not become a problem until industrialization and urbanization created the conditions that aided and abetted its transmission. By that time, new scapegoats (the tubercle bacillus in conjunction with poverty, overcrowding and unsanitary conditions), as well as the general acceptance of embalming, had eliminated the need for exhumation and heart-burning. As early as 1848, F. H. Davis noticed that consumption seemed to follow in the wake of industrialization:

> In the early settlements of this country, New England and the N. E. States were as free from consumption as are now the much vaunted far-western States and Territories. It was immediately consequent upon the change from an agricultural to a manufacturing population that the rapid increase in the death-rate from consumption is apparent in these States. Fifteen or twenty years ago Indiana, Illinois and the Lake region were the favorite resorts for consumptive patients. . . . Now we have a constantly increasing proportion of cases originating in this same region, not evidently from any change that has taken place in the climatic conditions, but from the change in the occupation and hygienic surroundings of the people.

These factors may help explain why only two cases of vampirism in North America have been reported outside of New England proper (Chicago, in 1875, and Ontario, Canada, sometime prior to 1893). Perhaps the following vampire account, published in 1898, and located at Lake Seneca, in the Finger Lakes region of

New York, can be related to the in-migration of Vermonters and other New Englanders in the late 1700s following the Revolution:

> The superstition of the vampire, that horror of the grave which was supposed to harbor the dead yet derive its sustenance from the living, had one illustration at least about Seneca Lake. Down the western shore not many miles from its head, in the early years the corpse of a young woman was exhumed, and the heart and other vital parts committed to the flames. The grewsome tale comports in a remarkable manner with the general sayings in regard to vampires. Of several sisters, all in succession had wasted away, until one remained and she was ill. Though in the grave for many months, the burned portions of the body were fresh in appearance. The living sister, undoubtedly from mental relief, recovered her health after the event.

The evidence establishing the existence of the vampire practice in New England seems incontrovertible: eyewitness accounts, old newspaper articles, local histories, journal entries, unpublished correspondence, genealogies, cemeteries, and gravestones, archaeological excavations, and oral traditions (including family folklore and local legends) suggest that the practice was widely accepted in the non–Puritan countryside. The documentation that has been preserved and has come to my attention probably represents a very small percentage of the exhumations that were carried out. I had never dared hope to find an official record that granted permission to exhume bodies or perform autopsies—a "smoking gun," if you will. The discovery of JB's skeleton in Connecticut was as serendipitous as possible.

Then, Ruth Herndon appeared in my office. Ruth was an acquaintance of mine who was completing her doctoral dissertation in history. Her topic was the role of women in colonial Rhode

Island as revealed in town records. Ruth and I were putting together some research to present at a forum on maritime traditions and, for some reason, I mentioned my vampire research (I admit, it is never far from my thoughts). Suddenly excited, Ruth leapt from her chair and shouted, "*That's* what it means!" She explained that, while searching town records, she came across an entry from the town of Cumberland that she found very puzzling. She described its contents and later mailed a copy of this entry from the town council meeting of February 8, 1796:

> Mr Stephen Staples of Cumberland appeared before This Council and Prayed that he Might have Liberty Granted unto him to Dig up the body of his Dofter [sic] Abigail Staples Late of Cumberland Single Woman Deceased In order to Try an Experiment on Livina Chace Wife of Stephen Chace Which Said Livina Was Sister to the Said Abigail Deceased Which being Duly Considered it is Voted and Resolved that the Said Stephen Staples have Liberty to Dig up the Body of the Said Abigail Deceased and after Trying the Experiment as aforesaid that he bury the Body of the Said Abigail In a Deasent Manner[.]

While reading this remarkable document, I shared Ruth's excitement and sense of discovery. I exulted in this concrete validation that the practice of exhumation was not entirely marginalized, but was part of the social fabric of a community.

This solitary record of the Staples case is so indefinite that someone not familiar with the vampire practice in New England would be hard pressed to decipher what kind of "experiment" Mr. Staples might be seeking permission to try. But, what else could it be? As vague as this entry is, neither Ruth nor I could come up with any other possible interpretation. Could anyone expect such a grisly matter involving individuals known in the community to be spelled out more clearly, given the circumspect nature of New Englanders, and bearing in mind that this is an *official* record that would be open for all to see, then and in the future. The entry includes enough detail to meet the requirements of maintaining a town record, but not enough to embarrass either Mr. Staples or the Town of Cumberland.

Cumberland, in the extreme northeastern corner of Rhode Island, is hilly with rocky and uneven terrain. The town's western boundary is the Blackstone River, named after the first white settler, William Blackstone. Although he arrived about 1635, when Cumberland was on the edge of Plymouth Colony, Massachusetts (site of a vampire exhumation about 1807), significant settlement did not begin until the eighteenth century. By 1747, when the town was annexed to Rhode Island and its name changed from the Attleboro Gore to Cumberland, there were just over 800 inhabitants. This number more than doubled over the next thirty years as family farms were cleared in the river valleys and less severe uplands, and small villages grew up around churches, shops, or grist mills and saw mills. Iron ore was mined in several locations, but the community was still rural and dispersed when Staples' request was granted by the Cumberland Town Council.

There is a death record for Stephen Staples of Cumberland in the *Providence Gazette*, showing that he died on April 8, 1815. Abigail Staples of Cumberland, child of Stephen and Susannah, is given a birth date of January 26, 1773. Had she died within the year of her exhumation, she would have been about 22 or 23 years old at the time of her death. Although permission was granted for the exhumation, there is no evidence that Abigail's corpse was indeed exhumed. Only days ago, I learned where the Staples family plot may be located, so I will still be following this trail in the years ahead.

A few years ago I had a conversation with a professor who was teaching a class in women's studies. She suggested that the vampire practice was the rest of New England's equivalent to the persecution of witches in Puritan Massachusetts. I responded,

"At least they were *already dead* when they became scapegoats." Like so many novelists, painters, and Medal of Honor winners, these individuals achieved renown only posthumously. While it is impossible to replace their hearts or restore their mutilated bodies, we *can* acknowledge their unwitting role in providing a measure of hope to desperate families.

In the final analysis, the anonymous poet who wrote—on the occasion of witnessing the exhumation of the bodies of an entire family in Plymouth, Massachusetts—that "the living was food for the dead" had it backwards. It was the *dead* who gave sustenance to the *living*.

Appendix A: Chronology of Vampire Incidents in New England

Date	Name of Vampire	Place
1793	Rachel Harris	Manchester, Vermont
1794 or 98	Reuben or Josiah Spaulding	Dummerston, Vermont
1796	Abigail Staples	Cumberland, Rhode Island
c. 1799	Sarah Tillinghast	Exeter, Rhode Island
c. 1799	Anonymous woman	Loudon, New Hampshire
c. late 1700s to early 1800s	JB	Griswold, Connecticut
1807	Anonymous sister	Plymouth, Massachusetts
1807	Frederick Ransom	Woodstock, Vermont
1810	Janey Denitt	Barnstead, New Hampshire
1827	Nancy Young	Foster, Rhode Island
c. 1830	Corwin brother	Woodstock, Vermont
c. 1847–62	Several anonymous	Saco, Maine
1854	Lemuel and Elisha Ray	Jewett City, Connecticut
1874	Ruth Ellen Rose	Exeter, Rhode Island
1875	Anonymous woman	Chicago, Illinois★
c. 1872–88	Anonymous sister(s)	West Stafford, Connecticut
1889	Nellie Vaughn	West Greenwich, Rhode Island
1892	Mercy Brown	Exeter, Rhode Island
c. before 1893	Anonymous	Ontario, Canada★
c. before 1898	Anonymous sister(s)	Seneca Lake, New York★

★ Incidents reported outside of New England

Appendix B: Children of Stukely and Honor Tillinghast

Child	Birth	Death
Anna	1763	?
Amos	1764	1858
Stephen	1766	1845
Amay (Amey)	1767	?
Honour (Honor)	1769	1866
Pardon	1771	1854
Hannah	1772	1800
Stukey (Stukely), Jr.	1774	1848
Mary	1776	1863
Sarah	1777	1799
Ruth	1780	1799
Andris (Aunstis)	1782	1799
Clark	1782	1832
James	1786	1799 or 1810

NOTES

Interview transcripts are taken from tape-recorded interviews that are housed at the Rhode Island Folklife Archive, Providence, Rhode Island.

NUMBER BEFORE ENDNOTE INDICATES PAGE IN BOOK

Chapter 1

10. "Rhode Island's past hides many . . . 'I don't know what I believe.' ": Paul F. Eno, "They Burned Her Heat ... Was Mercy Brown a Vampire?" *Narragansett Times* 25 October 1979, p. 1-SC.

Chapter 2

22. "The old superstition . . . called to attend him.": *Providence Journal*, 21 March 1892, p. 8.

22. For an overview of consumption, see Rene Dubos and Jean Dubos, *The White Plague: Tuberculosis, Man and Society* (Boston: Little, Brown and Company, 1952), p. 5.

23. For a summary of TB's history and treatment, see Ken Chowder, "TB: The Disease That Rose from Its Grave." *Smithsonian* 23, no. 8 (November 1992), pp. 180–94.

25. "In the future the fight . . . with a tangible parasite.": Mark Caldwell, *The Last Crusade: The War on Consumption, 1862–1954*, (New York: Atheneum, 1988), p. 160.

26. For an identification of competing medical paradigms, see Horacio Fábrega, Jr., *Evolution of Sickness and Healing*, (Berkeley and Los Angeles: University of California Press, 1997), p. 13.

27. For a discussion of the four "humors," especially blood, see Douglas Starr, *Blood: An Epic History of Medicine and Commerce*, (New York: Alfred A. Knopf, 1998), p. 5.

28. "It was heroic . . . the dangerous skill of physicians.": Bruno Gebhard, "The Interrelationship of Scientific and Folk Medicine in the United States of America Since 1850," in *American Folk Medicine: A Symposium*, edited by Wayland D. Hand, 87–98 (Berkeley: University of California Press, 1980), p. 91.

28. For a discussion of Samuel Thomson's *New Guide*, see J. Worth Estes, "Samuel Thomson Rewrites Hippocrates," in *Medicine and Healing*, edited by Peter Benes, Annual Proceedings of the Dublin Seminar for New England Folklife, 113–32 (Boston: Boston University, 1992).

29. The list of healing specialists appears in Peter Benes, "Itinerant Physicians, Healers, and Surgeon-Dentists in New England and New York, 1720–1825," in *Medicine and Healing*, edited by Peter Benes, Annual Proceedings of the Dublin Seminar for New England Folklife, 95–112 (Boston: Boston University, 1992), pp. 109–11.

29. "New Englanders gathered . . . from public acceptance and recognition.": Peter Benes, "Itinerant Physicians," p. 107.

29. For consumption and mortality rates, see Dubos and Dubos, *The White Plague*, pp. 9–10, and Sheila M. Rothman, *Living in the Shadow of Death: Tuberculosis and the Social Experience of Illness in American History* (Baltimore: The Johns Hopkins University Press, 1994), p. 2.

29. The progression of consumption's symptoms is described in Rothman, *Living in the Shadow of Death*, p. 4.

29. "Galloping" consumption is described in Dubos and Dubos, *The White Plague*, p. 205.

30. "feelings about evil . . . projected onto the world." Susan Sontag, *Illness as Metaphor* (New York: Farrar, Straus and Giroux, 1978), pp. 58–59.

30. "appears to be built up . . . enervating luxuries among the rich.": Dubos and Dubos, *The White Plague*, p. 197.

30. For Baron's geographic correlations, see John Baron, *Illustrations of the Enquiry Respecting Tuberculosis Diseases* (London: T. and G. Underwood, 1882).

31. The index list for "Therapeutics" appears in Rothman, *Living in the Shadow of Death*, p. 317.

31. "It is important to realize . . . they could do something, anything.": Starr, *Blood*, p. 30.

31. "consumptive patients are still . . . the fatal catastrophe.": Walter R. Bett, ed., *The History and Conquest of Common Diseases* (Norman, Oklahoma: University of Oklahoma Press, 1954), p. 433.

31. "a disease of incomplete civilization.": Dubos and Dubos, *The White Plague*, p. 219.

32. "The former high mortality . . . diminished by improved hygiene.": Edwin A. Locke, ed., *Tuberculosis in Massachusetts* (Boston: Wright & Potter, 1908), p. xi.

32. "are scarcely ever heard . . . regards this destructive disease.": Logan Clendening, comp., *Source Book of Medical History* (New York: Dover Publications, Inc., 1960), p. 434.

32. "epidemics do not usually . . . mythologize them in the same way.": Paul Barber, *Vampires, Burial, and Death: Folklore and Reality* (New Haven: Yale University Press, 1988), p. 121.

32. For a discussion of contagion, fear and vampires, see Barber, *Vampires*, p. 37.

33. "began to give evidence . . . his wife followed him later on.": Letter to the editor, *Pawtuxet Valley Gleaner*, 25 March 1892, p. 5.

33. For a description of the development of Colorado Springs, see Rothman, *Living in the Shadow of Death*, pp. 141–42.

33. "Our young fellow townsman, . . . the parents of Mrs. Brown.": *Pawtuxet Valley Gleaner*, 26 February 1892, p. 1.

34. "Watchers could administer medicine . . . if death seemed imminent.": Jack Larkin, *The Reshaping of Everyday Life, 1790–1840* (New York: Harper Perennial, 1988), p. 93.

35. "If the good wishes . . . restored to perfect health.": *Pawtuxet Valley Gleaner*, 26 February 1892, p. 1.

36. "the husband and father . . . any faith at all in the vampire theory.": Letter to the editor, *Pawtuxet Valley Gleaner*, 25 March 1892, p. 5.

37. "no confidence in the old-time theory.": *Providence Journal*, 19 March 1892, 3.

37. For a discussion of the concept of belief in relation to closely related "psychological verbs," see Rodney Needham, *Belief, Language and Experience* (London: Oxford University Press, 1972) pp. 93–94.

37. "several friends and neighbors . . . autopsy of the bodies.": *Providence Journal*, 21 March 1892, p. 8.

38. For a discussion of folk medicine and healing in the context of community, see Don Yoder, "Folk Medicine," in *Folklore and Folklife: An Introduction*, edited by Richard M. Dorson, pp. 191–215 (Chicago: University of Chicago Press, 1972).

38. "The shocking case of exhumation . . . have made scarcely any impression.": *Providence Journal*, 20 March 1892, p. 4.

Chapter 3

39. "not a word could he get . . . and died a fortnight later.": Thomas Robinson Hazard, *The Jonny-Cake Papers of "Shepherd Tom", Together with Reminiscences of Narragansett Schools of Former Days* (Boston: The Merrymount Press, 1915), pp. 247–48.

47. "How the tradition got to . . . and the neighboring towns.": *Providence Journal*, 21 March 1892, 8.

48. "corpse which comes from the grave at night and sucks blood.": Stith Thompson, *Motif-Index of Folk Literature: A Classification of Narrative Elements in Folktales, Ballads, Myths, Fables, Mediaeval Romances, Exempla, Fabliaux, Jest-Books and Local Legends*. Revised and enlarged ed. 1932–36 (Bloomington, Indiana: Indiana University Press, 1955–58), v. 2, p. 424.

48. "William Laudun, a brave English knight . . . recorded by William of Newburgh.": George Lyman Kittredge, *Witchcraft in Old and New England* (Cambridge, Massachusetts: Harvard University Press, 1929), p. 43.

49. "The German vampire . . . or demons in bird form.": Kittredge, *Witchcraft*, pp. 166–67.

49. Kittredge, *Witchcraft*, pp. 224–25.

50. George R. Stetson, "The Animistic Vampire in New England," *American Anthropologist* 9 (1896), p. 3.

50. "the vampire does not stop . . . the Rhode Island belief.": Stetson, "The Animistic Vampire," p. 5.

50. "By some mysterious survival . . . this remarkable superstition.": Stetson, "The Animistic Vampire," 7.

50. "The first visit in this farming community . . . adjoining villages in two families.": Stetson, "The Animistic Vampire," pp. 8–10

55. "A photograph we've seen shows him a big, husky young man.": James Earl Clauson, "Vampirism in Rhode Island," in *These Plantations*, 67–69 (Providence, Rhode Island: Roger Williams Press, 1937), p. 67.

56. "During the year 1854 . . . burned them there on the spot.": Montague Summers, *The Vampire in Europe* (New York: E. P. Dutton and Company, Inc., 1929), p. 116.

56. "*The Providence Journal* in 1874 . . . her surviving relatives.": Summers, *The Vampire in Europe*, pp. 116–17.

Chapter 4

58. The identification of Stoker's Dracula with Vlad is made in Raymond T. McNally and Radu Florescu, *In Search of Dracula* (Greenwich, Connecticut: New York Graphic Society, 1972).

59. "Count Dracula and Vlad the Impaler . . . so many about so little.": Elizabeth Miller, *Dracula: Sense & Nonsense* (Westcliff-on-Sea: Desert Island Books, 2000), p. 180.

59. Mercy Brown's case is included in Raymond McNally, *A Clutch of Vampires* (New York: New York Graphic Society, 1974).

59. "And in Peace Dale, . . . to deliver his 4 p.m. lecture.": Fritz Koch, "R. I. Latter-Day Transylvania?" *Providence Evening Bulletin*, 25 February 1975, pp. 1, A8.

60. "I know that William Rose . . . on which he performed sacrifices.": Raymond McNally, letter to author, 7 July 1994.

60. For a description of the beginnings of URI, see Carl R. Woodward, "Kingston's Cultural Heritage," *Rhode Island Yearbook* (1970), pp. 57–68.

61. "It was a warm summer night . . . not any more' ": "Campus Haunted by Ghost of Man Dead Since 1884," *The Good 5¢ Cigar* 5 (29 April 1975), p. 6.

63. "In 1874, according to . . . other members of his family.": Moncure Daniel Conway, *Demonology and Devil-Lore* (New York: Henry Holt and Company, 1879), p. 52.

64. "William C. [sic] Rose of Peace Dale . . . showed no record of the family.": James A.

Revson, "19th Century Rhode Islanders Lived in Fear of Vampire Attacks," *Westerly Sun*, 24 July 1977, p. 18.

64. "Obituary of Ruth Ellen Rose." *Narragansett Times*, 15 May 1874.

65. "At the breaking out of . . . took place to recover.": Sidney S. Rider, "The Belief in Vampires in Rhode Island," *Book Notes* 5, no. 7 (1888), pp. 37–39.

69. For dream motifs, see Stith Thompson, *Motif-Index of Folk Literature: A Classification of Narrative Elements in Folktales, Ballads, Myths, Fables, Mediaeval Romances, Exempla, Fabliaux, Jest-Books and Local Legends*. Revised and enlarged ed. 1932–36 (Bloomington, Indiana: Indiana University Press, 1955–58), v. 6, p. 228.

69. For death and misfortune heralded by dreams in folk narrative, see Lowry Charles Wimberly, *Death and Burial Lore in the English and Scottish Popular Ballads*, University of Nebraska Studies in Language, Literature, and Criticism, no. 8. (Lincoln, Nebraska: University of Nebraska, 1927), p. 87.

69. "to dream that a tree is uprooted in your garden is regarded as a death warning to the owner.": Charlotte Latham, "Some West Sussex Superstitions Lingering in 1868," *Folk-Lore Record* 1 (1878), p. 58.

70. "The conditions here narrated . . . believe in them.": Sidney S. Rider, "The Belief in Vampires," p. 39.

71. Sidney S. Rider, "Exeter Notes," unpublished notes in *Rider Collection* (Rider Collection, housed at John Hay Library, Brown University, Providence, Rhode Island), Box 300, no. 6, [c. 1887].

72. "lucrative business in rum and molasses . . . known as 'Molasses Pardon.' ": J. R. Cole, *History of Washington and Kent Counties, Rhode Island* (New York: W.. Preston & Co., 1889), p. 686.

72. For a discussion of the Hazard family's nicknames, see Wilkins Updike, *A History of the Episcopal Church in Narragansett, Rhode Island*, 2d ed. (Boston: The Merrymount Press, 1907), v. 1, p. 282.

74. "one of the leading antislavery . . . in the nineteenth century.": Joseph Conforti, "Samuel Hopkins and the Revolutionary Antislavery Movement," *Rhode Island History* 38, no. 2 (1979), p. 39.

74. "disinterested benevolence, . . . pursuit of his own salvation.": Conforti, "Samuel Hopkins," p. 39.

76. "A person who has experienced . . . social prestige, becomes decisive.": Lauri Honko, "Memorates and the Study of Folk Beliefs," *Journal of the Folklore Institute* 1 (1964), pp. 3–19.

77. "besieged on all sides . . . faith in the old theory.": *Providence Journal*, 19 March 1892, p. 3.

Chapter 5

81. "Another tale of vampirism . . . and watching for you.' ": James A. Revson, "19th Century Rhode Islanders Lived in Fear of Vampire Attacks," *Westerly Sun*, 24 July 1977, p. 18.

82. "But the biggest irritant, . . . dig up the coffin.": Richard C. Dujardin, "An Unusual Tradition at an Unusual Church," *Providence Journal-Bulletin*, 9 October 1982, p. A7.

85. "to exhume a body . . . spirit restless forever.": Harry Middleton Hyatt, *Folk-Lore from Adams County, Illinois*, edition no. 2 revised. 1935 (New York: Memoirs of the Alma Egan Hyatt Foundation, 1965) #15414.

94. "Many in [North Kingstown] know . . . unearthing these haunting tales.": Chris Carroll, "Local Haunts," *North Kingstown Villager*, October 1995.

98. " . . . Nelly is trying to vindicate . . . that she is somehow evil.": Charles Turek Robinson, *The New England Ghost Files: An Authentic Compendium of Frightening Phantoms* (North Attleboro, MA: Covered Bridge Press, 1994), p. 193.

99. "If one's grave sinks very much, another member of the family will die soon.": Wayland D. Hand, ed., *Popular Beliefs and Superstitions from North Carolina*, Vol. 6–7 of *Frank C. Brown Collection of North Carolina Folklore* (Durham, North Carolina: Duke University Press, 1964), #s 5526–27.

99. "If the grave is sunk . . . transformed himself into a vampire.": Quoted in Paul Barber, *Vampires, Burial, and Death: Folklore and Reality* (New Haven: Yale University Press, 1988), p. 69.

100. For a discussion of supplying the dead with money, see Sir James George Frazer, *Fear of the Dead in Primitive Religion*, 1933–36 (New York [London]: Arno Press, Macmillan, 1977), p. 193.

100. For examples of "paying the spirit," see Harry Middleton Hyatt, *Hoodoo, Conjuration, Witchcraft, Rootwork*, Memoirs of the Alma Egan Hyatt Foundation (Hannibal, Missouri: Western Publishing, Inc., 1970–78), v. 4, pp. 3316–23.

100. The Romanian examples are in Barber, *Vampires*, pp. 47–49.

100. "Another thing my mother . . . have money on his way.": Hyatt, *Folk-Lore from Adams County*, #15200. See also Hand, *Popular Beliefs and Superstitions*, #5424, and Vance Randolph, *Ozark Magic and Folklore*, original title of work: *Ozark Superstitions*, 1947 (New York: Dover Publications, Inc., 1964), p. 313.

104. " . . . just before dark, we . . . at least 10 miles away.": Kevin Sullivan, "A Journey Through Old Rhode Island: Quietly but in Vain, the Rural Areas Try to Fend Off Modernity," *Providence Sunday Journal*, 27 May 1990, p. A-1.

104. "Two couples out for . . . upon the opened grave.": George E. Trafford, "Four Looking for Vampire Find Casket, Opened Grave," *Providence Journal-Bulletin*, 2 November 1993, p. B8.

107. "You can't stop these . . . what they want.": Norine Dresser, *American Vampires: Fans, Victims, Practitioners* (New York: W.. Norton & Company, 1989), p. 68.

107. James A. Merolla, "Vandals Steal Mercy Brown's Gravestone," *Providence Journal*, 16 August 1996, pp. B-1&3, and Merolla, "Mercy Brown Grave Marker Recovered," *Providence Journal*, 21 August 1996, pp. B-1&3.

108. The Tillinghast genealogical connection is made in *Pardon's Progeny: A Publication of the Tillinghast Family in America* 10, no. 1 (Spring 1983), pp. 2–3.

Chapter 6

119. "William Potter purchased the sawmill . . . "haunted" in the 1885 census.": Rhode Island Historical Preservation Commission, *Statewide Historical Preservation Report P-F-1: Foster, Rhode Island* (Providence, Rhode Island: Rhode Island Historical Preservation Commission, 1982), p. 69.

Chapter 7

141. The reprinted article about Nancy Young is Casey B. Tyler, "Interesting Notes of Foster in 1827: Capt. Young's Purchase," *Pawtuxet Valley Gleaner*, 8 October 1892, p. 4.

148. For the interaction among tradition, community and personality in the legend process, see Linda Dégh, "Processes of Legend Formation," in *IVth International Congress for Folk-Narrative Research in Athens: Lectures and Reports*, edited by Georgios A. Megas, 77–87. Athens, 1965.

148. For the collective nature of legends, see Patrick B. Mullen, "Modern Legend and Rumor

Theory," *Journal of the Folklore Institute* 9 (1972), p. 102; for the combining of traditional and popular elements in local legends, see Ronald L. Baker, "Legends About Spook Light Hill," *Indiana Folklore* 3 (1970), p. 172.

148. For a discussion of recounting what *should have* occurred, see Lauri Honko, "Memorates and the Study of Folk Beliefs," *Journal of the Folklore Institute* 1 (1964), pp. 3–19.

149. The 1979 article referred to is C. Eugene Emery, Jr., "Did They Hear the Vampire Whisper?" *Providence Sunday Journal Magazine*, 28 October 1979, pp. 6–7, 10, 12–13.

150. For a discussion of lights that appear over the graves of murder victims, see Lowry Charles Wimberly, *Folklore in the English and Scottish Ballads*, 1928 (New York: Dover Publications, Inc., 1965), p. 82.

150. The blue glow is discussed by Paul Barber, *Vampires, Burial, and Death: Folklore and Reality* (New Haven: Yale University Press, 1988), p. 70.

150. "Suddenly, away on our ... in a moving circle.": Clive Leatherdale, ed., *Dracula Unearthed* (Westcliff-on-Sea: Desert Island Books, 1998), pp. 44–45.

151. "There has lately a ... these six weeks past.": Peter Kalm, *The America of 1750: Peter Kalm's Travels in North America*, the English version of 1770, edited by Adolph B. Benson (New York: Dover Publications, 1966), p. 669.

Chapter 8

158. "A strange and almost incredible ... enlightened and christian [sic].": "Strange Superstition," *Norwich Weekly Courier*, 24 May 1854, p. 2.

159. "the plight of the young man ... undergone such horrors.": Maria Hileman, "Reporter's 'Stakeout' Puts Bite on Vampires," *Norwich Bulletin*, 31 October 1976, p. 24.

159. "Unfortunately there is neither ... had saved his life." David E. Philips, *Legendary Connecticut: Traditional Tales from the Nutmeg State*, 2d ed. 1984 (Williamantic, Connecticut: Curbstone Press, 1992), pp. 245–46.

161. "In the old West Stafford ... performed during that year.": J. R. Cole, *The History of Tolland County, Connecticut* (New York: W. W. Preston & Co., 1888), p. 499.

165. "Almost every family has ... may have been the graves.": Henry I[ngersoll] Bowditch, *Consumption in New England and Is Consumption Contagious?* 1862 (New York: Arno Press, 1977), p. 50.

166. "No person shall remove ... permission of the Board of Health.": "Majority Report on Establishing a New Board of Health," Boston City Document No. 108, 1872, pp. 13–14.

166. A description of the excavation of the Walton Family Cemetery is in Nicholas F. Bellantoni, Paul S. Sledzik, and David A. Poirier, "Rescue, Research, and Reburial: Walton Family Cemetery, Griswold, Connecticut," in *In Remembrance: Archaeology and Death*, eds David A. Poirier and Nicholas F. Bellantoni, 131–54 (Westport, CT: Bergin & Garvey, 1997).

167. "consumptions ... proved to be mortal to a number": Bellantoni, Sledzik, and Poirier, "Rescue, Research, and Reburial," p. 149.

167. "Regardless of the specific infectious ... by 19th century rural New Englanders.": Paul Sledzik and Nicholas Bellantoni, "Brief Communication: Bioarcheological and Biocultural Evidence for the New England Vampire Folk Belief," *American Journal of Physical Anthropology* 94 (1994), p. 271.

168. "the physical arrangement ... desecrated at the cemetery.": Bellantoni, Sledzik, and Poirier, "Rescue, Research, and Reburial," p. 146.

168. "others in which the skull was present but separated from the trunk.": Paul Barber, *Vampires, Burial, and Death: Folklore and Reality* (New Haven: Yale University Press, 1988), pp. 78–79.

168. Descriptions of Romano-British and pagan Anglo-Saxon cemeteries are in M. Harman, T. I. Molleson, and J. L. Price, "Burials, Bodies and Beheadings in Romano-British and Anglo-Saxon Cemeteries," *Bulletin of the British Museum of Natural History (Geology)* 25, no. 3 (1981), pp. 162–65.

169. "To remedy the evil . . . for the plague ceased.": Sir James George Frazer, *Fear of the Dead in Primitive Religion*, 1933–36 (New York [London]: Arno Press, Macmillan, 1977). v. 2, p. 83.

169. For murderers and vampires receive the same treatment, see J. A. MacCulloch, "Vampire," in *Encyclopaedia of Religion and Ethics*, vol. 12, edited by James Hastings, 1908–26, 589–91 (New York: Scribner's Sons, 1928), p. 590.

169. "then its head was cut off, . . . the heart taken out.": Barber, *Vampires*, p. 13.

169. "In East Prussia . . . paid out in kind.": Frazer, *Fear*, v. 2, p. 83.

170. "the soul was believed . . . boots elsewhere in the grave.": Ralph Merrifield, *Archaeology of Ritual and Magic* (New York: New Amsterdam, 1987), pp. 75–76.

170. "liberate the spirit and remove any fear of haunting.": Merrifield, *Archaeology*, pp. 105–06; see also Barber, *Vampires*, p. 158 and George Lyman Kittredge, "Disenchantment by Decapitation," *Journal of American Folklore* 18 (1905), pp. 1–14.

170. "digging up the corpse . . . and then reburying him.": Louis C. Jones, "The Ghosts of New York: An Analytical Study," *Journal of American Folklore* 57 (1944), p. 252.

171. Criteria for skeletal evidence discussed in Paul S. Sledzik, Nicholas Bellantoni, and Allison Webb Willcox, "Skeletal Evidence for Tuberculosis and Vampirism in 18th and 19th Century New England," unpublished paper presented at the Paleopathology Annual Meeting (Toronto, Ontario, 1993).

171. "profane and uneducated . . . ignorant and vicious.": Quoted in Faye Ringel Hazel, "Some Strange New England Mortuary Practices: Lovecraft Was Right," *Lovecraft Studies* 29 (1992), p. 17.

172. Quotes from *Lucas Whitaker* are in Cynthia DeFelice, *The Apprenticeship of Lucas Whitaker* (New York: Farrar Straus Giroux, 1996).

173. "It is sort of homeopathic magic, . . . current scientific thinking.": David Brown, "Uncovering a Therapy from the Grave," *Washington Post*, 25 October 1993, p. A3.

174. Excerpts from "Carrick Hollow" are in Jan Burke and Paul Sledzik, "The Haunting of Carrick Hollow," in *Crime Through Time III: A New Collection of Original Historical Mysteries*, edited by Sharan Newman, with an introduction by Anne Perry, 242–67 (New York: Berkley Prime Crime, 2000).

176. The article that inspired the poem is Sam Libby, "Cemetery Holds Tales of Vampires," *New York Times*, 16 February 1992, p. CN8.

176. Michael J. Bielawa, "The Griswold Vampire," *Dead of Night* (Summer 1995).

177. Bellantoni was quoted in Peggy McCarthy, "Unearthing Clues to the Past: Bones Found in Lost Conn. Graveyard Give Clues to Life in Colonial Times," *Boston Sunday Globe*, 13 September 1992, p. 45.

Chapter 9

179. Ernest W. Baughman, *Type and Motif-Index of the Folktales of England and America*, Indiana

Notes

University Folklore Series, no. 20. (The Hague: Mouton and Company, 1966), motif E251.3.3(a).

179. For a discussion of Skinner as a source of folk legends, see Richard M. Dorson, "How Shall we Rewrite Charles M. Skinner Today?" in *Folklore: Selected Essays*, R. M. Dorson, 177–98 (Bloomington, Indiana: Indiana University Press, 1972).

179. "In a cellar in Green Street . . . picture is no more.": Charles M. Skinner, *Myths and Legends of Our Own Land* (Philadelphia: J. B. Lippincott Co., 1896), v. 1, pp. 76–77.

181. "Shunned House" citations taken from H. P. Lovecraft, "The Shunned House," in *At the Mountains of Madness and Other Tales of Terror*, 1924, 111–38 (New York: Ballantine Books, 1971).

185. It seems doubtful that Lovecraft used Summers' version of the Jacques Roulet incident since Lovecraft's manuscript for "The Shunned House" shows that it was written in October, 1924 (ten years before the publication of Summers' book), even though the story wasn't published until 1937.

186. "In the remote and wild . . . of the case are not clear.": Montague Summers, *The Werewolf* (New York: E. P. Dutton and Company, Inc., 1934), pp. 230–31.

187. For discussions of the French Huguenots in Rhode Island, see Thomas Williams Bicknell, *The History of the State of Rhode Island and Providence Plantations* (New York: American Historical Society, 1920), v. 2, pp. 557–62 and Carl R. Woodward, *Plantation in Yankeeland: The Story of Cocumscussoc, Mirror of Colonial Rhode Island* (Chester, Connecticut: Pequot Press, Inc., 1971), pp. 49–52.

188. "most of the more academic . . . and feasted ravenously.": H. P. Lovecraft, *The Case of Charles Dexter Ward* (New York: Ballantine Books, 1971), pp. 72–73.

189. "About the hidden churchyard . . . of less describable origin!": H. P. Lovecraft, "Letter to Helen V. Sully, 17 October 1933," Letters of H. P. Lovecraft in *Lovecraft Collection*, housed at John Hay Library, Brown University, Providence, Rhode Island.

190. "Poe knew of this place, . . . visits here 90 years ago.": H. P. Lovecraft, "Letter to Frank Utpatel, 15 February 1937," Letters of H. P. Lovecraft in *Lovecraft Collection*, housed at John Hay Library, Brown University, Providence, Rhode Island.

196. "very cosmopolitan . . . a complete alien.": S. Foster Damon, *Amy Lowell: A Chronicle*, 1935 (Hamden, CT: Archon Books, 1966), pp. 709–710.

196. "The last case of digging . . . Doesn't it seem extraordinary?": Damon, *Amy Lowell*, p. 711.

196. "Even in New England . . . as on Woodstock Green.": Jeremiah Curtin, "European Folk-Lore in the United States," *Journal of American Folklore* 2 (1889), pp. 56–59.

198. Death omens found in L. E. Chittenden, "A Note on an Early Superstition of the Champlain Valley," *Journal of American Folklore* 4 (1891), pp. 272–74.

198. "the falling of a picture . . . of the same individual.": Pamela McArthur Cole, "New England Funerals," *Journal of American Folklore* 7 (1894), pp. 217–23.

198. For a discussion of the Lamia, see Maria Leach, ed., *Funk & Wagnalls Standard Dictionary of Folklore, Mythology, and Legend* (New York: Funk & Wagnalls, 1949–50), v. 2, p. 602.

200. Calmet's recounting of the Arnod Paole incident appears in Augustine Calmet, *Dissertation on Those Persons Who Return to Earth Bodily, the Excommunicated, the Oupires or Vampires, Vroucolacas, Etc.*, vol. 2 of *The Phantom World: Or, the Philosophy of Spirits, Apparitions, Etc.*, 1746 (London: Richard Bentley, 1850).

200. This version of the Arnod Paole incident was taken from Paul Barber, *Vampires, Burial, and Death: Folklore and Reality* (New Haven: Yale University Press, 1988), 16.

200. A good summary of the literary vampire in relation its folk counterpart can be found in M. M. Carlson, "What Stoker Saw: An Introduction to the History of the Literary Vampire," *Folklore Forum* 10 (1977), pp. 26–32.

201. Lord Ruthven and other Gothic vampires are discussed in Rondald Foust, "Rite of Passage: The Vampire Tale as Cosmogonic Myth," in *Aspects of Fantasy: Selected Essays from the Second International Conference on the Fantastic in Literature and Film*, edited by William Coyle, Contributions to the Study of Fiction and Fantasy, no. 19, 73–84 (Westport, Connecticut: Greenwood Press, 1986).

Chapter 10

203. "Frederick Ransom, the second son ... with that disease afterward.": This text is found in Jeremiah Curtin, Jeremiah, "European Folk-Lore in the United States," *Journal of American Folklore* 2 (1889), pp. 58–59 and Rockwell Stephens, "They Burned the Vampire's Heart to Ashes," *Vermont Life* 21, no. 1 (1966), p. 47 (reprinted as "The Vampire's Heart," in *Mischief in the Mountains: Strange Tales of Vermont and Vermonters*, eds Walter R. Hard and Janet C. Greene, 71–80 {Montpelier, Vermont: Vermont Life Magazine, 1970}, pp. 78–79).

204. "We may as well ... some smoke was emitted.": Stephens, "They Burned the Vampire's Heart," p. 47.

207. The cemetery statistics are from an unpublished paper delivered by John Sterling at a session entitled "The Preservation and Archaeology of Historic Cemeteries" at the annual Rhode Island Statewide Historic Preservation Conference, Providence, 21 April 2001.

208. "The cemetery is there, ... also used Cushing plots.": Stephens, "The Vampire's Heart," pp. 79–80.

209. "Although apparently entirely fictitious, ... safely long-deceased).": Walter R. Hard and Janet C. Greene, eds., *Mischief in the Mountains: Strange Tales of Vermont and Vermonters* (Montpelier, Vermont: Vermont Life Magazine, 1970), pp. 79–80.

209. " 'Curwen,' 'Carwin,' or 'Corwin,' ... Hawthorne's ancestor, John Hathorne.": Barton L. St. Armand, "Facts in the Case of H. P. Lovecraft," *Rhode Island History* 31, no. 1 (1972), p. 13.

209. This version of the Giles Corey story appears in Robert Ellis Cahill, *New England's Witches and Wizards*, Collectible Classics, no. 1 (Peabody, Massachusetts: Chandler-Smith Publishing House, Inc., 1983), pp. 19–20.

210. For a discussion of the vampire and the belief in life after death and the magical power of blood, see Clive Leatherdale, *Dracula: The Novel & the Legend* (Wellingborough: Aquarian Press, 1985), p. 15.

211. For the importance of blood in placating the dead, see MacEdward Leach, "Blood," in *Funk & Wagnalls Standard Dictionary of Folklore, Mythology, and Legend*, edited by Maria Leach (New York: Funk & Wagnalls, 1949–50), v. 1, pp. 148–49 and J. A. MacCulloch, "Vampire," in *Encyclopaedia of Religion and Ethics*, edited by James Hastings, (New York: Scribner's Sons, 1928), v. 12, pp. 589–91.

211. "the unending river of life.": Roy Pinchot, ed., *Blood: The River of Life*, The Human Body (New York: Torstar Books, Inc., 1985), p. 7.

212. "Then out and cam ... a' the life lay in.": M. J. C. Hodgart, *The Ballads*, 1950 (New York: W. W. Norton & Company, Inc., 1962), p. 125.

212. "He griped her fast . . . so stood up a knight.": Lowry Charles Wimberly, *Folklore in the English and Scottish Ballads*, 1928 (New York: Dover, 1965), p. 342.

212. The Egyptian "Tale of the Two Brothers" is taken from H. Clay Trumbull, *The Blood Covenant: A Primitive Rite and Its Bearing on Scripture*, 2d ed. (Philadelphia: J. D. Wattles, 1893), pp. 103–05.

213. "A strange and horrible Wendish . . . invariably escaped detection.": "Wendish Superstition," Notes, *Folk-Lore Record* 3, no. 1 (1880), pp. 137–38.

213. For "liquid blood," see Paul Barber, *Vampires, Burial, and Death: Folklore and Reality* (New Haven: Yale University Press, 1988), p. 114.

214. "Liquid is life" is discussed in Alan Dundes, "Wet and Dry, the Evil Eye: An Essay in Indo-European and Semitic Worldview," in *Interpreting Folklore*, edited by Alan Dundes, 93–133 (Bloomington, Indiana: Indiana University Press, 1980), p. 102.

214. "entering into communion . . . mixed with food or drink.": Sir James George Frazer, *The Golden Bough: A Study in Magic and Religion*, 3d ed. (London: Macmillan, 1911–15), v. 8, p. 156.

214. "sometimes the valuable qualities . . . ethereal process of fumigation": Frazer, *The Golden Bough*, v. 8, p. 166.

214. "just as the savage thinks . . . only against disease.": Frazer, *The Golden Bough*, v. 8, p. 158.

215. For removing and evil humors and calming the insane, see Douglas Starr, *Blood: An Epic History of Medicine and Commerce* (New York: Alfred A. Knopf, 1998), p. xii.

215. "Esquire Powel's second wife . . . eye witness of the transaction.": John S. Pettibone, "The Early History of Manchester," *Proceedings of the Vermont Historical Society* 1 (1930): p. 158.

216. The other source that gives the date of exhumation is Gerald W. McFarland, *The "Counterfeit" Man: The True Story of the Boorn-Colvin Murder Case* (New York: Pantheon, 1990), pp. 53–54.

217. "The Capt. Isaac Burton, . . . the town in his day.": Pettibone, "The Early History of Manchester," p. 148.

217. "nearly all the leading men of the first decades were immigrants.": David M. Ludlum, *Social Ferment in Vermont, 1791–1850*. (New York: Columbia University Press, 1939). p. 18.

217. "overbearing" and "high tempered.": Pettibone, "The Early History of Manchester," p. 165.

218. " "Dr. Gould, a graduate . . . Gould became a drunkard.": Pettibone, "The Early History of Manchester," p. 157.

218. "Three times in all, . . . ghost to the grave site.": McFarland, *The "Counterfeit" Man*, p. 49.

218. "strange dreams and unaccountable visions.": McFarland, *The "Counterfeit" Man*, p. 51.

218. "religious liberals: freethinkers, deists, and universalists." McFarland, *The "Counterfeit" Man*, p. 21.

219. "Although the children of . . . state of despondency to hopefullness [sic].": Mansfield, David.. "The History of the Town of Dummerston." *Vermont Historical Magazine* (1884).

220. Ballad of "Barbara Allen" taken from Hodgart, *The Ballads*, p. 124.

220. Passage from "Tristan and Iseult" taken from Joseph Bédier, *The Romance of Tristan and Iseult*, Translated by Hilaire Belloc and Paul Rosenfeld (New York: Vintage Books, 1965), p. 151.

221. For a discussion of the lasting embrace of plants, see Edwin Sidney Hartland, *Primitive*

Paternity: The Myth of Supernatural Birth in Relation to the History of the Family, Publications of the Folk-Lore Society, vol. 65 (London: David Nutt, 1909), p. 166.

221. Thorns or nettles on the grave is discussed in Hartland, *Primitive Paternity*, pp. 159–60.

221. German folksong examples are from Jacob Grimm, *Teutonic Mythology*, 4th ed., translated by James Steven Stallybrass (London: George Bell & Sons, 1883), v. 2, pp. 286–87.

221. For examples of the soul entering a plant, see Lowry Charles Wimberly, *Death and Burial Lore in the English and Scottish Popular Ballads*, University of Nebraska Studies in Language, Literature, and Criticism, no. 8 (Lincoln, Nebraska: University of Nebraska, 1927), p. 121, n. 208 and Francis James Child, ed., *The English and Scottish Popular Ballads*, 1882–98 (New York: Dover Publications, Inc., 1965), v. 1, p. 98.

221. The example of the dryads of classical mythology is taken from Grimm, *Teutonic Mythology*, v. 2, p. 653.

222. "the soul of the family-ancestor . . . tutelary spirit of the family.": James Hastings, ed., *Encyclopaedia of Religion and Ethics*, 1908–26 (New York: Charles Scribner's Sons, 1928), v. 5, p. 484.

222. "A tree that grows on . . . will be at his service.": Frazer, *Golden Bough*, v. 2, pp. 32–33.

223. "Mrs. Spaulding . . . age of nearly a hundred years.": Mansfield, "History of Dummerston," p. 25.

223. "Lt. Spaulding was the first . . . wounded in that skirmish.": Mansfield, "History of Dummerston," p. 25.

224. "The day it was fought, . . . nearly forty miles away.": Mansfield, "History of Dummerston," p. 25.

225. Reference to Thoreau's journal entry appeared in C. Grant Loomis, "Henry David Thoreau as Folklorist," *Western Folklore* 16 (1957), p. 97.

225. "If the lungs of a brother . . . affected with that disease.": John McNab Currier, "Contributions to New England Folklore," *Journal of American Folklore* 4 (1891), p. 253.

Chapter 11

226. " "Ugh!" says the person . . . and vinegar into the grave.": *Providence Journal*, 21 March 1892, p. 8.

229. "If a dead man doesn't . . . family is going to die.": Wayland D. Hand, ed., *Popular Beliefs and Superstitions from North Carolina*, Vol. 6–7 of *Frank C. Brown Collection of North Carolina Folklore* (Durham, North Carolina: Duke University Press, 1964), v. 7, #5477.

229. "A woman who was speaking . . . many years after that herself".": Charlotte Latham, "Some West Sussex Superstitions Lingering in 1868." *Folk-Lore Record* 1 (1878), p. 57.

230. "Our pagan ancestors believed . . . spirits of dead ancestors.": Thomas R. Brendle and Claude W. Unger, *Folk Medicine of the Pennsylvania Germans: The Non-Occult Cures*, 1935, Proceedings of the Pennsylvania German Society, vol. 45 (New York: Augustus M. Kelley, 1970), p. 17.

230. For blaming the ghosts of near relations, see Sir James George Frazer, *Fear of the Dead in Primitive Religion*, 1933–36 (New York [London]: Arno Press, Macmillan, 1977), v. 1, p. 144.

230. "to die," means . . . sickness of undiagnosed origin.": Franciso Demetrio y Radaza, comp., *Dictionary of Philippine Folk Beliefs and Customs*, Museum and Archives Publications, no. 2 (Cagayan de Oro City: Xavier University, 1970), v. 1, p. vii, fn. 6.

230. Discussion of the Wallachian *moroi* can be found in Carl-Ulrik Schierup, "Why Are Vampires Still Alive? Wallachian Immigrants in Scandinavia," *Ethnos* 3–4 (1986), p. 179.

231. "Like the legend . . . *vampire* is clouded in mystery.": Katharina M. Wilson, "The History of the Word *Vampire*," In *The Vampire: A Casebook*, edited by Alan Dundes (Madison, Wisconsin: University of Wisconsin Press, 1998), p. 3.

231. For vampires unable to drown, see Agnes Murgoci, "The Vampire in Roumania." *Folklore* 37 (1926), p. 332.

231. For a discussion of the "ordeal by swimming" see George Lyman Kittredge, *Witchcraft in Old and New England* (Cambridge, Massachusetts: Harvard University Press, 1929), pp. 232–38.

231. "she sucks the blood . . . and therefore incurable marasmus." Henry Charles Coote, "Some Italian Folk-Lore," *Folk-Lore Record* 1 (1878), p. 214.

232. "seek its former house and . . . precautions at death and afterwards": Schierup, "Why Are Vampires Still Alive?" p. 180. For a thorough discussion on ways to become a vampire, see Montague Summers, *The Vampire: His Kith and Kin* (London: Kegan Paul, Trench, Trubner & Co., Ltd., 1928), pp. 77–170.

232. "This reviving being, . . . if the course be not interrupted.": Calmet is quoted in Arthur H. Nethercot, *The Road to Tryermaine: A Study of the History, Background, and Purposes of Coleridge's "Christabel"* (Chicago: University of Chicago Press, 1939), pp. 69–70.

233. "[A] vampire might be defined . . . cause of that crisis.": Paul Barber, *Vampires, Burial, and Death: Folklore and Reality* (New Haven: Yale University Press, 1988), p. 125

233. "a folkloric means of . . . the mouth of a corpse.": Barber, *Vampires*, p. 131.

233. "A vampire is a body . . . dimension and color.": Barber, *Vampires*, p. 20.

233. "Our descriptions of revenants . . . buried for a time.": Barber, *Vampires*, p. 118.

234. "the fear of the revenant . . . as we have nowadays.": Barber, *Vampires*, p. 37.

235. "put a face on our fear . . . of life and death.": Annette Curtis Klause, "Soap Box: A Young Adult Author Speaks Out—Why Vampires?" *Voice of Youth Advocates* 21, no. 1 (April 1998), p. 28.

235. "I can see him hovering . . . down the corridor at night.": Betty MacDonald, *The Plague and I* (Philadelphia; New York: J. B. Lippincott Company, 1948), p. 160.

235. "Voice hoarse, neck slightly bent, . . . apparent like wings of birds.": Rene Dubos and Jean Dubos, *The White Plague: Tuberculosis, Man and Society* (Boston: Little, Brown and Company, 1952), p. 71.

236. "The emaciated figure strikes . . . to tell his complaints.": Dubos, *The White Plague*, p. 118.

237. "a tradition of the Indians.": *Providence Journal*, 21 March 1892, p. 8.

237. "Widespread as the vampire is . . . are quite another.": Alan Dundes, ed., *The Vampire: A Casebook* (Madison, Wisconsin: University of Wisconsin Press, 1998), p. 161.

237. "corpse which comes from the grave at night and sucks blood": Stith Thompson, *Tales of the North American Indians* (Bloomington: Indiana University Press, 1966), p. 357.

237. "In the olden days, . . . neighborhood of his home.": James W. Terrell, "The Demon of Consumption: A Legend of the Cherokees in North Carolina," *Journal of American Folklore* 5 (1892), pp. 125–26.

238. "The Ojibwa have . . . among the Cherokees.": George R. Stetson, "The Animistic Vampire in New England," *American Anthropologist* 9 (1896). p. 12.

239. "An old 'witch' was dead, . . . covered with fresh blood.": M. Raymond Harrington, "An Abenaki 'Witch-Story'," *Journal of American Folklore* 14 (1901). p. 160.

240. "it seems likely . . . consumption in the nineteenth century.": Faye Ringel Hazel, "Some Strange New England Mortuary Practices: Lovecraft Was Right," *Lovecraft Studies* 29 (1992), p. 15.

240. "Some fifteen years ago . . . and regained their health.": Murgoci, "Vampire in Roumania," pp. 324–25.

242. "I would like to know . . . the Swedes or Welsh?": George R. Stetson, "Letter to Sidney S. Rider," unpublished letter in *Rider Collection*, housed at John Hay Library, Brown University, Providence, Box 181, no. 32, 1895.

242. The article that suggested the French Huguenots who settled in East Greenwich is "The Vampire Tradition," Arnold Collection, housed at Knight Memorial Library, Providence, 87.

242. For German mercenaries in ths Revolutinary War, see W. H. Bruford, *Germany in the Eighteenth Century: The Social Background of the Literary Revival* (Cambridge, England: Cambridge University Press, 1935), pp. 38–39.

243. "disease . . . destroyed ten men for us where the sword of the enemy . . . killed one.": Henry Steele Commager and Richard B. Morris, eds., *The Spirit of 'Seventy-Six: The Story of the American Revolution as Told by Participants*, 1958 (New York: Harper & Row, 1967), pp. 38–39.

243. "Beginning in 1775, soldiers . . . in Connecticut and Pennsylvania.": Charles Royster, *A Revolutionary People at War: The Continental Army and America Character, 1775–1783* (Chapel Hill, North Carolina: University of North Carolina Press, 1979), pp. 131–32.

243. "war itself, then as always, . . . new ideas and institutions.": Commager and Morris, eds., *The Spirit of 'Seventy-Six*, p. 367.

244. "Rhode Island folklorist Michael . . . sounds a trifle far-fetched.": Paul Sieveking, "Consumed by Vampires," *Fortean Times* 80 (1995), p. 46.

244. "curious and interesting material . . . from the English colonial settlers.": Jeremiah Curtin, "European Folk-Lore in the United States," *Journal of American Folklore* 2 (1889), p. 58.

245. "I was a little shocked to . . . none whatever in his prescriptions.": C. A. Fraser, "Scottish Myths from Ontario," *Journal of American Folklore* 6 (1893), p. 196.

245. "A much-respected dissenting . . . an' put her in't".":G. F. Black and W. Thomas Northcote, *Examples of Printed Folklore Concerning Orkney and Shetland Islands*, Publications of the Folk-Lore Society (London, 1903), p. 151.

246. "was at last restored . . . through being witch-ridden.": William George Black, *Folk-Medicine: A Chapter in the History of Culture*, Publications of the Folk-Lore Society (London, 1883), p. 96.

246. For Hufford's features of being hagged, see David J. Hufford, *The Terror That Comes in the Night: An Experience-Centered Study of Supernatural Assault Traditions* (Philadelphia: University of Pennsylvania Press, 1982), pp. 10–11.

246. "When comparing the accounts . . . of this increasing fatigue.": Hufford, *Terror*, p. 231.

247. Summers reference is to Montague Summers, *The Vampire in Europe* (New York: E. P. Dutton and Company, Inc., 1929), p. 82.

248. "A horrible scene revealed itself . . . they burnt it.": Summers, *Vampire in Europe*, pp. 114–15.

249. "The Vampyres, which come out . . . all disturbances cease.": Colin McEnroe, "The Surprising Account of Those Spectres Called Vampyres," *Hartford Courant*, 24 October 1999, p. G13.

Chapter 12

253. "Sep 4th — . . . I went this afternoon, . . . no purpose to the Sick relation.": Enoch Hayes Place, *Journals of Enoch Hayes Place*, Transcriber William E. Wentworth (Boston: The New England Historic Genealogical Society and the New Hampshire Society of Genealogists, 1998). v. 1, pp. 1–2.

255. For illness and the supernatural in New England, see Richard M. Dorson, *American in Legend: Folklore from the Colonial Period to the Present* (New York: Pantheon Books, 1973), p. 25 and Don Yoder, "Folk Medicine," In *Folklore and Folklife: An Introduction*, edited by Richard M. Dorson, 191–215 (Chicago: University of Chicago Press, 1972.), p. 204.

256. "did not swallow wholesale . . . into beasts and birds.": Dorson, *American in Legend*, p. 32.

256. "castigated those well-meaning . . . and worked for his salvation.": Dorson, *American in Legend*, p. 33.

257. "God's greater power . . . manner as his victim.": Dorson, *American in Legend*, p. 24.

257. "a group of witches . . . the kingdom of the Devil.": Richard Cavendish, *A History of Magic* (London: Arkana, 1987), p. 118.

257. "being filled with . . . individualists one and all.": Thomas Robinson Hazard, *The Jonny-Cake Papers of "Shepherd Tom", Together with Reminiscences of Narragansett Schools of Former Days* (Boston: The Merrymount Press, 1915), p. 398, n. 18.

257. "was bred in the strictest . . . Connecticut in like contempt.": Hazard, *Jonny-Cake Papers*, p. xi.

258. A thorough description of the magic world view of this "other New England" is provided by D. Michael Quinn, *Early Mormonism and the Magic World View*, Revised and enlarged ed. (Salt Lake City: Signature Press, 1998).

259. "This mix of magic and religion . . . folk inheritance and his Christianity.": Quinn, *Early Mormonism*, p. 27.

260. "Without statistical sampling and . . . eve of the twentieth century.": Quinn, *Early Mormonism*, p. xiv.

260. "there are considerable elements . . . more than surprising.": *Providence Journal*, 20 March 1892, 4.

261. "it is a common belief . . . whole number within its limits.": George R. Stetson, "The Animistic Vampire in New England," *American Anthropologist* 9 (1896), pp. 7–8.

262. "The persistence of this vampire belief . . . likely to have upon Maine" (411).": Faye Ringel Hazel, *The New England Vampire Belief: Image of the Decline*, Rept. no. 05–92, Center for Advanced Studies, United States Coast Guard Academy (New London, Connecticut: United States Coast Guard Academy, 1992), pp. 2–3.

263. "In the notorious articles . . . march of American civilization.": Hazel, *The New England Vampire Belief*, p.3.

000. "Of all the images of . . . than that of the vampire.": Hazel, *The New England Vampire Belief*, p. 1.

264. "My bringing-up was very cosmopolitan, . . . to have it disappear.": S. Foster Damon, *Amy Lowell: A Chronicle*, 1935 (Hamden, CT: Archon Books, 1966), pp. 709–10.

264. " . . . he [Frost] is much more . . . with the country people.": Damon, *Amy Lowell*, p. 710.

265. "There is a quiet rural town . . . name of "Deserted Exeter".": "A Rhode Island Country Town," *Wickford Standard*, 6 May 1892, p. 2.

267."We think that some one ... Providence Journal." 'Nuff said".": Editorial, *Pawtuxet Valley Gleaner*, 22 April 1892.

267."It is probable that ... discussion and criticism.": *Providence Journal*, 21 March 1892, p. 8.

267. For the division between agricultural and industrial interests in Rhode Island, see George H. Kellner and Stanley J. Lemons, *Rhode Island: The Independent State* (Woodland Hills, California: Windsor Publications, 1982), pp. 39–41.

269."strange infatuation ... still sucking the blood.": John S. Pettibone, "The Early History of Manchester," *Proceedings of the Vermont Historical Society* 1 (1930), p. 158.

269. "A strange and almost incredible ... calling itself enlightened and [C]hristian.": C. A. Fraser, "Scottish Myths from Ontario," *Journal of American Folklore* 6 (1893), p. 196.

270."In that almost insulated part ... *was food for the dead!*": "Superstitions of New England," *Old Colony Memorial and Plymouth County Advertiser*, 4 May 1822, p. 4.

272."Sir— ... The writer indulges his imagination ... the generality of our race.": Letter to the editor, *Old Colony Memorial and Plymouth County Advertiser*, 11 May 1822, p. 7.

275. For a description of the worldwide distribution of prone burials, see Sir James George Frazer, *Fear of the Dead in Primitive Religion*, 1933–36 (New York [London]: Arno Press, Macmillan, 1977), v. 3, pp. 29–30.

275. For various interpretations of corpses turned face down, see Agnes Murgoci, "The Vampire in Roumania," *Folklore* 37 (1926), p. 327 and Frazer, *Fear of the Dead*, v. 2, p. 86.

275. "An old man with some soldiers ... to enter the bodies again.": Murgoci, "Vampire in Roumania," p. 345.

276. "rite of separation ... direction which it should travel.": Ralph Merrifield, *Archaeology of Ritual and Magic* (New York: New Amsterdam, 1987), p. 76. See also M. Harman, T. I. Molleson, and J. L. Price, "Burials, Bodies and Beheadings in Romano-British and Anglo-Saxon Cemeteries," *Bulletin of the British Museum of Natural History (Geology)* 25, no. 3 (1981), p. 168.

276. Barber discusses the ancient roots of these interrelated interpretations of face-down burials in Barber, *Vampires*, pp. 47–50.

277. "American intellectuals ... growing sense of alienation and loss.": Roger D. Abrahams, "Rough Sincerities: William Wells Newell and the Discovery of Folklore in Late-19th Century America," in *Folk Roots, New Roots: Folklore in American Life*, eds Jane S. Becker and Barbara Franco, 61–75 (Lexington, Massachussetts: Museum of Our National Heritage, 1988), p. 61.

277. "latent hostility between town and country became more overt": Jackson Lears, "Packaging the Folk: Tradition and Amnesia in American Advertising, 1880–1940," in Becker and Franco, ed., *Folk Roots, New Roots*, 103–40, p. 108.

277. "The ideal of an independent ... throughout the 19th century": Lears, "Packaging the Folk," p. 107.

277. "Once upon a time, there was ... the rise of modern society.": Lears, "Packaging the Folk," p. 103.

Chapter 13

281. "When people die of a ... they become vrykolakes.": D. Demetracopoulou Lee, "Greek Accounts of the Vrykolakas," *Journal of American Folklore* 55 (1942), p. 127.

282. For the rising popularity of embalming in the nineteenth century, see R. W. Habenstein and W. M. Laners, *History of American Funeral Directing* (Milwaukee: Bulfin Printers, 1962), esp. pp. 328–39 & 395.

Notes

282. For a discussion of the relation of embalming to vampires, see Paul Barber, *Vampires, Burial, and Death: Folklore and Reality* (New Haven:Yale University Press, 1988), pp. 84 & 174.

283. For the distinction between hard and soft news, see Gaye Tuchman, *Making News: A Study in the Construction of Reality* (New York:The Free Press, 1978), esp. pp. 46–47 & 98–99.

283. "the family and friends . . . causing his loss of strength.": Nancy Kinder, "The 'Vampires' of Rhode Island," *Yankee*, October 1970, p.167.

283. "It was a sudden deteriorating . . . to lose all his strength.": France Carrado Bolderson, "Horrible History at the Boston Boo-Centennial," *Providence Journal-Bulletin*, 11 October 1975, p. 10.

284. "Surely the fiend rested . . . spirit of her brother.": Bruce Fellman, "Things Still Go Bump in South County Night," *Providence Journal*, 31 October 1980, p.W4.

284. "The mother, Mary Brown, . . . anew every Halloween in Exeter.": Roy Bongartz, "When the Wind Howls and the Trees Moan," *Providence Sunday Journal Magazine*, 25 October 1981, p. 5.

284. "Let the scientists and . . .Vampires DO roam.": Bruce Fellman, "What Really Happened to Mercy Brown?" *Providence Sunday Journal Magazine*, 28 October 1979, p. 4.

285. "Mercy Brown died nearly . . . undead do . . . don't they?": C. Eugene Emery, Jr., "Did They Hear the Vampire Whisper?" *Providence Sunday Journal Magazine*, 28 October 1979, p. 6.

285. "We have something from the grave . . . she was a vampire.": "Vampires in Rhode Island," *PM Magazine*, 20 April 1982 (WJAR TV: Providence, RI).

286. "An investigation showed . . . a poorly made cassette.": Emery, "Did They Hear the Vampire Whisper?" p. 13.

287. "Do you believe it is . . . to disprove their existence.": Norine Dresser, *American Vampires: Fans, Victims, Practitioners* (New York:W.W. Norton & Company, 1989), p. 69.

287. "spirit belief specialists, . . . social prestige, becomes decisive": Lauri Honko, "Memorates and the Study of Folk Beliefs," *Journal of the Folklore Institute* 1 (1964), 99.17–18.

288. "nourishes legendry—providing it with fresh subject matter and speeding its dissemination.": Ronald L. Baker, "The Influence of Mass Culture on Modern Legends," *Southern Folklore Quarterly* 40 (1976), p. 367. See also Donald Allport Bird, "A Theory for Folklore in the Mass Media:Traditional Patterns in the Mass Media," *Southern Folklore Quarterly* 40 (1976), p. 286.

288. "tubal transmission . . . has become the tribal storyteller.": Dresser, *American Vampires*, p. 117.

289. For discussions of factors that play a role in shaping legends, see Linda Dégh, "The 'Belief Legend' in Modern Society: Form, Function, and Relationship to Other Genres," in *American Folk Legend: A Symposium*, edited by Wayland D. Hand (Berkeley, California: University of California Press, 1971), pp. 55–68 and Roberrt A. Georges, "Toward an Understanding of Storytelling Events," *Journal of American Folklore* 84 (1969), pp. 313–28.

290. "about sickness caused and . . . agencies of the supernatural world.": Linda Dégh, "Processes of Legend Formation." In *IVth International Congress for Folk-Narrative Research in Athens: Lectures and Reports*, edited by Georgios A. Megas, 77–87. Athens, 1965.

290. "The whole fearful matter started . . . when they died.": Karen Lee Ziner, "Was She a Victim . . . or a Vampire?" *Providence Journal-Bulletin*, 25 October 1984, p. 10.

291. "Once upon a time . . . *Que m'importe.*": Sidney S. Rider, *Book Notes* 9, no. 7 (1892), p. 1.

295. "sanitized and romanticized . . . and enjoys sexual freedom.": Dresser, *American Vampires*, p. 169.

Chapter 14

296. Statistics regarding current disease were taken from Gregory L. Armstrong, Laura A. Conn, and Robert W. Pinner, "Trends in Infectious Disease Mortality in the United States During the 20th Century," *Journal of the American Medical Association* 281, no. 1 (6 January 1999), pp. 61–66.

296. "I've think we've gone ... severity of the outbreaks.": Johns Hopkins University Center for Civilian Biodefense Studies (www.hopkins-biodefense.org/).

297. For a discussion of antibiotic-resistant bacteria, see Stuart B. Levy, "The Challenge of Antibiotic Resistance," *Scientific American*, March 1998, 46–53.

297. The World Health Organization statistics on tuberculosis were taken from "Tuberculosis," Fact Sheet No. 104, revised April 2000 (Geneva: World Health Organization).

297. "now attribute the decline of tuberculosis chiefly to socioeconomic changes": Barbara Bates, *Bargaining for Life: A Social History of Tuberculosis, 1876–1938* (Philadelphia: University of Pennsylvania Press, 1992), pp. 320–21.

298. Ewald provides his views on infectious disease in Paul W. Ewald, *Plague Time: How Stealth Infections Are Causing Cancers, Heart Disease, and Other Deadly Ailments* (New York: Free Press, 2000).

298. "cancer is now ... can turn paranoid.": Susan Sontag, *Illness as Metaphor* (New York: Farrar, Straus and Giroux, 1978), p. 69.

299. "In the early settlements of ... surroundings of the people.": Rene Dubos and Jean Dubos, *The White Plague: Tuberculosis, Man and Society* (Boston: Little, Brown and Company, 1952), p. 199.

300 . "The superstition of the vampire, ... her health after the event.": John Corbett, *The Lake Country: An Annal of Olden Days in Central New York* (Rochester, New York: Democrat and Chronicle Print, 1898), pp. 98–99.

WORKS CITED

Abrahams, Roger D. "Rough Sincerities: William Wells Newell and the Discovery of Folklore in Late-19th Century America." In *Folk Roots, New Roots: Folklore in American Life*, eds Jane S. Becker and Barbara Franco, 61–75. Lexington, Massachussetts: Museum of Our National Heritage, 1988.

Armstrong, Gregory L., Laura A. Conn, and Robert W. Pinner. "Trends in Infectious Disease Mortality in the United States During the 20th Century." *Journal of the American Medical Association* 281, no. 1 (6 January 1999): 61–66.

Baker, Ronald L. "The Influence of Mass Culture on Modern Legends." *Southern Folklore Quarterly* 40 (1976): 367–76.

———. "Legends About Spook Light Hill." *Indiana Folklore* 3 (1970): 163–89.

Barber, Paul. *Vampires, Burial, and Death: Folklore and Reality*. New Haven: Yale University Press, 1988.

Baron, John. *Illustrations of the Enquiry Respecting Tuberculosis Diseases*. London: T. and G. Underwood, 1882.

Bates, Barbara. *Bargaining for Life: A Social History of Tuberculosis, 1876–1938*. Philadelphia: University of Pennsylvania Press, 1992.

Baughman, Ernest W. *Type and Motif-Index of the Folktales of England and America*. Indiana University Folklore Series, no. 20. The Hague: Mouton and Company, 1966.

Bellantoni, Nicholas F., Paul S. Sledzik, and David A. Poirier. "Rescue, Research, and Reburial: Walton Family Cemetery, Griswold, Connecticut." In *In Remembrance: Archaeology and Death*, eds David A. Poirier and Nicholas F. Bellantoni, 131–54. Westport, CT: Bergin & Garvey, 1997.

Benes, Peter. "Itinerant Physicians, Healers, and Surgeon-Dentists in New England and New York, 1720–1825." In *Medicine and Healing*, edited by Peter Benes. Annual Proceedings of the Dublin Seminar for New England Folklife, 95–112. Boston: Boston University, 1992.

Bett, Walter R., ed. *The History and Conquest of Common Diseases*. Norman, Oklahoma: University of Oklahoma Press, 1954.

Bédier, Joseph. *The Romance of Tristan and Iseult*. Translated by Hilaire Belloc and Paul Rosenfeld. New York: Vintage Books, 1965.

Bicknell, Thomas Williams. *The History of the State of Rhode Island and Providence Plantations*. New York: American Historical Society, 1920.

Bielawa, Michael J. "The Griswold Vampire." *Dead of Night*, Summer 1995.

Bird, Donald Allport. "A Theory for Folklore in the Mass Media: Traditional Patterns in the Mass Media." *Southern Folklore Quarterly* 40 (1976): 285–305.

Black, G. F., and W. Thomas Northcote. Examples of Printed Folklore Concerning Orkney and Shetland Islands. Publications of the Folk-Lore Society. London, 1903.

Black, William George. *Folk-Medicine: A Chapter in the History of Culture*. Publications of the Folk-Lore Society. London, 1883.

Bolderson, France Carrado. "Horrible History at the Boston Boo-Centennial." *Providence Journal-Bulletin*, 11 October 1975, 10.

Bongartz, Roy. "When the Wind Howls and the Trees Moan." *Providence Sunday Journal Magazine*, 25 October 1981, 5, 7, 10, 14–15.

Bowditch, Henry I[ngersoll]. Consumption in New England and Is Consumption Contagious? 1862. New York: Arno Press, 1977.

Brendle, Thomas R., and Claude W. Unger. *Folk Medicine of the Pennsylvania Germans: The Non-Occult Cures.* 1935. *Proceedings of the Pennsylvania German Society,* vol. 45. New York: Augustus M. Kelley, 1970.

Brown, David. "Uncovering a Therapy from the Grave." *Washington Post,* 25 October 1993, A3.

Bruford, W. H. *Germany in the Eighteenth Century: The Social Background of the Literary Revival.* Cambridge, England: Cambridge University Press, 1935.

Burke, Jan, and Paul Sledzik. "The Haunting of Carrick Hollow." In *Crime Through Time III: A New Collection of Original Historical Mysteries,* edited by Sharan Newman, with an introduction by Anne Perry, 242–67. New York: Berkley Prime Crime, 2000.

Cahill, Robert Ellis. *New England's Witches and Wizards.* Collectible Classics, no. 1. Peabody, Massachusetts: Chandler-Smith Publishing House, Inc., 1983.

Caldwell, Mark. *The Last Crusade: The War on Consumption, 1862–1954.* New York: Atheneum, 1988.

Calmet, Augustine. "Dissertation on Those Persons Who Return to Earth Bodily, the Excommunicated, the Oupires or Vampires, Vroucolacas, Etc." Vol. 2 of *The Phantom World: Or, the Philosophy of Spirits, Apparitions, Etc.* 1746. London: Richard Bentley, 1850.

"Campus Haunted by Ghost of Man Dead Since 1884." The Good 5¢ Cigar 5 (29 April 1975): 6.

Carlson, M. M. "What Stoker Saw: An Introduction to the History of the Literary Vampire." *Folklore Forum* 10 (1977): 26–32.

Carroll, Chris. "Local Haunts." *North Kingstown Villager,* October 1995.

Cavendish, Richard. *A History of Magic.* London: Arkana, 1987.

Child, Francis James, ed. *The English and Scottish Popular Ballads.* 1882–98. New York: Dover Publications, Inc., 1965.

Chittenden, L. E. "A Note on an Early Superstition of the Champlain Valley." *Journal of American Folklore* 4, no. 14 (1891): 272–74.

Chowder, Ken. "TB: The Disease That Rose from Its Grave." *Smithsonian* 23, no. 8 (November 1992): 180–94.

Clauson, James Earl. "Vampirism in Rhode Island." *In These Plantations,* 67–69. Providence, Rhode Island: Roger Williams Press, 1937.

Clendening, Logan, comp. *Source Book of Medical History.* New York: Dover Publications, Inc., 1960.

Cole, J. R. *The History of Tolland County, Connecticut.* New York: W. W. Preston & Co., 1888.
———. *History of Washington and Kent Counties, Rhode Island.* New York: W. W. Preston & Co., 1889.

Cole, Pamela McArthur. "New England Funerals." *Journal of American Folklore* 7, no. 26 (1894): 217–23.

Commager, Henry Steele, and Richard B. Morris, eds. *The Spirit of 'Seventy-Six: The Story of the American Revolution as Told by Participants.* 1958. New York: Harper & Row, 1967.

Conforti, Joseph. "Samuel Hopkins and the Revolutionary Antislavery Movement." *Rhode Island History* 38, no. 2 (1979): 39–49.

Works Cited

Conway, Moncure Daniel. *Demonology and Devil-Lore*. New York: Henry Holt and Company, 1879.

Coote, Henry Charles. "Some Italian Folk-Lore." *Folk-Lore Record* 1 (1878): 187–215.

Corbett, John. *The Lake Country: An Annal of Olden Days in Central New York*. Rochester, New York: Democrat and Chronicle Print, 1898.

"Cumberland Town Council Records." *Town Council Meeting of 8 February 1796*. Cumberland, Rhode Island, 1796.

Currier, John McNab. "Contributions to New England Folklore." *Journal of American Folklore* 4 (1891): 253–56.

Curtin, Jeremiah. "European Folk-Lore in the United States." *Journal of American Folklore* 2 (1889): 56–59.

Damon, S. Foster. *Amy Lowell: A Chronicle*. 1935. Hamden, CT: Archon Books, 1966.

DeFelice, Cynthia. *The Apprenticeship of Lucas Whitaker*. New York: Farrar Straus Giroux, 1996.

Demetrio y Radaza, Francisco, comp. *Dictionary of Philippine Folk Beliefs and Customs*. Museum and Archives Publications, no. 2. Cagayan de Oro City: Xavier University, 1970.

Dégh, Linda. "The 'Belief Legend' in Modern Society: Form, Function, and Relationship to Other Genres." *In American Folk Legend: A Symposium*, edited by Wayland D. Hand, 55–68. Berkeley, California: University of California Press, 1971.

———. "Processes of Legend Formation." In *IVth International Congress for Folk-Narrative Research in Athens: Lectures and Reports*, edited by Georgios A. Megas, 77–87. Athens, 1965.

Dorson, Richard M. *American in Legend: Folklore from the Colonial Period to the Present*. New York: Pantheon Books, 1973.

———. "How Shall we Rewrite Charles M. Skinner Today?" In *Folklore: Selected Essays*, Richard M. Dorson. 1971, 177–98. Bloomington, Indiana: Indiana University Press, 1972.

Dresser, Norine. *American Vampires: Fans, Victims, Practitioners*. New York: W. W. Norton & Company, 1989.

Dubos, Rene, and Jean Dubos. *The White Plague: Tuberculosis, Man and Society*. Boston: Little, Brown and Company, 1952.

Dujardin, Richard C. "An Unusual Tradition at an Unusual Church." *Providence Journal-Bulletin*, 9 October 1982, A7.

Dundes, Alan. "Wet and Dry, the Evil Eye: An Essay in Indo-European and Semitic Worldview." In *Interpreting Folklore*, edited by Alan Dundes, 93–133. Bloomington, Indiana: Indiana University Press, 1980.

———, ed. *The Vampire: A Casebook*. Madison, Wisconsin: University of Wisconsin Press, 1998.

Emery, C. Eugene, Jr. "Did They Hear the Vampire Whisper?" *Providence Sunday Journal Magazine*, 28 October 1979, 6–7, 10, 12–13.

Eno, Paul F. "They Burned Her Heart . . . Was Mercy Brown a Vampire?" *Narragansett Times*, 25 October 1979, 1-SC.

Estes, J. Worth. "Samuel Thomson Rewrites Hippocrates." In *Medicine and Healing*, edited by Peter Benes. Annual Proceedings of the Dublin Seminar for New England Folklife, 113–32. Boston: Boston University, 1992.

Ewald, Paul W. *Plague Time: How Stealth Infections Are Causing Cancers, Heart Disease, and Other Deadly Ailments*. New York: Free Press, 2000.

Fábrega, Horacio, Jr. *Evolution of Sickness and Healing.* Berkeley and Los Angeles: University of California Press, 1997.

Fellman, Bruce. "Things Still Go Bump in South County Night." *Providence Journal,* 31 October 1980, W4.

———. "What Really Happened to Mercy Brown?" *Providence Sunday Journal Magazine,* 28 October 1979, 14–15.

Foust, Ronald. "Rite of Passage: The Vampire Tale as Cosmogonic Myth." In *Aspects of Fantasy: Selected Essays from the Second International Conference on the Fantastic in Literature and Film,* edited by William Coyle. Contributions to the Study of Fiction and Fantasy, no. 19, 73–84. Westport, Connecticut: Greenwood Press, 1986.

Fraser, C. A. "Scottish Myths from Ontario." *Journal of American Folklore* 6 (1893): 185–98.

Frazer, Sir James George. *Fear of the Dead in Primitive Religion.* 1933–36. New York [London]: Arno Press, Macmillan, 1977.

———. *The Golden Bough: A Study in Magic and Religion.* 3d ed. London: Macmillan, 1911–15.

Gebhard, Bruno. "The Interrelationship of Scientific and Folk Medicine in the United States of America Since 1850." In *American Folk Medicine: A Symposium,* edited by Wayland D. Hand, 87–98. Berkeley: University of California Press, 1980.

Georges, Robert A. "Toward an Understanding of Storytelling Events." *Journal of American Folklore* 84 (1969): 313–28.

Grimm, Jacob. *Teutonic Mythology.* 4th ed. Translated by James Steven Stallybrass. London: George Bell & Sons, 1883.

Habenstein, R. W., and W. M. Laners. *History of American Funeral Directing.* Milwaukee: Bulfin Printers, 1962.

Hand, Wayland D., ed. *Popular Beliefs and Superstitions from North Carolina.* Vol. 6–7 of Frank C. Brown Collection of North Carolina Folklore. Durham, North Carolina: Duke University Press, 1964.

Hard, Walter R., and Janet C. Greene, eds. *Mischief in the Mountains: Strange Tales of Vermont and Vermonters.* Montpelier, Vermont: Vermont Life Magazine, 1970.

Harman, M., T. I. Molleson, and J. L. Price. "Burials, Bodies and Beheadings in Romano-British and Anglo-Saxon Cemeteries." *Bulletin of the British Museum of Natural History (Geology)* 25, no. 3 (1981): 145–88.

Harrington, M. Raymond. "An Abenaki 'Witch-Story'." *Journal of American Folklore* 14 (1901): 160.

Hartland, Edwin Sidney. *Primitive Paternity: The Myth of Supernatural Birth in Relation to the History of the Family.* Publications of the Folk-Lore Society, vol. 65. London: David Nutt, 1909.

Hastings, James, ed. *Encyclopaedia of Religion and Ethics.* 1908–26. New York: Charles Scribner's Sons, 1928.

Hazard, Thomas Robinson. *The Jonny-Cake Papers of "Shepherd Tom", Together with Reminiscences of Narragansett Schools of Former Days.* Boston: The Merrymount Press, 1915.

Hazel, Faye Ringel. *The New England Vampire Belief: Image of the Decline.* Rept. no. 05–92. Center for Advanced Studies, United States Coast Guard Academy. New London, Connecticut: United States Coast Guard Academy, 1992.

Works Cited

————. "Some Strange New England Mortuary Practices: Lovecraft Was Right." *Lovecraft Studies* 29 (1992): 13–18.

Hileman, Maria. "Reporter's 'Stakeout' Puts Bite on Vampires." *Norwich Bulletin*, 31 October 1976, 24.

Hodgart, M. J. C. *The Ballads*. 1950. New York: W. W. Norton & Company, Inc., 1962.

Honko, Lauri. "Memorates and the Study of Folk Beliefs." *Journal of the Folklore Institute* 1 (1964): 3–19.

Hufford, David J. *The Terror That Comes in the Night: An Experience-Centered Study of Supernatural Assault Traditions*. Philadelphia: University of Pennsylvania Press, 1982.

Hyatt, Harry Middleton. *Folk-Lore from Adams County, Illinois*. Edition no. 2 revised. 1935. New York: Memoirs of the Alma Egan Hyatt Foundation, 1965.

————. *Hoodoo, Conjuration, Witchcraft, Rootwork*. Memoirs of the Alma Egan Hyatt Foundation. Hannibal, Missouri: Western Publishing, Inc., 1970–78.

Jones, Louis C. "The Ghosts of New York: An Analytical Study." *Journal of American Folklore* 57 (1944): 237–54.

Kalm, Peter. *The America of 1750: Peter Kalm's Travels in North America*. The English version of 1770. Edited by Adolph B. Benson. New York: Dover Publications, 1966.

Kellner, George H., and Stanley J. Lemons. *Rhode Island: The Independent State*. Woodland Hills, California: Windsor Publications, 1982.

Kinder, Nancy. "The 'Vampires' of Rhode Island." *Yankee*, October 1970, 114–15, 166–67.

Kittredge, George Lyman. "Disenchantment by Decapitation." *Journal of American* Folklore 18 (1905): 1–14.

————. *Witchcraft in Old and New England*. Cambridge, Massachusetts: Harvard University Press, 1929.

Klause, Annette Curtis. "Soap Box: A Young Adult Author Speaks Out—Why Vampires?" *Voice of Youth Advocates* 21, no. 1 (April 1998): 28–30.

Koch, Fritz. "R. I. Latter-Day Transylvania?" *Providence Evening Bulletin*, 25 February 1975, 1, A8.

Larkin, Jack. *The Reshaping of Everyday Life, 1790–1840*. New York: Harper Perennial, 1988.

Latham, Charlotte. "Some West Sussex Superstitions Lingering in 1868." *Folk-Lore Record* 1 (1878): 1–67.

Leach, MacEdward. "Blood." In *Funk & Wagnalls Standard Dictionary of Folklore*, Mythology, and Legend, edited by Maria Leach, 148–49. New York: Funk & Wagnalls, 1949–50.

Leach, Maria, ed. *Funk & Wagnalls Standard Dictionary of Folklore, Mythology, and Legend*. New York: Funk & Wagnalls, 1949–50.

Lears, Jackson. "Packaging the Folk: Tradition and Amnesia in American Advertising, 1880–1940." In *Folk Roots, New Roots: Folklore in American Life*, eds Jane S. Becker and Barbara Franco, 103–40. Lexington, Massachussetts: Museum of Our National Heritage, 1988.

Leatherdale, Clive, ed. *Dracula Unearthed*. Westcliff-on-Sea: Desert Island Books, 1998.

————. *Dracula: The Novel & the Legend*. Wellingborough: Aquarian Press, 1985.

Lee, D. Demetracopoulou. "Greek Accounts of the Vrykolakas." *Journal of American Folklore* 55 (1942): 126–32.

Levy, Stuart B. "The Challenge of Antibiotic Resistance." *Scientific American*, March 1998, 46–53.

Libby, Sam. "Cemetery Holds Tales of Vampires." *New York Times*, 16 February 1992, CN8.

Locke, Edwin A., ed. *Tuberculosis in Massachusetts*. Boston: Wright & Potter, 1908.

Loomis, C. Grant. "Henry David Thoreau as Folklorist." Western Folklore 16 (1957): 90–104.

Lovecraft, H. P. *The Case of Charles Dexter Ward*. New York: Ballantine Books, 1971.

———. "Letter to Frank Utpatel, 15 February 1937." *Letters of H. P. Lovecraft in Lovecraft Collection*. Lovecraft Collection, housed at John Hay Library, Brown University, Providence, Rhode Island.

———. "Letter to Helen V. Sully, 17 October 1933." *Letters of H. P. Lovecraft in Lovecraft Collection*. Lovecraft Collection, housed at John Hay Library, Brown University, Providence, Rhode Island.

———. "The Shunned House." In *At the Mountains of Madness and Other Tales of Terror*. 1924, 111–38. New York: Ballantine Books, 1971.

Ludlum, David M. *Social Ferment in Vermont, 1791–1850*. New York: Columbia University Press, 1939.

MacCulloch, J. A. "Vampire." In *Encyclopedia of Religion and Ethics*, vol. 12, edited by James Hastings. 1908–26, 589–91. New York: Scribner's Sons, 1928.

MacDonald, Betty. *The Plague and I*. Philadelphia; New York: J. B. Lippincott Company, 1948.

"Majority Report on Establishing a New Board of Health." *City Document No. 108*. Boston, 1872.

Mansfield, David.. "The History of the Town of Dummerston." *Vermont Historical Magazine* (1884).

McCarthy, Peggy. "Unearthing Clues to the Past: Bones Found in Lost Conn. Graveyard Give Clues to Life in Colonial Times." *Boston Sunday Globe*, 13 September 1992, 43, 45.

McEnroe, Colin. "The Surprising Account of Those Spectres Called Vampyres." *Hartford Courant*, 24 October [21 January] 1999, G13. 1765.

McFarland, Gerald W. *The "Counterfeit" Man: The True Story of the Boorn-Colvin Murder Case*. New York: Pantheon, 1990.

McNally, Raymond T. *A Clutch of Vampires*. New York: New York Graphic Society, 1974.

McNally, Raymond T., and Radu Florescu. *In Search of Dracula*. Greenwich, Connecticut: New York Graphic Society, 1972.

Merolla, James A. "Mercy Brown Grave Marker Recovered." *Providence Journal*, 21 August 1996, B-1,3.

———. "Vandals Steal Mercy Brown's Gravestone." *Providence Journal*, 16 August 1996, B-1,3.

Merrifield, Ralph. *Archaeology of Ritual and Magic*. New York: New Amsterdam, 1987.

Miller, Elizabeth. *Dracula: Sense & Nonsense*. Westcliff-on-Sea: Desert Island Books, 2000.

Mullen, Patrick B. "Modern Legend and Rumor Theory." *Journal of the Folklore Institute* 9 (1972): 95–109.

Murgoci, Agnes. "The Vampire in Roumania." *Folklore* 37 (1926): 320–49.

Needham, Rodney. *Belief, Language and Experience*. London: Oxford University Press, 1972.

Nethercot, Arthur H. *The Road to Tryermaine: A Study of the History, Background, and Purposes of Coleridge's "Christabel"*. Chicago: University of Chicago Press, 1939.

Works Cited

"Obituary of Ruth Ellen Rose." *Narragansett Times*, 15 May 1874.

Letter to the editor. *Old Colony Memorial and Plymouth County Advertiser*, 11 May 1822, 7.

Pardon's Progeny: A Publication of the Tillinghast Family in America 10, no. 1 (Spring 1983): 2–3.

Letter to the editor. *Pawtuxet Valley Gleaner*, 25 March 1892, 5.

Editorial. *Pawtuxet Valley Gleaner*, 22 April 1892.

Pawtuxet Valley Gleaner, 26 February 1892, 1.

Pettibone, John S. "The Early History of Manchester." *Proceedings of the Vermont Historical Society* 1 (1930): 147–66.

Philips, David E. *Legendary Connecticut: Traditional Tales from the Nutmeg State*. 2d ed. 1984. Williamantic, Connecticut: Curbstone Press, 1992.

Pinchot, Roy, ed. *Blood: The River of Life. The Human Body*. New York: Torstar Books, Inc., 1985.

Place, Enoch Hayes. *Journals of Enoch Hayes Place*. Transcriber William E. Wentworth. Boston: The New England Historic Genealogical Society and the New Hampshire Society of Genealogists, 1998.

Providence Journal, 19 March 1892, 3.

Providence Journal, 20 March 1892, 4.

Providence Journal, 21 March 1892, 8.

Quinn, D. Michael. *Early Mormonism and the Magic World View*. Revised and enlarged ed. Salt Lake City: Signature Press, 1998.

Randolph, Vance. *Ozark Magic and Folklore*. Original title of work: *Ozark Superstitions*. 1947. New York: Dover Publications, Inc., 1964.

Revson, James A. "19th Century Rhode Islanders Lived in Fear of Vampire Attacks." *Westerly Sun*, 24 July 1977, 18.

"A Rhode Island Country Town." Editorial. *Wickford Standard*, 6 May 1892, 2.

Rhode Island Historical Preservation Commission. *Statewide Historical Preservation Report P-F-1: Foster, Rhode Island*. Providence, Rhode Island: Rhode Island Historical Preservation Commission, 1982.

Rider, Sidney S. "The Belief in Vampires in Rhode Island." *Book Notes* 5, no. 7 (1888): 37–39.

———. *Book Notes* 9, no. 7 (1892): 1.

———. "Exeter Notes." *Unpublished notes in Rider Collection*. Rider Collection, housed at John Hay Library, Brown University, Providence, Rhode Island, Box 300, no. 6, [c. 1887].

Robinson, Charles Turek. *The New England Ghost Files: An Authentic Compendium of Frightening Phantoms*. North Attleboro, MA: Covered Bridge Press, 1994.

Rose, J. S. *Consumption Curable, a Practical Treatise to Prove Consumption a Manageable Disease*. Philadelphia: Crolius & Gladding, 1841.

Rothman, Sheila M. *Living in the Shadow of Death: Tuberculosis and the Social Experience of Illness in American History*. Baltimore: The Johns Hopkins University Press, 1994.

Royster, Charles. *A Revolutionary People at War: The Continental Army and America Character*, 1775–1783. Chapel Hill, North Carolina: University of North Carolina Press, 1979.

Schierup, Carl-Ulrik. "Why Are Vampires Still Alive? Wallachian Immigrants in Scandinavia." *Ethnos* 3–4 (1986): 173–98.

Sieveking, Paul. "Consumed by Vampires." *Fortean Times* 80 (1995): 46–47.

Skinner, Charles M. *Myths and Legends of Our Own Land*. Philadelphia: J. B. Lippincott Co., 1896.

Sledzik, Paul S., Nicholas Bellantoni, and Allison Webb Willcox. "Skeletal Evidence for Tuberculosis and Vampirism in 18th and 19th Century New England." *Unpublished paper presented at the Paleopathology Annual Meeting.* Toronto, Ontario, 1993.

Sledzik, Paul S., and Nicholas Bellantoni. "Brief Communication: Bioarcheological and Biocultural Evidence for the New England Vampire Folk Belief." *American Journal of Physical Anthropology* 94 (1994): 269–74.

Sontag, Susan. *Illness as Metaphor*. New York: Farrar, Straus and Giroux, 1978.

St. Armand, Barton L. "Facts in the Case of H. P. Lovecraft." *Rhode Island History* 31, no. 1 (1972): 3–19.

Starr, Douglas. *Blood: An Epic History of Medicine and Commerce*. New York: Alfred A. Knopf, 1998.

Stephens, Rockwell. "They Burned the Vampire's Heart to Ashes." *Vermont Life* 21, no. 1 (1966): 47–49.

———. "The Vampire's Heart." In *Mischief in the Mountains: Strange Tales of Vermont and Vermonters*, eds Walter R. Hard and Janet C. Greene, 71–80. Montpelier, Vermont: Vermont Life Magazine, 1970.

Stetson, George R. "The Animistic Vampire in New England." *American Anthropologist* 9 (1896): 1–13.

———. "Letter to Sidney S. Rider." *Unpublished letter in Rider Collection*. Rider Collection, housed at John Hay Library, Brown University, Providence, Box 181, no. 32, 1895.

"Strange Superstition." *Norwich Weekly Courier*, 24 May 1854, 2.

Sullivan, Kevin. "A Journey Through Old Rhode Island: Quietly but in Vain, the Rural Areas Try to Fend Off Modernity." *Providence Sunday Journal*, 27 May 1990, A-1, A-10, A-11.

Summers, Montague. *The Vampire: His Kith and Kin*. London: Kegan Paul, Trench, Trubner & Co., Ltd., 1928.

———. *The Vampire in Europe*. New York: E. P. Dutton and Company, Inc., 1929.

———. *The Werewolf*. New York: E. P. Dutton and Company, Inc., 1934.

"Superstitions of New England." *Old Colony Memorial and Plymouth County Advertiser*, 4 May 1822, 4.

Terrell, James W. "The Demon of Consumption: A Legend of the Cherokees in North Carolina." *Journal of American Folklore* 5 (1892): 125–26.

Thompson, Leslie M. "The Vampire in an Age of Technology." In *T is for Texas: A State Full of Folklore*, edited by Francis Edward Abernathy. Publications of the Texas Folklore Society, no. 44, 151–60. Dallas: E-Heart Press, 1982.

Thompson, Stith. *Motif-Index of Folk Literature: A Classification of Narrative Elements in Folktales, Ballads, Myths, Fables, Mediaeval Romances, Exempla, Fabliaux, Jest-Books and Local Legends*. Revised and enlarged ed. 1932–36. Bloomington, Indiana: Indiana University Press, 1955–58.

———. *Tales of the North American Indians*. Bloomington, Indiana: Indiana University Press, 1966.

Trafford, George E. "Four Looking for Vampire Find Casket, Opened Grave." *Providence Journal-Bulletin*, 2 November 1993, B8.

Works Cited

Trumbull, H. Clay. *The Blood Covenant: A Primitive Rite and Its Bearing on Scripture.* 2d ed. Philadelphia: J. D. Wattles, 1893.

Tuchman, Gaye. *Making News: A Study in the Construction of Reality.* New York: The Free Press, 1978.

Tyler, Casey, B. "Interesting Notes of Foster in 1827: Capt. Young's Purchase." *Pawtuxet Valley Gleaner,* 8 October 1892, p. 4.

Tylor, Edward B. *Primitive Culture: Researches Into the Development of Mythology, Philosophy, Religion, Language, Art, and Custom.* New York: G. P. Putnam's Sons, 1929.

Updike, Wilkins. *A History of the Episcopal Church in Narragansett, Rhode Island.* 2d ed. Boston: The Merrymount Press, 1907.

"The Vampire Tradition." Arnold Collection, housed at Knight Memorial Library, Providence, 87.

"Wendish Superstition." Notes. *Folk-Lore Record* 3, no. 1 (1880): 137–38.

Wilson, Katharina M. "The History of the Word Vampire." In *The Vampire: A Casebook,* edited by Alan Dundes. 1985, 3–11. Madison, Wisconsin: University of Wisconsin Press, 1998.

Wimberly, Lowry Charles. *Death and Burial Lore in the English and Scottish Popular Ballads. University of Nebraska Studies in Language, Literature, and Criticism,* no. 8. Lincoln, Nebraska: University of Nebraska, 1927.

———. *Folklore in the English and Scottish Ballads.* 1928. New York: Dover Publications, Inc., 1965.

Woodward, Carl R. "Kingston's Cultural Heritage." *Rhode Island Yearbook* (1970), 57–68.

———. *Plantation in Yankeeland: The Story of Cocumscussoc, Mirror of Colonial Rhode Island.* Chester, Connecticut: Pequot Press, Inc., 1971.

Yoder, Don. "Folk Medicine." In *Folklore and Folklife: An Introduction,* edited by Richard M. Dorson, 191–215. Chicago: University of Chicago Press, 1972.

Ziner, Karen Lee. "Was She a Victim . . . or a Vampire?" *Providence Journal-Bulletin,* 25 October 1984, 10.

INDEX

Index

Index

ABOUT THE AUTHOR

Michael E. Bell was awarded a Ph.D. in Folklore from Indiana University at Bloomington, where his dissertation topic was African-American voodoo practices. He also has an M.A. in Folklore and Mythology from the University of California at Los Angeles, and a B.A. in Anthropology and Archaeology from the University of Arizona, Tucson. Since 1980, Bell has been the Consulting Folklorist at the Rhode Island Historical Preservation & Heritage Commission in Providence, Rhode Island. He has also taught folklore, English, and anthropology at several colleges and universities. Dr. Bell has served as a scholar or consultant on numerous projects, particularly those concerned with folklore, folk art, oral history, and humanities programs for young adults. These projects have taken a variety of forms, including primary research and fieldwork, exhibits, publications, school curricula, workshops and lectures, festivals, performances, and media productions. In addition to many state and local grants, project funding sources have included the National Endowment for the Humanities, the National Endowment for the Arts, the American Folklife Center at the Library of Congress, and the Smithsonian Institution. Bell has completed a variety of publications and media productions on topics ranging from local legends and the magical black cat bone to the occupational folklife of the shell fishing industry of Narragansett Bay. Michael E. Bell currently serves as Chairman of the Cranston Historic District Commission, and lives with his wife, Carole, near Providence, Rhode Island. Their family includes daughters, Meighan and Gillian, and son, Brendan.